Contents

Letting Them Lead

Adventures in Game-Based, Self-Directed Learning

Laurie Block Spigel

Mountain Ash Press

This book is dedicated to the innovative educators who came before me and whose shoulders I stand on. Some of these teachers I was fortunate to meet and work with in person and many whom I never met have inspired me with their body of work. The list includes my parents Elaine C. Block and Haskell M. Block (my earliest teachers), Sylvia Ashton Warner (pioneer in child-led learning), Viola Spolin (the mother of improvisation), Carol Sills, Aretha Sills, Lynda Barry, Kenneth Koch, Daniel Judah Sklar, and others. This book is also dedicated to all the children and students I have encountered, including my sons, who were my greatest teachers.

Most especially, this book is for the children.

We learn through experience and experiencing, and no one teaches anyone anything. This is as true for the infant moving from kicking to crawling to walking as it is for the scientist with his equations.

~Viola Spolin, *Improvisation for the Theater*

Preface

I stood in front of the blackboard in a Long Island college classroom facing rows of desks, every seat occupied by an alternative educator. Teachers from democratic schools, homeschool learning centers, and other unconventional learning environments stared at me. More filed in the door and stood in the back. I was speaking at the Alternative Education Resource Organization (AERO) Conference of 2015 on Child-Led Learning in the Classroom. I explained how self-directed learning wasn't just a one-on-one experience. It could happen in groups anywhere that allowed for a flexible approach to curriculum. I showed images of classes where students joined together to play games and create unique projects. The audience laughed at a photo of kids vying to teach their chosen topic in a game called Stump the Class and another of me bending with my head tilted to listen closely to one child over the din of activity in a room full of board-game makers working on the floor and at tables, using books, computers, and art supplies. That image of happy chaos was a dramatic contrast to the AERO Conference classroom with neat rows of desks with everyone sitting face-forward.

At the end of my lecture, I opened the floor for questions. Hands went up, and I called on one young teacher. "You say that you approach each class with a plan that you are willing to change. Tell us a time when you changed your plan." Everyone leaned forward to hear my answer. I realized this was information they needed.

"Why, it happens all the time, probably in every course, certainly every year. The plan might change in the middle of a class when an idea appears that gets us excited." I related two anecdotes, one that occurred in an elementary age class and another with a group of teens. That question at the end of that lecture became the inspiration for this book. The two anecdotes I told that day are included here, in the section "Planning to Be Surprised," a phrase I consider a personal motto that describes my approach to teaching. I arrive at each class with a Plan A and a Plan B, and sometimes I even have a plan C, but my real hope is that I won't use any of those plans. My secret hope is that I will be surprised and we will create a new plan in the moment, a plan hatched by the entire class, not just me.

Self-directed (also called child-led or student-centered) learning happens when the student's interests, learning style, personality, and needs are placed at the center of the educational plan (curriculum). An impersonal education is rigid, standardized, and uniform. In his AERO keynote speech of 2012, Sir Ken Robinson declared that the key to transformation in our educational system and in our children is personalization.

I started adopting a more personalized, child-led approach with my own homeschooled kids simply because it worked better than any other approach. Putting their interests at the center of their learning kept them engaged instead of bored. Recalling my own childhood education, school was crushingly boring, yet I loved learning, read voraciously, and sought out meaningful learning experiences that inspired me. My education came from my parents and the world around me, not from school.

I homeschooled my two children, each starting at age nine even though they are five years apart. In *Letting Them Lead*, I recount a few of my sons' homeschooling experiences because they were formative for me as an educator.[1] *Letting Them Lead* is intended for alternative educators, although homeschoolers will also find plenty of helpful information.

Teaching experiences recounted in this book occurred between 1990 and 2022 in person in New York City, the state of Maine, and Sydney, Australia and via video conference with students in the USA and other countries. Students, mostly homeschoolers, came from widely differing backgrounds, countries, religions, races, and economic statuses. Naturally, they possessed individual attitudes, values, personalities, learning differences, and talents. This diverse mix made for rich learning experiences, for me as well as the children. All student names have been changed in this book (unless otherwise requested and except where work is quoted) in order to protect their privacy.

The academic content in my classes is predominantly language arts, social studies, and theater arts. However, all subjects enter the room when taking a student-directed, thematic approach. Science takes a central place in an animals course, where all activities relate to animals. Math, science, history, geography, art, and music have all been used as topics in a board game class that develops research and writing skills. In an interview course, any and all subjects are likely to come up when students interview people in professions that interest them while aiming at a final project in language arts and social studies.

When teachers and homeschooling parents consider taking a child-centered approach, people often ask how they can determine a child's interests. I suggest asking them! But sometimes, a child won't tell us with words. If we look and listen carefully, we can see it in their eyes, their body language, and physical reactions. Notice what they glance at and look at again. Learning choices don't have to be deep interests; curiosity is enough. It is my honor and delight as an educator to help feed that curiosity.

---

1. *If you want to know more about my reasons for homeschooling and our homeschooling journey, I wrote about that in detail in my book, *Education Uncensored*, where I also explain how and what's wrong with our current educational system and provide an overview of education for homeschooling parents.

Definitions

with the Author's Interpretations and Usage

*C**hild-led*** — A child-led approach to learning places the child's interests, needs, learning style and personality at the center of the curriculum or educational plan. The adult remains the leader but takes their cue from the child. Synonyms: *self-directed, student-centered, personalized.*

Common Core — Standardized curriculum in the USA for K-12 that was adopted by all states except for four. It is possible to find the Common Core Curriculum for any state online. Many educators (myself included) feel the Common Core has low standards.

curriculum — A curriculum is an educational plan. Many people mistakenly think this word means *enforced, standardized, required curriculum.* Plans are an essential part of life (just try getting through your day without one), but plans become problematic or even dangerous when you are forced to stick with a plan that isn't working well. Curriculum (like any plan) is a problem when it is inflexible and cannot be changed. It's important to make plans but even more important to be able to change or amend those plans.

democratic school — A school where students have no required courses and can learn what they want to learn. The school operates democratically: everyone has a say or a vote in the on-going process, even the hiring of new teachers. Examples include the A. S. Neill Summerhill School in Suffolk, England and Sudbury Valley School in Framingham, Massachusetts.

deschooling — 1. Synonym for *unschooling*. 2. The decompression period or adjustment period children need after leaving traditional school as they transition to a less standardized, more personalized education. Some homeschoolers estimate that the period of time needed for *deschooling* or decompression is one month for every year the child has been in school.

homeschooling — Homeschooling is a legal alternative to school, available in every state in the USA, with regulations that vary from state to state. Homeschoolers have more freedom than schools and school teachers in choosing curriculum resources, changing curriculum at any point in time, and taking a child-led, personalized approach. Other countries' homeschooling laws vary, sometimes making homeschooling illegal.

self-directed — Synonym for child-led or student-centered, often used to describe the independent learning of teens and adults. The word *directed* does not imply authoritarian direction; a self-directed learner may seek out different teachers and experiences that provide direction.

side-coaching — Side-coaching is a technique used by the teacher to increase the student's focus without disrupting the student. Students do not stop and face the teacher but hear the side-coached suggestions while continuing to play so they can respond within the game. Side-coaching is something we can do for ourselves, using our inner voice to help us maintain focus.

standardized curriculum — A grade-level, one-size-fits-all curriculum designed for all students K-12 with the same basic content to be delivered in the same way. This approach does not take into account the innate differences in each student or the fact that no one is average or at "grade level" in everything all the time. People are not standardized!

teacher-led — A teacher-led or teacher-centered or teacher-centric classroom is where the curriculum (educational plan) is created by the teacher. The teacher is free to take a less standardized, more creative approach and create their own lessons. This approach may or may not take into account the interests and needs of the children and often focuses on the teacher's interests. One example is the Fairytale Curriculum created by Elba Marrero for her 3rd grade class at Hunter Elementary School. As a girl, I would have loved this enchanting curriculum, but it might not suit a nonfiction reader who dislikes fantasy.

unschooling — This term is used to refer to a child-led approach yet may also have other meanings. One definition of *unschooling* is *learning without using a curriculum*, yet I question this (see definition of *curriculum*) and instead suggest *education with a focus on experiential learning that does not rely on standardized curriculum*. Another definition of *unschooling* is that all learning is experiential. Yet, I question that too since many unschoolers are serious readers and some, given the freedom, choose to take a traditional textbook approach for their own reasons. Because of the wide variety of definitions for this term and because the word itself expresses what it is not rather than what it is, I prefer to use *child-led* or *self-directed*.

Introduction

The Empowerment Of Self-Direction

My approach to education is holistic and child-centered, placing the student's interests and needs at the center of a flexible curriculum that is co-created by teacher and students. The child-led, self-directed approach puts students in charge. Having the freedom to choose implies students have choices. In fact, the choices are vast. Students must weigh the options and think about what resonates. In this way, they learn to discern what matters to them. They become thoughtful learners who delight in choosing each new direction. They wear their learning like custom-made garments with unique style. Comparatively, standardized learning feels like bargain basement, off-the-rack clothing that resembles everyone else's. In a rigid school environment with an authoritarian structure, students often feel unable to be themselves. A rigid, standardized environment can thwart learning, stall individual empowerment, and kill creativity. Students need an open, safe environment with the freedom to make personalized creative choices and selected bargain-basement bits can mix with customized, crafted, stand-out educational experiences.

Every teacher and every parent with more than one child can tell you how different children are from each other. My own sons were almost opposite in interests and personality; one loved theater and art, the other loved science and the ocean. I knew from the start that they would end up in different professions, even different lifestyles. If children have such different paths in life, why should their education be the same? Why not tailor their education towards those goals? That personalization of learning can feed an inner calling. Children who grow up with the freedom to learn what matters to them often become experts on a chosen topic long before college and may find direction at an earlier age than expected.

Prioritizing the interests and strengths of the child boosts their self-confidence and helps them thrive. More importantly, a holistic focus with a sense of well-being as the primary goal yields better results. Pleasure, even joy, is apparent in work that takes a personalized, noncompetitive approach.

The Essential Games

In the finite arena of standardized curriculum, required subject material is often plugged into games like Bingo or Jeopardy for the purpose of memorization and retention of information. But my goal as a teacher is not the retention of information; I am not training students to pass an exam. Rather, I seek to expand their horizons both internally and externally. What if games taught us how to think differently? What if games expanded our consciousness? The games I primarily use are theater games created by Viola Spolin and traditional children's games cataloged by Neva Boyd. These games build communication skills, sharpen the senses, and open minds to new ways of thinking and understanding.

Moreover, the games bond the group. Playing together, students learn to trust each other and the space. We create a safe, relaxed atmosphere that is ripe with awareness. A constant give and take between players keeps them alert, ready to help each other, as they watch each other's backs and jump in to assist a struggling player at a moment's notice. This sense of belonging and togetherness lasts beyond the classes. My students maintain friendships with each other and with me, visiting years later as lifelong friends.

Focus On Play, Not Problems

"In striving for excellence, freedom and spontaneity are almost inevitably sacrificed. Interest tends to be centered in self and competition is over emphasized." ~Neva Boyd, *The Theory of Play*

My focus is not to fix or remove problems in children, to replace flaws with perfection, or to achieve high marks. A focus on excellence is common in the traditional schools that most of us attended. Teachers and parents are often stuck in the mindset that their job is to fix whatever is "wrong" with the child. Yet, by placing a magnifying glass on what's "wrong," the child is apt to feel like a failure. It is more practical and beneficial to focus on a child's strengths and seek an overall balance in which the child's strengths are developed to support and compensate for weaknesses.

I have had many students on the autism spectrum and many with learning and behavioral challenges. I never asked a parent for a diagnosis and often told parents not to bother giving me one. I have met parents who feel exhausted by the focus on their child's problems, who meet me with a long lists of apologies and explanations before I have even met the child. I interrupt them and ask about their child's strengths and interests instead. I want to lead with what is working from the child's point of view. Knowing that the child will reveal all to me in time, I want to take a positive approach that I can share with the child so that we can start as a team and the child can feel that I am on their side. I have no training in special education, no background in autism, yet I have had success working with these children, often finding the right game or creating a game for them that helps them to overcome their obstacles. I begin by being open with the child and meeting them where they are, whatever that means. Students need to be accepted for who they are, even celebrated for who they are, if they are to shine.

It's easy for a parent or teacher to feel concerned about problematic or disruptive behavior and find it hard to accept the whole child. Any classroom is likely to have a wide variety of behavioral and learning issues. One child may be overactive, another prone to anxiety, another shy to the point of not speaking, and another unable to stop talking, and these are just a few examples. In my experience, the solution to assisting each child is not to focus on their problem or even to point it out, which often makes the child feel awful, like an example to others of what not to do. Rather, the solution is for the group to play games, especially the games of Neva Boyd and Viola Spolin. These games build skills in communication, perception, and focus and help the students bond. Spolin game evaluations are non-judgmental and ignore good or bad, allowing for the whole person to play and learn with less anxiety. (Specific games are listed in the resource section of this book that address certain problems.)

In the playing of games, children are motivated to abstain from disruptive behavior because they want the game to continue and disruptive behavior puts the game at risk of ending. Each game also gives them new awareness that offers the ability to see and correct what they are doing. The child who self-corrects a problem feels strengthened by the process. They are able to look back on how they used to be and feel good about how they have changed instead of feeling bad because a problem that persists was highlighted by the teacher. Whenever possible, step back and be patient. Let the children and the games show you what is possible.

As parents and teachers, we can create an environment of learning that offers safety, comfort, creative freedom, and the ability to feel seen and heard. Through the use of improvisational games that help to access the intuition, we can create an environment in which students relax and learn and allow their true selves to emerge.

Non-Authoritarian Leadership

My husband used to protest, "It's child-led, not child-ruled!" when people implied that our children or my students were fully in charge. As teacher or parent, I am the clear leader, but I take a non-authoritarian attitude. The first class of the year I am liable to call out, "Let's get this party started!" I am both

host and participant at the educational party of my dreams, where we get to learn and play and teach with passion, intuition, and creativity. This kind of fearlessness needs friendly encouragement away from the critical eye of a stern authority figure. We need to be able to play together! When we play together, the child's perspective on the teacher changes. I become a fellow player, not someone to be wary of.

In a non-authoritarian setting, the teacher is free to say, "I don't know," to any question. I often follow that remark with, "How do you think we could find out?" This makes finding the answer or solution a team effort, a lesson and adventure by itself.

The teacher's job is primarily to help the student learn how to learn and to encourage independent learning. This is done by utilizing a wide variety of resources in a safe, creative, playful environment. Collaboration and discourse are encouraged, respecting individual choices and points of view. Non-judgmental feedback is practiced, with the focus on the problem not the person. In this way, students learn to stop being afraid to make mistakes. Instead, they learn to evaluate themselves honestly, eventually gaining a sense of artistic detachment that makes self-evaluation possible and constructive, never punitive.

Work and play occur simultaneously. Play heightens focus, and a sense of play makes the students want to keep going. Play is an essential part of any creative process and yields new perspectives and solutions to problems. A playful attitude helps bond students together and dissolve walls between participants. Taking a playful attitude, especially when combined with good listening skills, the teacher becomes a friend.

Time pressures and arbitrary deadlines imposed by the teacher are absent in a child-led classroom and are replaced by real life deadlines or consequences. Students are likely to finish a project for a major event such as a performance or fair. When the project isn't finished on time for such an event, the partial work can still be displayed or the work can be read in progress to avoid disappointments and to celebrate all students' work. Students work hard for real life goals and for peer respect, but they rebel against arbitrary deadlines. When there are no real life consequences, deadlines can be absent, resulting in shorter or longer projects. Undue pressure that leads to anxiety can be avoided, replaced with open-ended projects, creative inspiration, and personal goals.

Learning happens not just to complete a project or assignment but for the sheer love of the experience. The lasting reward is personal growth. When a student learns something that matters to them, or develops a skill they are proud of, or opens their eyes to seeing the world in a new way, they end up seeing themselves anew as well. Taking a deep dive into a personalized world of learning, they are forever changed.

Practical Considerations — Age Range and Duration of Classes

Age Range Of Groups

The age range of students I taught was 5-19, with classes typically divided into groups with a three to four-year "suggested" age range:

- lower elementary - ages 6-8

- upper elementary- ages 8-11

- middle school - ages 11-13

- high school - ages 14-19

Age ranges were flexible and often changed. The Board Game class in Australia was for ages 8 to 12 but included one 7-year-old. Playwriting or Improv for Teens might include ages 12-19 combining middle and high school. Groups tended to be small, as few as four or five students and as many as sixteen or twenty. I also worked one-on-one, tutoring in unconventional ways using games and creative outcomes. In large classes, parent volunteers or former students assisted, keeping the adult-student ratio low.

Grade Level

I have found grade level to be a false assumption that often limits and frustrates students. I try to make sure that materials are appropriate for the age group present. For example, teens want to discuss books with adult issues while younger children prefer less serious fare. But I do not limit book selections to a certain level of vocabulary nor do I refrain from discussing complex ideas with younger students. Very often students elect to read or study something more advanced, or easier, than their supposed level. In reality, each student brings their own level with them, and that level is always changing. Partly for this reason, it is best for students to have a hand in the selection of materials with the teacher's guidance available as needed or requested.

Time Length Of Classes

Playing games takes time. One hour isn't long enough to do much, so my class sessions range from ninety minutes to three hours. Determining the time length for a class can depend on the number of students and their age. A smaller or younger group may require less time; a larger or older group may need more and may be able to stay focused for longer.

It is difficult to estimate the time each activity will require, so flexibility is important in planning. I keep a list of games on hands that can replace a longer or shorter game or fill a gap near the end of class or at the start if we are waiting for students to arrive. Midway through class, I may swap out a game for a variety of reasons, time being one of them. I may schedule an activity near the end that can be completed later at home or at the start of our next class. I plan more than we will have time for, so flexible choices are ready.

A suggested range of time for a course is stated at the top of each curriculum syllabus in this book. It is advantageous to spend more time if you can. More time equals more learning, increased awareness and perspective, more time to digest ideas, ask questions, make connections, and complete projects in greater detail. A lack of urgency removes undue pressure. Children need time! They must gather their thoughts, search for the right words, change their minds, and figure things out before they can even speak. Pressure can freeze a child's intuition, creativity, productivity— the child's mind and body can become immobile. Students need time to breathe! And eat! And play! And laugh! The more relaxed and playful a child is the more spontaneous they can be, which increases the pace of learning. If you find yourself with extra time at the end of class, play another game!

Classroom Set-Up

The standard grid with rows of desks and chairs is to be avoided. Eight or so can sit around a single large table. As the teacher, I avoid sitting at the head of a long, rectangular table. That position places me farthest away from whoever is seated at the opposite end and it separates me from the group by placing me at an end. With a rectangular table, I prefer to be in the middle of one side where I can almost touch everyone else. This is the most powerful table position for the teacher because it is within reach of everyone, and it is also more democratic, friendlier, and less imposing than sitting at the head.

For playwriting or improv, my preferred set-up is a circle or semi-circle of chairs for teacher and students. In this way, we are positioned as equals, and the curve (instead of a straight row) allows everyone to see everyone else. Students do not need desks because they can write in notebooks or pads and can move to the floor if needed. Chairs are easily repositioned to clear the space for a game or place the chairs in a semi-circle for audience members to view players who stand to perform. There are times when I put myself in the center of a semi-circle so I can see everyone at once, especially if I need to side-coach a game they are playing while seated. Art projects like bookmaking require work tables, but a simple semi-circle of chairs is best for playing games. It also creates a casual, relaxed feeling that a grid of desks and chairs seems to disallow.

Assessment and Evaluation

In traditional schools, assessment (the gathering of information for the purpose of evaluation) is done by numbers— test scores, amount of homework completed, and classes attended. Evaluation is often a process of comparing student assessments with an end result of ranking. Students at the top get a lot of perks and big bragging rights, so this system supports competition between peers and focuses on the self. It also amplifies the anxiety and sense of failure felt by students with a low ranking.

In a student-centered environment where tests are absent, teachers never have to judge or rank. Evaluations are not imposed by authority figures. Non-judgmental practices can be taught so students learn to self-evaluate as a life tool. Information can be gleaned directly from the student's work rather than from test scores and numbers. Students can participate by creating a personal portfolio or presentation of work and by writing a narrative self-evaluation. This evaluation can turn into a poetry exercise about growth and change (Example: I used to think (or feel or do) _____, but now I _____) or a personal essay about how students see themselves differently.

As often as possible, evaluations and outcomes are real world results such as an audience's applause of student plays or visitors having fun playing student-made board games. Success comes not in the form of a judgement or an authoritarian determination such as a score or ranking but from the reactions of family, friends, guests, and peers and from the student's self-awareness and personal sense of self-worth.

As adults we must guide ourselves and avoid relying on the value judgements of others, which are so often based on subjective opinions. If evaluation is always imposed on us by others, how are we to learn that skill? (A non-judgmental feedback guide can be found in the Curriculum and Resources section in this book.) Spolin games are often followed by evaluation questions that ask the players and the audience what was communicated. Additional questions include what happened when players were in focus. These questions help the participants to explore their experience without labeling it as good or bad.

Through the use of non-judgmental self-examination, we can develop a sense of artistic detachment that will serve us well throughout our adult lives. Self-assessment is a skill that can start at an early age, when a parent might ask a child what it felt like to color a picture or sweep the room. Ask questions about focus and process such as, "Was there a moment when you felt more connected [to the activity]? Did something different happen then?"

When assessment and evaluation are done by teacher and student in partnership, the evaluation process becomes a learning experience. When both student and teacher use non-judgmental practices, the results can be empowering instead of nerve-wracking or humiliating. The focus can be on real growth, which is far more valuable and lasting than a high score.

Curriculum

Curricula in this book was created by me, combining techniques and activities from many other sources with a view towards self-directed, creative learning. These are projects that defy grade level and take a flexible, child-centered approach. In this book, there are over 75 classroom hours of detailed lessons, and the ingredients to make endless variations of child-led, game-based learning experiences for and with your students.

- Multicultural Geography Syllabus, ages 9-13, 20 hours

- Puppetry Workshop Syllabus, ages 6-12, 2 days or 12 hours

- Make Your Own Board Game Syllabus, ages 8-13, 20 hours

- Interview Course Syllabus, ages 9 and up, 20 hours

- Playwriting for Teens, Workshop on Repressed Desire, 3 hours

- Literature Discussion Curriculum Guidelines for middle and high school

Chapters in the section "Planning to Be Surprised" chronicle examples of this curricula in action. These chapters are organized by student ages from younger to older with elementary school classes first, then middle school, and finally high school. However, all lessons and experiences are adaptable to younger or older ages, and each lesson or course can be shortened or extended. Guidelines and additional resources are provided to help the user expand any curriculum, by, for example, making multicultural geography a course that lasts a year or even several years or perhaps a single workshop with a focus chosen by a particular group.

In addition to curricula and resources, a Discussion Guide for *Letting Them Lead: Adventures in Game-Based, Self-Directed Learning* is included after the final chapter in "Planning to Be Surprised." This discussion guide can be used in groups or by the lone reader. These discussion questions can act as a starting point for further exploration and application. Choose the questions that interest you. Feel free to rephrase and expand on them. Add your own topics and questions for further discussion and your own activities that explore self-directed learning in a personal way.

My Journey to Self-Directed Learning

Chapter One

I Swore I'd Never Teach

"Never! Never ever!" I shook my head back and forth. "It'll be over my dead body!"

"Me too! Uh uh! Not on your life!" My younger sister giggled as she, too, shook her head. Sitting cross-legged on my Brooklyn bed one teenage summer afternoon, my sister and I wrapped our pinky fingers together and swore to each other. Locking eyes, we chanted, "I'll never be a teacher! I'll die first!" This mutual promise bonded us to our adolescent shared dislike and distrust of our parents, both professors, as we promised ourselves an unknown future far from schools and the world of academia.

How often we laugh over this memory! My sister became an occupational therapist with the local Board of Education paying her tuition in exchange for her promise to work for the New York City school system, where she ended up staying. She wasn't a teacher, but she spent her weekdays in a school working closely with children.

I resisted the family business of teaching, secure in the knowledge that without a college degree or teaching certification I was safe. When I started homeschooling my children, I created group classes that sparked a growing wave of teaching opportunities for me outside of traditional schools. Then at age 50, I felt a calling impossible to refuse and threw myself into the world of playwriting and theater games for children. Teaching had become my passion.

When I swore I'd never teach, I did not know that educational freedom was possible. I was familiar with overcrowded classrooms in public schools and couldn't bear the thought of being cooped up in one. I just knew I'd be climbing the walls and pulling out my hair by 3:00. Yet in my 50s, over 35 years after openly cursing the prospect of being a teacher, teaching was all I craved. I could never have predicted that I would work with small groups in open spaces, comfy living rooms, leafy parks, rec rooms in community centers, and church basements with rules we created for ourselves. As a teen, I couldn't imagine academic classes that included games and creative expression or an environment where every child felt safe, comfortable, and able to have their say. Yet with homeschoolers, I could do all of this. I could be flexible, abandon lesson plans when they weren't working and replace them with activities and goals suggested by the students themselves. Instead of feeling constricted by overcrowding and a standardized approach, I could expand the idea of what learning is. I could practice educational freedom.

As an educator, I am always learning and often attend professional development workshops, where I meet other teachers. If the group is small enough, we start by introducing ourselves, saying where we teach, the subject and age group. I am always the only teacher in the room working with homeschoolers, the only one teaching K-12, the only one not bound to a single subject and grade level. The other teachers ask me what it's like (mostly because they want to leave the public school system and are curious if they can find a way into the homeschooling community). I boldly tell them that I am on the luxury cruise liner of teaching jobs while other teachers have to make do with a leaky rowboat. When I say this, they look at me curiously as I try to explain.

First, imagine that you never have to fail a child. Teachers blink as they entertain this alien thought. Not only do I never have to fail a child, I never have to grade a child. I never compare one child to another or make a child feel bad because they are not "up to par." I never have to test a child! Testing, evaluation, and all reporting on homeschoolers in New York State is the job of the parent or legal guardian. Since I don't have to test, I don't teach to a test. Imagine no test prep! Already, teachers are stunned. But that's just the beginning.

I am never evaluated by a superior. My teacher friends have told me what it's like when an administrator enters their classroom without warning, clipboard in hand, assessing everything said and done as they check boxes off on their worksheet. At the end of the hour, the (possibly award-winning) teacher is told they failed to cover the desired number of items (not enough boxes were checked), maybe because they spent too much time allowing the children to ask questions or share ideas or because they focused on one point in depth rather than skirting over many or offered the same information in a variety of ways to accommodate learning differences. Often lesson plans are scheduled to the max without any allotted time for these activities, leaving children and teachers frustrated. School evaluations are about a checklist, not about what's happening in the room and inside children's minds.

My teacher evaluations happen naturally with students and parents with their letters of thanks and requests to hire me again or with their absence as they seek a different learning environment more suited to their needs. Homeschooled students are not forced to stay with a person assigned to them; they do not have to stick out the year. They have the freedom to choose where they get their learning and when, the methods, approach, materials, and resources. If something isn't working, they don't have to wait to change it.

As a teacher of homeschoolers, I am not bound to use a standardized curriculum or follow the Common Core, which, in my opinion, has awfully low standards. This decline in education is evident in the lack of basic skills in many young adults. The Common Core curriculum, enforced in most of the USA, has shockingly poor goals and results when compared to a fully engaged student learning what they love. Children growing up with Common Core standardized curriculum often say they hate learning. I've heard students say they never read a book in school that they liked. Working outside of the system, I am not limited to a single subject with points I am forced to cover. If a lesson or topic choice or approach is not working, I will change it. When the approach works, I will do more of it. This ability to choose and choose again is something that most school teachers don't experience. I can combine arts and sciences with literature and history, creating interdisciplinary, ever-changing curriculum influenced and guided by the students. We can do what excites us! More engagement equals more learning.

The ultimate capper, the icing on the cake, is that the child wants to be there. As I tell other teachers this, they look stunned as if what I've just said is unimaginable. They might have spent years in a classroom setting where hardly any children want to be. I remember sitting in fourth grade, looking longingly out the window, thinking if only I could fly out the window and leave this dull place. Having to sit there day after day was heartbreaking. Children often compare school to prison. Most teachers I meet have grown up in the same kind of classroom environment where they now teach, stuck in a stifling atmosphere for their whole lives. They cannot imagine a classroom where *every child actually wants to be*, a classroom that feels *alive*.

A teacher seated next to me in an educator's workshop, a slim fellow working in a New York City public high school, engaged me in conversation. "So, what is your goal with your students? I mean, do you teach drama?"

"Well, yes, and other subjects as well. But my goal is never curriculum."

His eyebrows went up. "What do you mean?"

"Don't get me wrong. There's a lot of curriculum involved, a lot of information and activity and writing happens, but curriculum is just a means to an end, never the end itself. My real goal, to be honest, is nothing short of a personal awakening for every student."

My new friend sits quietly, soberly thinking. I wonder if I've upset him. "Did I say something wrong?" I ask.

"Oh no," he answered and then added softly with his head low, "it's just... well..." softer still, "I don't do that." I felt sympathetic. Most teachers haven't experienced the kind of freedom that I have. Their job is likely overly demanding with constant pressure. They feel a weight on their shoulders.

Paolo Freire, author of *Pedagogy of the Oppressed* and the "Banking Concept of Education," wrote about the misconception of the teacher as the sole source of learning, a myth prevalent in American schools. In our current system, students regard the teacher as the well that contains all knowledge. They must approach the well and, with permission, draw from it in order to gain this precious knowledge. But that is not the truth! The truth is the world is the well; teacher and student go to the well *together* and draw from the well together. The world is an endless resource, a bottomless well, and we do not need permission but guidance and assistance at learning to draw from various resources in order to expand the learning experience. We need to learn how to learn! Resources abound, from the park on the corner (a naturalist's paradise), to your neighbors (with their own history and expertise), to museums, historic sites, concert halls, commemorative events. Research and resources exist far beyond libraries and the Internet; they include observation of anything and communication with anyone, even people you pass on the street. Resources in a classroom include every child's family and every child!

Today, I am grateful for my parents' work, which influenced me deeply, sometimes showing me what to do and sometimes showing me what not to do. My sister is now retired, relieved to no longer be working in the public school system, an environment she felt was draining and burdensome instead of supportive. Even now, we joke about our fervent teenage promise made repeatedly. We wanted to forge our own paths and not follow in our parents' footsteps. In the end, I grew into the teacher I never had and always wanted. I became a teacher I never could have imagined. My classes are the opposite of my childhood schooling— not boring but exciting! I get to fully participate in that excitement. We play! Create! Explore! Discover! Learn! Together!

Chapter Two

You Pick Two; I'll Pick Two

My three-year-old son and I peered up the wide staircase of the St. Agnes branch library, an old brownstone building on Manhattan's Amsterdam Avenue, and grabbed the heavy wooden banister as we ascended to the children's room. The high ceilings and walls heavy with woodwork cast a spell on my quiet son, even though he was typically shy. I am always comfortable in a library, perhaps because I grew up surrounded by books. My father was a professor of comparative literature, and books in many languages filled our spacious Victorian-style home in Brooklyn. Weekend afternoons often found us browsing used bookstores and wherever we traveled, to my delight, we visited libraries. I secretly hoped my children would inherit my love of books, but they both seemed uninterested.

"You pick two, and I'll pick two," I told my son. He barely reached the height of the second lowest row of shelves, with his head still in uncut curls bobbing down a long row of picture books. I placed two on a table by an empty child's chair, a fairytale and humorous rhymes of Dr. Seuss. He glanced at them and moved on. I waited, having made my choices, until he solemnly handed me his, a board book on whales and a selection of Aesop's Fables.

That evening, we read the four books during our bedtime reading ritual, and after that, the choice was his. He asked for *What is a Whale?* every single evening. By midweek, I ached for our next library visit when we would trade it in for something else. I was so bored reading that little book over and over! Finally, we went back to the library and, you guessed it, he renewed that book on whales. From then on, every time we went to the library, one of his two picks was a book on whales.

My older son had discovered his favorite section of the library years earlier and always made a bee line for the drawing books. He loved to draw and looked for new techniques to sketch his daily animals and superheroes. He also liked graphic novels and comics, opting for Tintin rather than grade-level readers, even though the vocabulary was more difficult.

I felt strongly about exposing them to my selections, books they would not normally have chosen, and believed that honoring their freedom of choice would help them connect to the library and to reading. It was only in hindsight years later that I realized their choices far outweighed my own. I thought I was teaching them, but they were actually teaching me. Their book choices revealed deep inner interests that sustained them for much of their lives. This was my first hands-on view of a child-led academic learning experience, and it took a long time for me to recognize its true value. By age 11 or 12, each of my sons mentioned college programs, respectively in art and marine biology, programs that I had no knowledge about. I was stunned. What 11-year-old brings up college? Years later, they pursued these very interests at their first-choice colleges, New York University (NYU) Film School and College of the Atlantic with a focus on marine sciences. Those early library selections, made before they could even read, were indicators of a child's innate process of discovering a unique path.

Chapter Three

A Unique Revolutionary War Experience

I started homeschooling my older son when he was age nine while my youngest was attending preK. The standard United States history school curriculum for fourth grade includes the Revolutionary War Era. To make the subject fun, I chose a comic book for the main text, Stan Mack's *Real-life American Revolution*. Other materials included *The History of US* by Joy Hakim, issues of Cobblestone Magazine, and *Johnny Tremaine* by Esther Forbes (historic fiction set in Boston in the Revolutionary War era). Naturally, we started with the comic book.

My son sped through all the material in a few short months. In December, he announced he was done. I suggested that he do a final project using the knowledge he gained. He thought for a moment and asked, "Can I make a gun?"

This was my son testing me because we didn't have toy guns in the house. He loved arguing with his mom! I thought for a moment, and then I watched his eyes go wide in surprise as I said, "You can make it out of wood or cardboard or any other material you think best. When it's done, you can show us what kind of rifle or musket it is and tell us where and when it was used. In fact, I think it would be a good project."

Suddenly, he lost interest in making a gun. He suggested, "What about a comic book? My own comic history of the Revolutionary War." I told him that was also an excellent idea. He went straight to work, drawing as he did every day, but this time it was comics about the Revolution.

This project allowed him to retell the story from a creative point of view. He displayed what he had learned through humorous drawings and amusing dialogue, which kept him fully engaged. In one comic, fish were seated at a table on the ocean floor calmly playing poker while sipping cups of tea as more tea spilled over the side of a boat docked in Boston Harbor, depicting the notorious Tea Party from the fish's point of view. In another panel, Ethan Allen and his Green Mountain Boys took over Fort Champlain in a dawn attack, surprising the British general who stood half-dressed in a striped pajama top and boxer shorts covered with big red hearts. Here was my son's love of art and humor, along with a detailed understanding of major events of the Revolution, with a focus on strategy and battle. Using his imagination to express these ideas revealed his depth of understanding. He remembered all of those facts because he had fun with them!

The rest of the year we learned history from field trips and reading. That spring, we went to Boston and walked the free, self-guided Freedom Trail starting in Boston Commons. Thanks to our reading *Johnny Tremaine*, the trail came to life for my son. He leaped in the air when he saw a plaque for The Green Dragon Tavern. "Look!" he pointed at the tavern unable to contain his excitement. "This is where the Sons of Liberty hatched their plans!" Outside of the Paul Revere House, he stretched to his full height, trying to peer into the windows before taking the tour. He sang and danced around the Old North Church Tower where the lights had hung and reminded us that Dawes, not Revere, actually finished the famous ride. Our walk along the Freedom Trail capped this curriculum, which we finished with a fabulous family dinner at an Italian Restaurant in Boston's North End.

Five years later, I was glad I had saved all those materials when I started homeschooling my younger son, about to enter fourth grade. We opened up Stan Mack's comic book history and just a few pages in encountered the famous quote, "The pen is mightier than the sword."

"How can that be?" my son asked, perplexed. "How can a pen be more powerful than a weapon in battle?"

My almost-nine-year-old asked this question every day for over a week. We ended up talking about the value of free speech and why some world leaders fear it. We went around the globe, exploring different kinds of governments with varying levels of freedom of speech and freedom of the press. Finally, after days of discussion, he said he understood how words could be more powerful than weapons. Then we turned the page.

At the top of the next page were facts about Roger Williams, who founded Rhode Island because he believed in the separation of church and state. My son was curious. "Separation of Church and State? What's that? Why should they be separate?" Down we went into another question rabbit hole, spending the next week or more exploring a single idea.

After a year of study, we had explored a fraction of the same material that had lasted just a few months with his older brother. Yet, we went beyond the content of the books, exploring ideas behind the Revolutionary War at such an intense level that sometimes it felt like a high school or university course, definitely not fourth grade. My son's questions led us to a course in the philosophy and thought of the era rather than military strategy and how America won the war.

In a typical classroom, both of my sons would have felt dissatisfied and had a comparatively poor learning experience. Homeschooling allowed them to focus on what interested them most. They were each free to ask questions that would have been ignored in a traditional classroom or to make jokes and be silly, all which would have been viewed as disruptive or a nuisance instead of creative engagement. The boys moved along at an individual pace, rare in most classrooms, and found what they needed from a wide variety of resources. I was unprepared for their unique takes on the subject and amazed that they each had a dramatically different learning experience using the same materials.

This was an important learning experience for me: the child, not the material, dictated the approach and material learned. If there was a required standardized outcome of a written essay or exam, both might have done poorly. If there had been a test on mundane facts, they would not have been motivated to study. Yet, they surpassed my expectations. Using their curiosity, questions, and responses to guide their direction, they achieved a deeper level of understanding, with attention to detail and a surprising level of retention of information.[1]

---

1. Find history resources in E – Historical Fiction Syllabus.

Chapter Four

Whale And Animal Curriculum

A round age six or seven, my older, artistic son started making board games that were full of mazes leading to imaginary worlds. He was also writing and illustrating handmade books about mouse adventures. His younger brother grew up in awe of his older sibling and when he was six-going-on-seven decided to make his own board game. But I knew his would never be a maze to Gnome Land. I encouraged him to follow his natural inclination as a nonfiction reader and lover of ocean mammals and suggested a game about whales.

We cut index cards in half, the perfect size for fact cards. My son researched facts on his own and dictated to me while I did the writing. I had little to no knowledge about whales, but that didn't hinder the project. My son never assumed that an adult would act as the sole resource for information on whale facts or any subject for that matter. He could learn on his own, beyond me, simply because I created a safe space where he could. He watched videos at home on ocean life, browsed books on whales for children and adults, and found his own resources for whale information.

As a makeshift game board, we used four strips of cardboard laid on a table-top in the shape of a rectangle; the cardboard strips formed a four-sided path like the rim of the board in Sorry or Monopoly. With a black marker, we drew lines that sectioned the cardboard strips into squares and wrote game instructions in some of the squares such as "pick a card" or "roll again" or "move back two spaces." Game instructions were now part of the game board path. The deck of handmade whale fact cards was placed in the center of the open rectangle with dice at the ready. Any age could play. The questions and format were easy, even though a lot of work went into writing, drawing, and figuring out the math and strategy before the game was complete. My son had gone over and over what it took to win, creating a final loop where some players could get stuck having to move back two or three spaces again and again and adding a rule that you had to roll the exact number needed to reach the winning square.

A few years later, my whale-obsessed son, now about age eight, said the questions had become too easy, so he made a second, more advanced deck of cards. Players could freely choose from the easy deck or the advanced deck. I was able to answer all the easy questions, like "What is the world's largest whale?" (the blue whale) but was stumped by questions in the advanced deck such as how much does an average adult blue whale weigh (I still have no idea). For years, my son entertained family and friends with this game.

New York Home Educators Alliance (NYCHEA), the largest homeschool support group in New York City, hosts an annual science fair for homeschoolers. I suddenly realized the fair was only a few weeks away, so I asked my son, now age 11, if he wanted to make an exhibit. He thought there wasn't enough time, so I suggested he take out the whale board game he had made when he was younger and see if he could polish up the project.

He had already improved the questions when he made an advanced deck; now, he decided to improve the board and the playing pieces or pawns. We copied a world map of the northern hemisphere and glued it onto a large sheet of foam board. He penciled four different migratory paths across the oceans. Each path had the same number of spaces that stretched across the board, making four separate, equal paths instead of one that ran around the circumference of the board. I helped him make four different cardboard whales, each about an inch high, one for each species that migrated on each path, four miniature whales. He titled his game "The Whale Race Game." Each player drew cards and answered questions that helped their whale race from warm breeding areas to winter feeding grounds and back again. Some whales raced across the Pacific Ocean, some across the Atlantic. This was the first board game I saw other than Risk that was a map, but the Risk map is not accurate; the Whale Race Game borrowed its map from a world atlas. The game taught science as well as geography and was a big hit at the Science Fair. All the kids wanted to play, imagining their little cardboard whales coursing through ocean waves with each move.

Through my son's board game project, he learned to do research, take notes, apply facts to a game, decorate the board and game pieces, write instructions, and engage others to learn from his research. His learning went beyond biology and writing. He studied world geography in the migratory paths of whales as well as cultural history and practices related to whale hunting and preservation. He used math to predict possible outcomes of his game and edited the game instructions to make it more difficult to win. In the end, every major academic subject had been employed in the making of this game.

As part of his research process, I introduced my son to the specialized library in the American Museum of Natural History in New York City, where he browsed research material published by scientists employed by the museum. Though he was in sixth grade, he poured over pages written by university professors for graduate students. When you are motivated to learn, grade level ceases to matter. My son wasn't daunted by the material. Instead, he was excited to try and answer his own questions such as how are baby whales raised and how do we know? Can scientists observe whale behavior in the ocean's depths?

One summer we had the chance to take a family vacation. Discussing possible destinations, our youngest, usually quiet, piped up. "I've never walked on a beach," he said softly. How could that be? All the New York City culture we had at our fingertips suddenly seemed small compared to the simple delights of walking on a beach. "And I've never seen a whale...." That clinched it. I checked out whale watching opportunities from New York City to Canada and discovered Tadoussac in Quebec. Two great rivers, the St. Lawrence and the Sagaunay, meet there. Opposing currents of the rivers churn up krill from the bottom, giving whales a picnic on the surface. Scientists and tourists come from all over the world to watch the show.

We arrived in Tadoussac on a river ferry and drove through the mist to a sprawling white-walled, red-roofed hotel. We had the feeling that we had stepped into a storybook world. Our first task was to arrange whale watching. We opted for a small boat rather than a large, more protected vessel because we didn't want to see the whales through a thick window. We craved a close-up experience where we could feel the spray. The weather stalled us, but just two days later, we were up early to get a front row seat on a small boat with no protection other than the heavy boots and wet weather gear supplied by the guide. Our boat chased whales for over an hour without luck, and the captain was about to give up when two minke whales and a humpback showed up looking for dinner.

Unfortunately, our ocean-loving son gets seasick, we discovered, but he bore it well and never complained. He kept his eyes closed, resting his head, until he heard oohs and aahs from fellow passengers and then, holding his queasy stomach, he stood up wide-eyed and leaned over the edge to watch, never once taking his eyes away from the show.

Whales leaped into the air with water dripping from their baleen and then slammed their bodies on the water's surface, slapping the krill down their throats in a single movement before lifting their giant heads up as water dripped from their mouths, only to do it over again. Maybe it was the easy pickings and no-effort swallowing that gave the whales an aura of jubilation. Maybe that sense of jubilation was just a reflection of how every passenger felt. The whales leaped and danced on the water! My son was rapt, as if he was holding his breath. We had front-row seats to the best show on earth!

Another highlight of the trip, even better than walking on the beach and eating fresh-caught river salmon for supper, was our visit to the Marine Mammal Interpretation Centre, a museum devoted to whales. Interacting with exhibits on the science and history of whales, my son pondered the ancient nature of this animal. He asked me, "If whales are the oldest mammals, do they know the oldest stories?" This question grabbed my imagination. Who knows where a learning journey will go? Who knows what will strike a note of inspiration? His question led me to write the following poem, a memory of a shared learning experience, a give and take between a parent and a child in love with the mystery of whales.

What Stories Do the Whales Tell?

What stories do the whales tell?
From what ancient weather bell?
What seasons of old, what climes retold,
In how many ice ages did they dwell?

What magic figures did they know?
What gnomes, what sprites, what elfin foe?
What wizards told them where to go
When they moved from land and snow?

What tales are told to baby whales
By mammals of the widest girth?
What legendary truths evolved
From the oldest creatures of the earth?

Do humpbacks hum their teachings
To their children in a rhyme?
What stories do the whales tell
In their wisdom of all time?[1]

---

1. For Animal-Themed Curriculum, see I – Animal Themed Curriculum

Chapter Five

High School Theater All-Subject Curriculum

When my first-born was ten or eleven, he announced that he would become a costume designer. I hate to admit that I laughed out loud. "You? A costume designer? You're going to spend hours at a sewing machine when you can't sit still for five minutes?"

"Oh, Mom, you don't understand. I'm going to have my costumes sewn *for me.*"

Exasperated, I asked, "What is it about costume design? Why choose that?"

I could see his frustration as he explained what was obvious to him. "See Mom, every day in my sketchbooks I draw superheroes with their super-pets and super-vehicles. Then one day, I noticed that I was making all the heroes the same shape. I'd created a template that I drew over and over again for each hero. What defined each one was their costume! When I realized the costume was creating the character, that's when I knew," he clenched his fist with determination. "I have to be a costume designer!"

I was stunned. He had won me over. The costume defined the character! I had witnessed a profound realization by an artist at work, an insight that refined his direction.

Every year, I asked my kids to choose someone to interview. My younger son had met whale scientists and marine biologists, peppering them with carefully-researched questions. Now, my older son asked to meet designers and costumers. In interviews with a wardrobe master and, later, a costumer designer, he asked how they found their way to that job. One day, he returned from an interview and commented, "I didn't know that Boston University has a costume program. It must be so cool to go there!"

Halloween became his personal passion, starting new designs every year in early November. He delighted himself and his younger brother with wizard capes and Merlin hats. One year, he wore fake body armor as a wounded explorer and was stopped by people on the street who actually thought he was hurt. In his teens, he transformed himself into a devil with red horns growing out of his hair, ready to go out on Halloween and offer someone "whatever they wanted, for a small price, only your soul!" as he cackled.

In his high school years, he pursued mask making at the School of Visual Arts in their Continuing Education Department that had no age minimum. Masks crowned his costumes! He attended medieval fairs, where appearing in costume got you a discounted ticket and lots of attention. Once he went as a black bird, obscured by a beaked mask and a massive black feathered cloak that he had spent months making.

At age 16, he volunteered to design and build a set for an Off-Off Broadway play. After a long day of set building, he came home exhausted, head hanging, with news that he was no longer aiming at costume design. He explained that he had spent over an hour talking the director out of painting the entire set bright orange. He groaned, "Now I know it's not enough to be a costume designer. *I have to be the director!*"

By 11th or 12th grade, he said he was done with traditional academics. "All I want to study is theater. Just theater."

"But how will you fulfill your requirements for college? What will you study for history this year?"

"I'm just doing theater."

"How about the history of theater?" He gave a nod to agree.

For literature, he read plays, starting with the ancient Greeks and going around the world. He read Japanese Noh puppet theater plays, medieval plays of Europe, anti-apartheid plays of South Africa, all the way to contemporary plays produced in London and New York.

He learned about the history of the theater, the stage and the director, discovering the earliest directors and how the shape and design of the stage changed over time. He explored the work of great directors and attended plays with experimental direction. We saw an unforgettable production of *Hamlet* directed by Peter Brook with an international cast. Our seats were on floor cushions in the first row, where we witnessed up close a single cardboard box used as a throne, a bed, a grave, and a table. We watched the skull of poor Yorick become animated like a talking puppet on a stick.

Pursuing set design, he wanted to learned about design blueprints. With the help of his math tutor, a manual, and set of tools, he soldered circuitry and read and created blueprints. He then designed a miniature theater set made to scale using the metric system and Autocad, software for set designers that I had never heard of. Math and science are not requirements for New York homeschoolers in grades 11 and 12, but these activities had us reporting those subjects for all high school years.

Art and theater were his focus, so my son developed a portfolio for college admissions to an Arts or Theater Department with drawings and photographs of his set designs, masks, and mask-making process. His writing was screenplays and essays. He studied film as well, comparing adaptations to original works, noting directorial styles and techniques, and learning about the history and social impact of movies and movie-making.

My son learned far more history this way than he would have with a traditional approach. I was amazed at how comprehensive his theater curriculum became not only including every required subject but also preparing him for the future he desired. This ease and flexibility with fulfilling requirements can be applied to any interests and any part of the schooling or life path, allowing the individual to enrich their inner world while learning from the outer world. Examples I have seen with other homeschooled teens include swapping the standard high school chemistry requirement for neuroscience or the earth science requirement with astronomy or botany and foraging. The flexibility to address curriculum and requirements any way you like at the individual's chosen pace and direction with the ability to pick and choose along the way teaches empowerment, clarifies direction, and strengthens sense of self.[1]

---

1. See H – Theater Themed Curriculum

Chapter Six

Student-Led Social Studies in Elementary and High School

Homeschooling my sons led me to offer classes so they would have group experiences. That led to working with other groups as well as doing tutorials. Five-year-old Frankie, the younger sister of two other students, visited me to make art projects. She bounced into my apartment, her caramel skin glowing with excitement, dark brown eyes peeking out from behind a mass of chocolate corkscrew curls. Giggling, we munched on blueberries while we made art. When her new cousin was about to be born, she decided to make him an alphabet book. Each page had one letter, collaged from recycled trash. The result was a foldable accordion book made of foam board, an alphabet board book full of color and texture that a baby could touch and read. There were no words so the alphabet could be used to introduce words in any language.

Frankie had resisted learning Spanish even though her family was bilingual. Instead, she asked for French! The next gift she wanted to make for her beloved baby cousin was a French dictionary. Knowing her cousin would grow up with

Spanish and English, I suggested a trilingual dictionary. Frankie chose a handful of words she thought were important for babies to know, like *ball* and *blueberry*, and we glued in pictures of each item. On the cover were the words for each language in red, blue, and green, color coding the words in the book in the same color as the language. Only a handful of pages long, this is the only trilingual dictionary I've ever seen, even more unique since it was for a baby!

Years later, I got a call from Frankie, now in her first year of high school (ninth grade), asking if she could visit. I wondered if she wanted to talk about homeschooling. Regardless of the reason, I told her to come right over. She arrived armed with notes, ready for a serious discussion on homeschooling. She had attended public school for most of her childhood and was now in a specialized art school in New York City. She found the art program satisfying but the academics were sorely lacking ("Boring!"), and even though she'd made friendships she thought would last, the social scene was rife with bullying and meanness. But before she talked to her parents about homeschooling, she wanted to have a plan ready.

"I don't want this to be any more work for them," she said, concerned. "Their first question will be about my art, and I've already figured that out." The Art Students League had a good deal on classes, where she could not only maintain the level of instruction she'd been getting but raise the level and increase the hours. She knew her parents would give her permission to take adult classes, and she was excited about the courses. So we set out to plan her academic subjects. I asked her what period of history and part of the world she wanted to study for social studies.

There was no hesitation. "I want to know the truth about Black history, African and African-American."

"Well, you're in luck because there's a great series called *Africa's Great Civilizations*, hosted by Henry Louis Gates, Jr. It aired on PBS, and now it's streaming."

"Oh!" Excited, she scribbled down the title.

"When you watch the series, take notes. Write down any questions you have. Then choose one aspect or fact to research more about."

Frankie agreed.

Periodically, Frankie visited me with her questions and research. After African history, she moved to Afro-Latina history, exploring her family's cultural heritage.

Week after week, I asked if she had new questions, and every week she repeated the same one: "Why do teachers lie to you?"

That's a big question! I explained that the short answer is they don't know any better, but I encouraged her to ask more probing questions such as why did these lies appear in the first place and how and why are they perpetuated? Frankie's question implied another question: Why is history (or social studies) so boring in the classroom when it's about us, our world, and our history? This question is particularly nagging when you discover the many complicated layers in history, often hidden from us, and the truth that it's not boring at all. The standardized, traditional approach to history is worse than boring; it's crushing! Limiting students to standardized resources, often presented as the "right" resources, ultimately serves to lessen a student's sense of self and prevents them from having a sense of history. That lack of history creates a greater potential for intolerance and misunderstanding. Only through learning the truth of our own history can we understand our heritage and know more about who we are. This leads to more than personal insights. The knowledge of self adds to a student's internal strength, outward awareness, and ability to communicate and learn from others. We cannot share our heritage until we know it ourselves.
1

---

1. See E – Historical Fiction Syllabus

Chapter Seven

Finding Your Genre

Two families I had met on my travels to Australia met me in New York City. With mixed emotions, we greeted with deep hugs. We had lost a mutual friend the year before, the man who had introduced us, and they made this trip in his honor. Two moms with three kids piled into a walk-up apartment on Manhattan's upper west side chosen because it was near my improv classes. We spent as much time together as we could.

One evening we sat and talked at my apartment in the Bronx, where I served them a home-cooked dinner of baked salmon and cherry pie. After dinner, the older kids went into reading mode, but the youngest, Tessa, was bored. I showed her a bookcase of children's books and encouraged her to browse. After scanning each shelf, she asked if I had more. I led her to shelves full of young-adult historical fiction arranged by time and place. She pored over these but found nothing appealing. Finally she asked, "Do you have any Edgar Allen Poe?"

Tessa was seven or eight, so her question surprised me. I had given away most of my mysteries, but surely I had some Poe somewhere. I found it in a short story anthology for college students. Tessa now had her bliss as she settled into a chair with her nose in the book, oblivious to distraction.

What third grader asks for Poe or even knows about Poe? One who loves mysteries! This was Tessa's favorite genre. I suggested to her mom that she learn everything through this genre that she loved so much. Science could be forensics. Reading would include books adapted into Hitchcock movies and other mysteries with a film viewing after each reading and a discussion comparing book with movie. Math would include logic and strategy with word problems based on detective stories. History would include historical fiction mysteries and archeology from a detective's point of view.

Before this incident, I had not realized that a genre, rather than a topic, could be the personalized focus of an all-subject curriculum. The devilish delights of a good mystery can lead everywhere! The same is true for other genres. It is possible to learn American history entirely through popular music, world history through great art, and the growth of any civilization through short stories and novels. [1]

---

1. Mystery-themed curriculum resources available at LaurieBlockSpigel.com/resources

Chapter Eight

Finding Your Setting

A massage therapist who was a lifelong student of her profession told me how she discovered her direction. As a teenager, she was asked what environment she wanted to work in. This was the first time the question was posed with a focus on the setting rather than the profession itself. She had heard many times, "What do you want to be when you grow up (or leave school)?" but had always felt stumped for an answer. This was the first time she heard, "Where do you want to be?" Where! Instead of what or who!

Instantly the idea of working in a hospital popped into her head. She did not feel any urge to become a doctor or nurse or take on any traditional hospital role, but when asked to focus on a setting, she suddenly found a hospital appealing. That was where she found her first jobs: in a local hospital. Her exposure to that environment led her to look at alternative therapies and, eventually, to massage. It still amused her that she had felt no attraction to health-related professions, yet she was drawn to hospitals.

Sometimes, we overlook the obvious and neglect to ask ourselves an important question in different ways that might help us to see something in a new light. Each environment is a place of learning that is more involved than a classroom can be. Choosing a workplace environment and offering to volunteer or intern can result in a free or paid education, often leading to employment in a place that continues to inspire and educate.

If the environment permits it, anyone can learn whatever he chooses to learn; and if the individual permits it, the environment will teach him everything it has to teach. ~Viola Spolin, Improvisation for the Theater

Chapter Nine

I'll Prove It To You

My son met his future wife in college on the shores of Frenchman's Bay in the Gulf of Maine, a perfect setting for romance. Both fair, reasonable people, they tend to be easygoing, but while they were getting to know each other, there were bound to be disagreements.

One day she asked him, "What makes you think you can do whatever you want?"

"What are you talking about?" he furrowed his brow.

"Do you think you can do whatever you want to?"

"Well, yeah...."

"What makes you think that? What makes you so special?"

"What are you talking about? Anyone can do what they want to do."

"No, you're wrong. Everyone can't. I can't make my living on the water, on boats. I can't make my living on a farm. I can't do what I want to do! What makes you think *you* can?"

The world has many ways of implying that we can't do the things we want to do. No one had expressly told her that she could never do these things, but it was strongly implied. She grew up in a landlocked area, so how could she work on the ocean? Her grandfather nearly lost everything farming. How could farming be a realistic goal?

"But anyone can do what they want," he insisted. "I'll prove it to you."

The next year, they took a term off to go to Ireland and work on a farm they found through WWOOF (Worldwide Opportunities in Organic Farming, which offers room and board in exchange for farm work). They got full school credit since they were fulfilling a college requirement of a ten-week internship. After two weeks on a horse farm, they spent ten weeks on a goat farm run by a blind farmer. They learned so much! Then, in their senior year, they spent 12 weeks at sea with the Ocean Classroom, working alongside crew members while studying marine biology (once again earning full college credit) while sailing from Maine to the Caribbean.

My son had chosen his college for ocean studies. He learned to scuba dive, handle boats, and identify whale sounds. He created a museum exhibit on whale sounds and presented a paper on whales at an international conference on cetaceans. After graduating, my son became... a blacksmith! We were surprised, but this was what he wanted to learn next. He apprenticed to a blacksmith, studied metal-making techniques, and attended the New England School of Metalwork, where he learned how to make knives and tools from scratch. Then he wanted to learn how to build houses so he took a job with a local contractor.

After graduating, my future daughter-in-law worked as a deckhand for the Portland Schooner Company. For nine summers, she climbed the rigging, tucked in the sails, and swung by a rope (called a line) onto the dock, taking tourists over the waters of Casco Bay on beautiful, antique wooden schooners. After nearly a decade of sailing professionally, she explored new directions, working at other things she wanted to learn.

Through experience, my son proved to his beloved what he had always known. Yet, they went a step further. Now they not only know that they can do whatever they want; they also know how to get paid to learn it!

Both my sons taught their traditionally-schooled wives to feed their own curiosity. These young men proved to their wives that we can all learn and pursue what we want. Even if you don't know your purpose and are unsure of what is in your heart, you still have the freedom to search and try to find out. Through that search, we discover more than knowledge and skill. We discover ourselves!

Chapter Ten

Ten Reasons Why Self-Directed Learning Works So Well

A fter applying what worked with my own kids to individual students and classroom experiences, I realized there are many reasons why a child-led approach has surprisingly good results.

1. When interest and curiosity are present, LEARNING IS ALREADY HAPPENING.

2. When the student is genuinely interested, learning is fun.

3. When learning is fun, the mind is playful and fully engaged.

4. With full engagement and playfulness, creativity, problem solving, and research are more enjoyable and ultimately fruitful.

5. Interest equals motivation. Self-directed learning is intensified, deeper,

and more meaningful than imposed or forced learning. More information is learned and applied; there is a greater retention of information.

6. Unexpected results, often surpassing expectations, happen when curiosity is alert and allowed to lead.

7. Actively following one's own interests results in connecting with others of like mind regardless of age, background, and geographical location.

8. The pursuit of what we love endures, leading to extended learning experiences. This results in opportunities, confidence, and expertise.

9. Self-directed learning allows us to be ourselves, encourages self-discovery, and leads to self-awareness. Self-realization is the ultimate learning experience for all of us.

10. Ultimately, we each choose our own direction in work and in life. Self-directed learning gives us an early start. Others suffer through a standardized enforced education, waiting for their "real" learning to begin.

The Heart of the
Process

Chapter Eleven

Hearing and Listening

I walked down the sidewalk with my six-year-old son as he ran ahead, then behind, then hurried to catch up. We slowed as we approached his new school, a two-story brick building with a playground overlooking the water. It seemed an idyllic setting for a public school. Inside, our footsteps echoed down dark halls. We entered the office to register for the coming year, where we met the principal, a robust woman with a loud voice. "You're so lucky!" she boomed. "You have Mrs. Berg for your teacher. She's the best! She could pick any grade she wanted, and she chose first! Why, there she is now!"

Just outside the office we ran into Mrs. Berg, a short woman with close-cropped hair, her arms full of papers. "This is your new teacher," I introduced her to my son. He looked up at her slyly with a half-smile and suddenly fell backwards to the floor in a mock faint, swooning with one hand across his forehead. He lay there, his closed eyes flickering open to see if he had entertained his teacher. Mrs. Berg was not smiling. She eyed my ham of a son with a stony glare. *Uh oh*, I thought. *This could be a tough year.*

Parent-teacher orientation was a week away. That would be my only chance to ask a question if I got lucky enough to ask one. It took me a day to decide what was most important to my son, a single topic I could ask about. I spent the rest of the week thinking about how to phrase the question.

The day arrived with a room full of parents squeezed into children's seats, each seat attached to a desk, allowing little room for an adult to breathe. The moment came for questions; my hand went up, and I was given the nod so I spoke. "What are your goals for the creative expression of each child this year?" I knew that my son would put up with a lot of nonsense and hardship if he could express himself creatively. By asking the question in this way, I presumed that the teacher had such goals.

Without hesitation, she replied, "Mrs. Spigel, in a class of 34 children, there's no room for creative expression." I felt like she had just thrown me a medicine ball that hit me in the gut. Then she mumbled, "Oops, that didn't come out quite right," and pointed to the next parent for another question.

I silently promised myself that I would volunteer to teach creative writing. At home, my son was dictating his dreams and adventure stories, turning them into little illustrated books. I could bring that energy into his classroom and not only give my son the chance to express himself but also give it to every child in the room. I waited for a few days of school to pass so things could settle down before I asked Mrs. Berg if I could volunteer to teach writing.

"Mrs. Spigel, what we really need is someone to watch recess and wear a whistle."

"You can get someone else to do that. I can teach creative writing."

"Mrs. Spigel, we don't need that right now. We need someone wearing a whistle."

But I persisted. Every day when I walked my kid to school, I stopped by again to offer writing help. Finally, Mrs. Berg said yes. I could come one morning a week and sit in the back, working with one child at a time. I couldn't wait.

On my first day, I was shown to a round table in the back, large enough for four or more children to sit around. Two chairs were positioned before a huge lined pad that lay on the table with a black marker next to it. I sat in one of the chairs, and a round-faced, red-cheeked boy was brought to the table to sit beside me. I realized quickly that working with this boy was not going to be easy. The teacher had started me with her most problematic child. He was hesitant to speak, and his language skills were poor. I was prepared to take dictation from first graders but wondered if this child would be able to dictate to me. I asked him what he wanted to write about, and he shrugged. Then I asked him what he liked to do on the weekend, and he grinned. Tilting his face up, he told me about his big brother who visits on weekends and plays ball with him. I picked up the marker and uncapped it so I could write. Suddenly, he grabbed the marker out of my hand and put it to the top of the page, struggling with the first letter, *M*, for "My brother." He paused to ask me how to spell each word and then changed his mind to choose a better word, *exciting* instead of *fun*, fussing over the x and c to make sure he got it right.

Just then the paraprofessional came by to observe us. An immigrant woman who spoke with an accent, untrained as a teacher, she worked in this classroom every day and knew the children. She interrupted us, speaking to me in a low voice. "Harold, he is very slow. He is soooo slow," she clucked sympathetically and shook her head back and forth.

Harold's body tensed, the gripped marker froze mid-word, mid-letter. I shot up out of my chair and looked her in the eye, our faces inches apart. "He is doing just fine! He is doing *great!*" I sat down immediately, prepared to ignore further interruption. The assistant moved on.

I was concerned about how Harold felt overhearing a demeaning remark about him. But he wasn't ashamed or sad. He glowed at me, beaming a look of adoration. My anger at the assistant vanished. I hadn't expected to see hero worship on a child's face. From that moment on, Harold would have done anything for me. Minutes later, he had filled the page, ending on the very last line. He regarded his work, and me, with pride.

Whenever I visited the class, children called out, "Pick me, Mrs. Spigel! Pick me!" They would reach out and touch my clothes as I walked between rows of desks to the round table in the back. I had no control over who was chosen; that was up to the teacher. When a child returned to their seat, others whispered, "What did she ask you to write about?" The answers were always different. "What you did on the weekend." "Your favorite animal." "Your mom and dad." This is because I never actually asked them to write about anything specific.

Instead, I listened to them talk about what mattered, which was different with each child, and I encouraged them to write about that.

The children loved working with me because I listened. The assistant teachers' demeaning comment, said directly above the child's head while he was trying to work, is an example of someone who had never really listened to a child in their care and who continued to ignore him. She never once glanced at him when she made that cutting remark. She had overlooked his strengths as if his weaknesses obliterated them. Harold may have had language difficulties, but he worked as hard or harder than any other student I have ever had. Harold was impressive!

At the end of the morning, when the children left for lunch and I got ready to go home, I handed large pages of handwritten student work to the teacher. Both teacher and paraprofessional marveled at the pages, and they asked me, "How did you get them to do it?" This question left me speechless because I never *got* them to do anything! I *let* them do it! I let them write what they wanted to write. I didn't push them or tell them what to do. Instead, I created an environment that felt safe and supportive, that empowered the student to share what mattered most. I made them feel supported in their choice, which added to their sense of safety. If I had tried to force the process, I doubt if much writing would have resulted. My method was to sit back, listen, and allow them to connect with what they were doing. They always put a piece of their life on the page.

At home, I tried to explain to my husband what was happening in that first grade classroom, perhaps in an effort to explain it to myself. Sometimes I wondered if I was doing anything at all! "It's as if I sit there, and they grab the pencil and start to write, and I continue to just sit. In those moments, I imagine there's an invisible window or small door hanging in the space between us, floating above the middle of our table, shimmering in the air above the enormous lined pad where the child is writing. No one sees the invisible window or door but me. And no one sees that I have unlatched it, and it's swung open. There it hangs, an invisible open door, existing in the space above and between me and the child. And I sit and wait. While I wait, the child writes and works to express something on the page. And all of a sudden, without any warning, I imagine the child leaps through the open door. No one sees the leap but me. Yet, I know it happened. I see it and feel it, a shift in the air between us. I recognize the child's pride of effort and achievement, the acquiring of new skill, and their satisfaction of self-expression. Somehow, the child takes a leap through an invisible door while I sit back and watch. What do I do? Nothing. I unlatch an invisible door and wait. The child does all the work." How could I explain such a mysterious phenomenon? I couldn't understand it myself because all I did was listen to the children and let it happen.

Listening is different from hearing since it requires more thought and added patience; it is never used to coerce. Hearing is often done shallowly on purpose as we try to ignore unwanted noise or daydream while pretending to listen to someone boring or ignore the world at large when we are on the phone or in a conversation where hear only what we want to hear because in that moment we are only listening to ourselves.

Many games are available that focus on listening skills, notably theater games created by Viola Spolin that heighten sensory awareness. Children and adults alike love these games, including "Listening to the Environment," "Sending Hearing Out," "Adding Color," and "Dubbing," a game where voices and sound effects are created for silent players. A traditional children's game called "Dog and Bone" demands full auditory attention from all players. The most overactive, noisiest kids have begged for this game! Normally, it might be hard for them to exercise this level of control, but in a game it becomes a worthwhile challenge. Antsy children with ADHD remain stock still, and nonstop talkers maintain silence. The child playing the dog hopes to catch the thief before they steal the bone to keep the game going while the thief works to steal the bone soundlessly so they can be the dog in the next round. When I hear teachers and parents say, "These children just don't listen!" I think that all they have to do is play "Dog and Bone," and just like magic the children will be listening.

Yet, perhaps **children don't listen because they don't feel listened to.** Children who have challenges or difficulties are listened to less. Children who are talkative and demanding are listened to less. Children in a traditional classroom setting with over 20 students in a room with one teacher are listened to less. If you want children to listen to you and give you respect, first you must listen to them and give them respect!

There is a serious need for parents and teachers to play these games. We need to sharpen our sensory awareness when working with children. We must listen outwardly and inwardly to our intuition and our impulses. Spolin games teach us how to access intuition through play. Actively playing the games, we transform into intuitive learners and teachers.

Sometimes, I have to reflect on what I have heard in order to listen more deeply. A new student attending a class held in my home asked me, "Can I look through all of the cupboards and drawers?" Short, dark-haired Etan behaved shyly, but his question was bold and direct. I said no without hesitation and felt slightly wary. Afterwards I thought about Etan's question. Instead of reacting personally, worried he would go through my belongings, I asked myself what his question said about him as a person. At our next class, I told Etan, "You must be very curious to want to know what is behind every door and drawer, and being curious is a sign of intelligence." Immediately, he looked at me with new respect. From that moment, Etan dropped his guard and started to express himself creatively. He wrote and illustrated stories about a cowboy pencil whose antics made the class laugh. Once he felt understood and appreciated, he relaxed and found his voice.

New students often feel wary at first. I offer them the choice to watch or participate. They can play or observe. I met Ireni in a middle school playwriting class. On the first day she joined the circle for a warm-up game of "Pussy Wants a Corner" (or "Kitty Wants a Corner"), but stood still, arms crossed in front of her chest, refusing to make eye contact with anyone. She occupied a physical spot in the game yet didn't play. I thought to myself, "We'll see how long this lasts" and let her do as she liked while the rest of us played around her. Suddenly, Ireni broke her pose and joined in the fun. Her unannounced observation had lasted mere moments. She was now an integral member of the class.

Avery was a new student in my writing class. His mother let me know that he had been shamed in school and every day had come home with his head hanging lower. She warned me that Avery was a non-writer and to keep my expectations low. I told her not to worry, whatever he did was fine with me. That first day, I told Avery he could watch and join in whenever he felt like it. I was prepared for him to not write for weeks, but at the second class, he showed up with a draft of a story. It took only one class, where he felt no pressure and witnessed no one being pressured or judged, to relax and start to write.

Listening requires patience, respect, and a suspension of all judgement. I catch myself presuming to know what comes next, mentally finishing a student's sentence and thinking, erroneously, that I know what they mean. When those sentences were finally completed, we all had an awakening.

When a student has difficulty or experiences a lack of motivation, I reflect on the problem, seeking a deeper level of listening. In meditation, I ask my inner self, or I ask the student in my mind, to show me the problem and perhaps offer a solution. The meditation process quiets the anxiety I feel when things don't go well. It helps me to suspend judgement and not take the situation personally. I gain insight, partly because my emotions are tabled so my feelings don't get in the way. When I next see the student, I can take a more thoughtful approach. If I'm not sure what to do, I have learned it is best to back off, watch and listen, and refrain from pushing or even asking. Let the child ask or show me in some other way what is needed. Perhaps through their body language or my noticing where their focus is and how it changes, I will see a path we might take together as student and teacher.

I met Yasmin when she was 11 or 12 and came to observe a class in my home. She had left school because she was bullied for believing in fairies. Yasmin's wavy dark hair bounced down her back, and her solid shape settled into the circle of literature discussion students. She introduced herself in a soft, high-pitched voice and sat with her head held high, almost defiant. She looked down the walls of my living room, lined with floor-to-ceiling bookcases, and asked me about the contents of my library — the first and only student to do so. I was charmed.

Yasmin signed up for my classes that fall, including playwriting. Remembering a sensitive, imaginative, intelligent girl, I looked forward to her work. But her first draft was incoherent, and the preliminary assignments were unfinished.

When she shared her work in class, the other students found it confusing and wanted to know why she had ignored the guidelines. As the students chimed in, her work became an example of what not to do. This was unfortunate. Her face twisted as she held back the tears. If only she had sent me her work in advance, as requested, I would have been able to discuss it with her outside of class.

Later, when I meditated on Yasmin, I saw tiny, invisible fairies dancing around her face. They sped past her eyes with a mischievous glee, spinning in colors, encircling her head. They giggled, delighting in distracting her. Was this why Yasmin couldn't focus on her work? Because fairies were constantly dancing in front of her eyes?

Years earlier, when my son's fake faint distressed his first grade teacher, she was not charmed. She often complained that 34 children is too many (I agree), which affected the children. My son mimicked her voice and attitude at home, saying, "Thirty-four children is too many," and then in his own voice he threw up his hands, "so I'll just stay home, and she'll have 33 and be happier without me!" Mrs. Berg may have been too overwhelmed by her students to attempt to understand them. She did not listen and often yelled, sometimes scaring her young charges. She took my son's fainting scene as a personal affront and judged his behavior on the spot.

When he was four or five, my son came into my bedroom one morning and asked me, "Mom, are leprechauns real?" He leaned against the doorframe looking up at me wistfully, waiting for my reply. I had overheard parents at his preschool say that fairytales gave children a skewed sense of reality and that they should be exposed only to nonfiction, to prevent confusion. I was shocked to think that children's minds could be so misunderstood and that imagination could be sacrificed when it is needed to deal with reality. I felt a flood of relief when the preschool teacher disagreed and continued to read folktales and fairytales to the class.

Now, my son wanted to know if leprechauns were real. I thought about the canon of fairytale literature from cultures all around the world, with ubiquitous pixies, genies, angels, gnomes, leprechauns, and more. What right did I have to say that they didn't exist when their stories had been told and retold for hundreds, even thousands of years?

I donned a storyteller character and spoke with an Irish lilt and smiling eyes. "Well now, who do you think makes the milk turn sour when it goes bad? And who scares the cat in the wee hours of the night? And who makes the branches sway when there's no wind? Who do you think? Why the Little People, that's who!" And he giggled and leaped into the air as he ran back to his play space. What right, after all, did I have to take away a child's imagination? I have never seen or encountered fairies to my knowledge, but I am not so arrogant to say that only what I know and experience exists. To quote Shakespeare, "There are more things in heaven and earth... than are dreamt of in your philosophy."

Having made the decision years earlier to treat fairies as real, I had no problem believing that fairies were influencing my young student. Yasmin had told me that fairies showed her magical spots in the woods where she always found four-leaf clovers, and the right branches and leaves to make fantastic fairy furniture that delighted her friends. But my meditation had shown me that the same fairies could also divert her attention, confuse her, and get her into trouble. I invited Yasmin and her mother to come over for a talk.

Yasmin's face was puffy as if she had been crying. She thought I was going to talk about her incoherent draft, and she sat stiffly on the edge of her seat. When I said that I wanted to talk about fairies, she relaxed and sank into her chair. Her mom, about the same height as her daughter with darker hair and a dimpled smile, perked up. Neither had expected this topic. I told them about my meditation and what I had seen. I suggested that fairies could be delightful friends, but they could also be mischievous children. When you are with friends who make mischief, you have to be careful. "What if you meet a little boy who doesn't believe in fairies and he insults them, and then the fairies say to you, 'Let's *get* that kid!' What would you do?"

Her mother laughed, her dimples grinning. "Laurie, have you been spying on us?" Apparently a situation like this happened at the beach the previous summer when Yasmin chased a little boy for this very reason. Now Yasmin was almost a teenager, on the threshold between childhood and adulthood. I told her that when fairies or any beings around her act like irresponsible children she might have to act like an adult and make some mature decisions. She became quiet and thoughtful. This was a turning point for her. Yasmin's experience was being validated, and her world was expanding.

From that day on, Yasmin focused in class. She finished her work, gave and received feedback, and was aware of what happened in the room. Fairies no longer blurred her vision though she continued to make amazing fantasy furniture from items found on nature walks. She returned to playwriting in successive years and in her teens experienced a burgeoning growth as a writer, artist, and performer.

Rather than low expectations or high expectations, I aim for no expectations at all. I try to keep my mind open to new ideas, alert for cues from the students. A sense of uncertainty is essential for true listening, where anything becomes possible. We must be present, not assuming that we know the next word, not rushing to predict what the student will say or do. Children are less predictable than adults and need more time to find their words and express their thoughts. We must be gentle, easygoing, alert, open, unassuming and non-judgmental.

In *Native Plant Stories*, told by Joseph Bruchac, he writes:

> We are often so busy scanning the horizon, looking for big things coming from far away, that we fail to notice those things closest to us. We do not notice the grass—or the flowers—beneath our feet; we do not listen to the songs of the leaves. We take for granted the rooted, growing plants that are all around us, and we fail to recognize or remember that all life on this planet depends on them.

As parents and teachers, we often take our children for granted without realizing it. We focus on big problems that loom ahead, worrying about their college entrance when they are in elementary or middle school, spending our energy paying bills and maintaining the home. We fail to hear the unspoken yearnings of our children. We do not listen to their songs. Yet, the future of our world is in the hands of our children. To urge them to sing is not enough; urging does not motivate. We must first **listen closely with the heart and the mind. This makes all future milestones more attainable. Listen well so they know they are heard.**

Tips for Listening:

1. Relax. Breathe deeply and relax your body. Have you noticed that sounds seem to get louder just before you fall asleep? Hearing becomes more acute when the body is relaxed.

2. Make eye contact. This is important for the speaker too. If you can't make eye contact, it may help to close your eyes.

3. Visualize what you hear. Use your imagination and try to see the words or the story. This technique also helps when speaking.[1]

---

1. See J - Listening, and Listening/Hearing Games

Chapter Twelve

Giving and Taking

Inwood Hill Park, down the street from the apartment of the host parent, always welcomes my fairytale writing class whenever the weather is good. At the start of the course, I met the children at the apartment and we walked over together, but then a parent volunteered to greet the kids in the park earlier, where they played until I arrived. I walk along the park path and spy the gaggle of giggling girls sitting on the grass. I join them and out come the pads and pencils, books and pillows, and we write, relaxed, alert, and content. It feels more like a family gathering than a class. Suddenly, it dawns on all of us that we are writing fairy stories in a place where fairies live.

During our writing sessions, I usually write along with my students. In one park session, I wrote about this new awareness of writing about fairies while sitting in their world.

Fairytale Class in the Park

I hear the children laughing as I'm walking through the park.
Their double dutch jump ropes move in ever-larger arcs.
With pads and pencils in my bag I take a seat nearby,
Slowly they surround me and I greet them eye to eye.
Fairy tales and books come out and stories beg for telling.
Then we realize we are working in the midst of fairy dwellings.

Tiny winged creatures could be living in the trees.
They could be smaller than a petal, floating on the breeze,
Or spinning on a leaf or gliding down a blade of grass
To gather drops of dew or eavesdrop on our class.
Now the children say goodbye and I gather up my things.
Fairies flutter off on silver fairy wings.
What a perfect place to teach fantasy and lore,
A place of peace, where young imaginations can explore.
At night the fairies gather here to cast their magic glow.
They dance in circles on the grass and put on quite a show.
Come morning they have vanished leaving only fairy dew
And tiny springtime flowers, waiting just for you.

At the end of each class, we share voluntarily. The girls read their stories and poems, and if there's time, I read mine. We work together, share together, toss ideas back and forth. It's like a game of Give and Take.

Viola Spolin writes, in *Theater Games for the Classroom: A Teacher's Handbook*, that the purpose of Give and Take is "To be in a state of nonverbal agreement" while the focus is "On listening/hearing ... to know when to give and take." This unspoken agreement, with respectful attention within the group, allows for a constant flow of back and forth. Like an invisible ball that is tossed from one player to another without ever falling to the floor, ideas move back and forth, elevated by each response, kept afloat, moving from one player to another. Even when students turn to their notebooks and write quietly, the flow continues. Ideas invisibly travel across the space, inspiring stories and poems onto the page.

An absence of Give and Take happens when there is a lack of listening and respect. The result may be students feeling ignored with one person dominating the room. There is no flow, no sense of true sharing in the space. Most students don't feel like they are participating — they are only giving to the one who is taking, forced to wait, never taking their turn. In my classes, we all give and take;

we all remain alert and respectful of each other and work to maintain a flow. We play together, brainstorm together, write and read and laugh together.

At the end of the year, we do a final project to crown our hard work. Often, we make handmade books of our stories and have a reading for family and friends. One year, the all-girl group asked to perform stories they had written. I reached out to one of my mentors, Kathy Hendrickson, who had given me curriculum guidance before. A serious actor with a solid sense of humor, Kathy was running a children's theater in Jersey City, performing folktales and teaching children. I told her my problem: the students wanted to perform their original stories, but I had not prepared them with any theater games and now there was no time. "Just play Give and Take," she advised. "One good game of Give and Take, and they can play anything." I was nervous, but I trusted Kathy. It was the last day of the course. With no planning or preparation, I guided the children in a game of Give and Take in the host's living room.

In the game of Give and Take, any player who makes a sound and/or movement is Taking. All other players are in a state of waiting to move, and while they wait (or hold) for their opportunity, they are Giving. They Give to the player who Takes. The player who takes continues to take until someone else starts taking. When the inevitable moments of overlap occur, with two people taking simultaneously, one stops and holds, silently giving to the other player who is taking. Seen from the audience, it can look like only one player moves at a time with a continuous flow of movement that leaps from one player to another, perhaps from opposite sides of the room. Increased awareness occurs as players listen keenly for sound or movement when backs might be turned, holding still in mid-movement at the moment another starts taking. Players remain alert to give or take at any moment, sometimes rescuing another player from having to take for too long or finding a way to take when they've been giving for a long time.

The game of Give and Take symbolizes life, family, relationships, and even the planet we live on. **Every interaction or conversation is a form of Give and Take.** A family or team that coexists well has developed a flow of give and take. In a larger sense, we spend our lives taking and have an implicit responsibility to give back in return. Families pitch in and help each other, share the work and give support. We care for our children when they are young and for our parents as they age. As we age, we consider our legacy, what we can give back and what we might leave behind. For the planet, we can respect the circle of life and try to honor what we have been given by protecting our natural resources. We can help those less fortunate. In small ways, in daily life, we create a Give and Take exchange. From greeting the mail carrier to returning a phone call, we know that how we treat others will come back to us, and we will all have our turn.

The girls' first and only game of Give and Take was mesmerizing. Each was Giving while another was Taking with overlaps so brief that movement and sound seemed to flow from one player to another across the room like graceful choreography instead of an improvised game. It was as if a magic wand moved from one player to another, igniting one to move and utter sound while stilling the others, an endless flow from one player to another until the game ended.

Then the students spontaneously chose characters and scenes from each other's stories, working together seamlessly just as they had in the game. Scenes were unscripted, unrehearsed, and beautifully performed. How was this possible with just one preparatory game? In retrospect, I realized that our classes were like a game of Give and Take.

In a traditional, standardized classroom the teacher is doing all of the Taking, and the students are rarely allowed to Take and even then only under the limitations of the teacher who is always in control. Yet the illusion, to teachers and society, is that this is not Taking but Giving. Teachers by the very nature of their profession, impart knowledge to students, leading, educating and guiding them in service to the class. Yet teachers demand their students' full attention. They stand or sit at the head of the room, towering over smaller humans, and expect all eyes on them. In theater terms, this is someone doing all of the taking, a scene stealer who prevents or stifles ensemble work. **Too much taking by the leader impedes or halts the natural flow of give and take necessary for a community to thrive and for students to learn.** Yet in traditional schools, the teacher assumes the role of Taker, and students submit to ceaseless Giving to comply with teachers' demands. Still, it is possible for a teacher's attitude to shift and for Taking to transform into a Give and Take. A difficult or disappointing situation can be turned around if those involved keep an open mind and are willing to adapt, change, and exchange.

An example of a turn-around happened with my son's piano teacher. With high expectations, my young son and I entered the music school room, where a sleek baby grand piano with gleaming keys dominated the space. I sat in an armchair on the far side of the room behind my son and his new teacher, a fair-haired, gentle young man, who shared the piano bench. My shy son was secretly eager. This was his first time in a music school and with someone he'd heard was a concert pianist. The teacher introduced the instrument, touching keys, then chords. He opened a music book and showed my son the staff with musical notation, repeating keys and chords. Then he played a simple scale and asked my son to copy him, correcting his arm and hand positions. My son complied but kept glancing at the round, black and white clock on the wall, watching the minute hand inch through the allotted time. With repeated glances at the clock, the teacher became nervous and uncertain and started to repeat himself. The question evident in his face was, "What am I doing wrong?"

After we went home, I called the school to ask if there was a penalty for cancelling lessons and if it was possible to change teachers. I explained that a special rapport was necessary, which I hadn't seen. Reassured that there was no penalty, I said, "Don't worry. I'll give the teacher another chance, and I'll speak to him before the next lesson."

When we walked in, the teacher slouched in his seat and wore a worried look. Obviously, a superior had warned him that I was displeased. We spoke while my quiet son listened attentively. I explained, "I registered my son as a beginner because he's had just six months of lessons, but at home, he loves to practice. He enjoys a challenge. He kept glancing at the clock, not because he was impatient for the lesson to end but because he was waiting for it to *begin*."

Suddenly aware of his student in a new light, the teacher turned his head towards the child sharing his bench. "What kind of music do you like?"

My son blinked and replied with a childish lisp, "Tchaikovsky and Scott Joplin."

The teacher's eyes widened. "Really!"

I interrupted their conversation. "He was in the Nutcracker last year, and his first piano piece was the theme to *Swan Lake*. Just recently, he heard Joplin for the first time. He likes the syncopated rhythm. It's good to dance to."

"How about this?" The teacher spontaneously played a few bars of Joplin's "Maple Leaf Rag." My son's face lit up. "Do you like that one?" My son nodded, eyes on his teacher. That day, he didn't glance at the clock once.

At home, with a new music book of easy rags, my son practiced ragtime to his heart's delight. The next week, he played for his teacher, received guidance, and a surprise.

"I was going through my repertoire and the rags that I know," the teacher said softly to my son with a smile, "and came upon one that I had wanted to learn. So I worked on it this week. What do you think?" He played a beautifully complex Scott Joplin rag that we had never heard. The two of them looked like they might be younger and older versions of the same person, two slim, soft-spoken guys sitting on the same bench, one tall and one small, softly bobbing and swaying to the rhythm.

Later that month, one of the music school heads stopped me in the lobby to ask how things were going. "Great!" I smiled broadly. "My son loves the music he's playing, Scott Joplin rags. His teacher was inspired by his love of ragtime and learned a new rag that he shared with us."

"Really!" The head of the school looked at my son and asked, "He learned a new rag to share with you?" My son nodded seriously while the school head grinned. A good Give and Take between student and teacher is rare and worth noting. My son remained inspired by this teacher for years, and the teacher was often inspired by my son. All it took was a moment to open the teacher's mind to see the individual, for the teacher to have a shift in attitude, and ask questions of the student instead of presuming the answer.

I tell my students I'm not like other teachers. "I work for you; you don't work for me," I say. My job is to help them learn what they want to learn and to help them pursue their own aspirations. In order to do this, I must listen more than I speak. **I must Give (in support and in waiting) more than I**

Take, just as I would in any circle of friends or any community. I must share the time and space and encourage others to share it. The last thing I want to do as a teacher is listen to myself talk all the time. My students want to speak, play, and share their lives. They want to ride on the flow of energy between players (classmates) and the creative flow within themselves, to discover and absorb new ideas and knowledge. I do not expect nor want silent children who sit still, eyes forward, hands on desks, seated in rows. Shutting down natural tendencies to move and respond also shuts down parts of the brain, which shuts down learning. If a student is tired, I suggest they close their eyes and rest. If they are antsy, I urge them to get up and move. I advise students to doodle, scribble, and draw, which enhances focus whenever anyone else is speaking. If they take notes, I suggest that they doodle around their notes.

My classes begin with a brief group conversation, setting a casual tone. The conversation is followed with a game. In a Zoom class, I number each student. In person, we sit or stand in a circle. Players take turns moving quickly to keep the game going. The conversation and the game introduce ideas that may be used later. This process also establishes a group sense of Give and Take at the start of every class. A sense of silent group agreement implies mutual support and naturally leads to questions, ideas, and sharing.

In this environment, even though I am the teacher, I do not have the burden of doing the majority of Taking. I listen and respond as an appreciative audience member, offering guidance or asking a question to keep the ideas in the air, side-coaching to keep the players focused. At the end of class, if there's time, we play another game. If I'm not on a tight schedule, I offer extra time to play another round, and the kids shout, "Hooray!"

Giving to each other, we are taking turns as "teacher," each having a moment in the spotlight, each finding a way to lead and shine within the group. A good class is like a good game of Give and Take. It turns out Kathy Hendrickson was right. It can prepare you to do anything!

Proof of our Give and Take is that we inspire each other. Here is another poem I wrote in the park with this same group to introduce the idea of Going Inside.

Inside

Inside of a golden palace
Is a silver moon.
Inside of the silver moon
Sits a princess in dazzling white.
Inside of the princess
Is a beautiful lullaby being sung.
Inside of the lullaby
Is my poetry class.
Inside of my poetry class
Is a herd of elephants,
Deep blue lagoons with swaying palms,
Sapphire meteorites glowing in the heavens,
And warm apple pie.
And me. I am there too.
And inside of me is
An endless universe,
Crystalline tears,
And untold joy.

The following essay by a student in this class was also written in the park at the same time that I shared my poem.

"Laurie" by Caoilin

I am in my imagination, in the shade, in the park, on the blue, floral blanket surrounded by trees, grass, leaves, clover plants, and creative friends.

And Laurie is also there, in the lawn chair, laughing in the distance, which pulls me out of my imagination and back down to earth, and I glance at her sitting there contently in her shorts, pretty sandals, and the flowery tee-shirt she got from Hawaii. Hawaii, the place she describes as being "Aloha."

But this glance of the woman, her hair, usually cascading down to her shoulders, but now pulled up in a bun, and her leg crossed over her other, doesn't leave me blank, out of my imagination, for long. Laurie has seemed to put a spell over every girl there, as they are all absorbed in their worlds, like I am. But now, even though we are all imagining in unique universes, our universes are the same, harmonizing and blending like the blue sky and clouds through the treetops. We are all together.

This lets us imagine the strangest, most wonderful things, such as Frankfurt the mouse, who was betrayed by the evil bird, who was really his wife, who was really his mother, or such as the fantastic binomial in which the clock and piano were spewing mucus and regurgitating due to a certain food poisoning.

Laurie can make anything come alive and enchant you, or even jump off the page at you! She has a way of pulling one's real self out of them, plopping them down on the blanket, and saying,

Hello! Welcome; this is life!

But, of course, she doesn't often have to do this, for we are imagining already, all cozy in our universes, and once we are there, we have nothing to conceal.

For instance, when I have an open mind and travel to my imagined world, I sometimes visit the woods with a brook trickling through it. I tingle with sensation when I dip my toes in the cold morning water, but I sit back and watch the sunlight peek through the dancing treetops.

Then, I slip my socks back into my shoes and start venturing deeper into this unexplored world. Pushing vines out of my way and ducking between bushes, I come upon a clearing. Grass and wildflowers are growing plentifully, and the warm sunlight is beaming down on the earth.

But Laurie is talking to us, and I realize she is reading one of her poems, one about us, and a princess "in dazzling white." And warm apple pie, I realize with a smile. She has succeeded in intriguing me once again, and to do it many more times.

Here is evidence of Giving and Taking, where mutual awareness and group inspiration create a unique state of being within an individual. As Caoilin put it, "...even though we are all ... in unique universes, our universes are the same, harmonizing and blending like the blue sky and clouds through the treetops. We are all *together*." This is the definition of Give and Take. We are always Giving or Taking, waiting or moving/speaking, sharing the same world, existing in the same space. With conscious awareness and an activated flow, we become a connected group of individuals where each has a voice while working *together*.[1]

---

1. See J – Resources on Listening, Giving and Taking, and Games.

Chapter Thirteen

Games: My Not-So-Secret Weapon

"Play is the only way the highest intelligence of humankind can unfold." ~Joseph Chilton Pearce, *Magical Child*

"Dog and Bone?" Liam, a skinny, nervous boy looks up at me with pleading eyes.

"Yes! Dog and Bone!" the others cry out almost in unison.

"Get in a circle," I smile, allowing the game to begin. Hands shoot into the air to volunteer as the first dog. Liam is given the honor and moves to the center, crouching down, eyes closed. I silently indicate which child will try to steal the bone first, a soft, soundless toy that I drop on the floor in the circle, halfway between the dog and the circle of potential thieves. The game begins. The first thief stands noiselessly and tiptoes in stocking feet towards the bone. Liam's ears remain as alert as an animal listening for prey, his eyes covered, his body curled up and still as a stone so he can listen all the better.

I side-coach the game, amazed at Liam's self-control. Normally, he can't sit still. As if he has nervous leg syndrome, his limbs constantly quiver and shake. He speaks often, crowing his words, jumping up and down to accent their meaning. He noisily demands attention and never seems to rest. Yet, here he lies as still and quiet as anyone could be.

The "thief" gets pointed out as Liam's arm reaches in that direction, and a new thief is chosen. Liam is unmovable, intent on discovering the next thief. He stays frozen for countless minutes until finally, after several attempts, the bone is stolen. Liam sits up, eyes bright with the light, and faces the circle of players who all have their hands behind their backs. He grins and tries to point out the thief one last time. When he fails, everyone's hands are shown so we see which player holds the puffball. That thief becomes the "dog," and another round begins.

What makes a game addictive? Why do we want to play even when the skill required is difficult and not yet attained? How can we play the same thing over and over and not feel bored? I wondered about these questions as I watched Liam stay still and silent, two things he was usually unable to do, knowing he would ask for this game again. Liam was addicted to Dog and Bone, which was fortunate since it taught him some of the most challenging things he needed to learn.

Games were the turning point in my own transformation. I spent two years looking for the right source and three more years getting there before I experienced that turning point. My playwriting mentor, Daniel Judah Sklar, placed Viola Spolin's seminal book *Improvisation for the Theater* into my hands when he released me from his instruction. After many sessions with long hours of writing in his tiny West Village apartment, he told me, "You are ready to teach playwriting. But you'll need this." I held Spolin's book in my hands for the first time and sensed he was right. "But I can't teach you that," he added. "You'll have to find that somewhere else."

The search to practice Spolin games began. I took trial classes at several New York City improv clubs but always left dissatisfied. I felt a pressure there to speak quickly and deliver funny lines, which didn't come naturally to me. It was nothing like the games in the book. The Wisconsin Theater Games Center, founded by Paul Sills, son of Viola Spolin, had exactly what I needed, but it was in a remote corner of Wisconsin. Eventually, I found my way there, to an open barn with a blue circle painted on the floor, purple dragonflies buzzing through the August air, and a bat or two hanging from the rafters. It was the first day of a five-day intensive course in theater games with Aretha Sills, Viola Spolin's granddaughter.

After a warm-up game of "Pussy Wants a Corner," Aretha told us to get up and walk in and out of the space. What did she mean? Walk in and out of the blue circle? Walk through space? I wondered as I moved across the floor, experimenting with the sensation in my mind of what it felt like to move in and out of the space. Aretha, fair-faced with a level gaze, moved among us, side-coaching us to have full contact with the space, full-body, head-to-toe involvement and interaction with the space. We contacted the space with our knees, our backs, our noses, our hair. I encountered space all around me, behind, beneath, and above, and that's when I had the first epiphany of many during my time in that blue circle.

I suddenly realized that until that moment I had minimized my awareness of space, my contact with space, and my connection to it. Space was no longer an empty thing that could be ignored. It was now present, palpably so, and available. We didn't just interact with the space; the space interacted with us. I awoke to the fact that I'd been wearing blinders like a horse forced to only see ahead. Suddenly, I saw all around me in every direction. My sense of what a performance space was would never be the same. Most plays I had seen were performed on a typical proscenium stage with three walls and an open "fourth wall" facing the audience. I assumed actors were trained to face the audience and plays were choreographed or "blocked" with that view. Now, moving in slow motion in the blue circle, playing with the space, my stage awareness was 360 degrees — not just 360 degrees around my middle but around me in all directions spherically. My prior view of a performance space contained less than 180 degrees, maybe narrowed to 95 degrees, from the actor's point of view and the audience's. In that blue circle, my preconceptions exploded and vanished. Not only would I never see a performance space the same way, I would never see the world or myself the same way again. My universe had cracked open. My former view felt like a sliver of what I was beginning to comprehend.

I had started my role as a teacher and parent thinking that games were a way to make learning fun. I believed learning, especially for children, should not be a dry, boring task but an exciting adventure. I also knew of games as ice breakers, ways to relax and get to know each other, often used as party entertainment. Then I discovered the power of math games, and my children played their way to becoming adept at numbers in ways I had never imagined. Was the learning happening because it was fun? Or was the learning greater, the thinking deeper, because of the games?

As a poetry teacher, I was inspired by the work of Kenneth Koch (*Wishes, Lies and Dreams,* and *Rose, Where did You Get That Red?),* and Gianni Rodari (*The Grammar of Fantasy*). In my classes, I introduced sensory games as a prelude to writing poetry. Children listened with eyes closed and created words for sounds, touched hidden objects and wrote words for textures, smelled scents in bottles with covered labels and described the aromas. I did this with my own children at home, sitting on the kitchen floor opening spice jars with my hands covering the labels while my five-year-old told me that cinnamon smelled like Christmas. Rodari's "Fantastic Binomial" game, combining unlikely words into amusing pairs, proved to be a fire-starter for writing poetry and stories. Children jumped and cheered when they heard we were going to play this game. Games had become doorways to the senses and portals to creativity.

My use of games reached a deeper, greater level after being introduced to the work of Viola Spolin. The breadth of Spolin games includes sensory games, "Where" games and "Who" games, games that foster communication and help connect players to the space, to each other, or to the story. Yet, every game contains something greater that its focus. This is the player's connection to intuition. The expanded use of intuition opens the mind and increases the ability to understand and experience. Through the intuition, learning skyrockets.

> Experiencing ... means involvement on all levels: intellectual, physical, and intuitive. Of the three, the intuitive, most vital

to the learning situation, is neglected. The intuitive ... comes bearing its gifts in the moment of spontaneity, the moment when we are freed to relate and act, involving ourselves in the moving, changing world around us. Through spontaneity we are re-formed into ourselves. ... It is the time of discovery, of experiencing, of creative expression. ~Viola Spolin, Improvisation for the Theater (Chapter 1)

The first year I taught playwriting, games might have made up 15% of the course with writing the other 85%. After ten years, that ratio had reversed, and the course had become 85% games with most of the writing started in class and finished at home. During this ten-year period, the frequency and number of games increased in all of my classes, regardless of subject. The intuitive result of playing Spolin games gave each student a creative and intellectual boost and dramatically enhanced communication and connection between students.

The traditional approach to a writing course is all table work. Everyone sits down to write. Reading or sharing is done aloud while seated, and revisions occur at the same tables or desks. In such a traditional writing environment, I might see a student take a leap in skill over three or four months of effort. But with the games, I saw it happen right away. Before my eyes, the students came alive. Their faces lit up with new ideas and new ways of communicating. When groups were divided into audience and players, the audience also acted as valued players, responding to and learning from the others. Everyone in the room watched and supported each other. As students experimented, they discovered character, developed plot and setting, created conflict and climactic moments, and found new, personalized forms of expression. Students improvised scenes for their fellow playwrights and had their written scenes improvised by fellow players. Writing and revision happened eagerly as they responded to ideas that surfaced in the playing. Shakespeare famously wrote, "...the play's the thing (*Hamlet*), " but I learned *the game's the thing!*

Peter Gray, psychologist and author, writes about how before there was written language all humans learned through play. He has documented how hunter gatherers learned through play and how elders taught children through play and story. All knowledge was once acquired through play.

Brain scientists have proven that nothing lights up the brain like play, especially free-form, unstructured play. Once, I was sitting at a picnic table with a group of parents having lunch after teaching a workshop with their children. While we ate, the children played. Two boys fashioned swords from branches and squared off, challenging each other, engaging in mock swordplay. They argued as one of their mothers, sitting next to me, watched. She wanted to get up but hesitated, unsure if she should intervene. I leaned over and whispered in her ear, "Look at those two, standing there, learning everything they need to learn just by trying to figure out how to play the game and how to keep the game going. Right now, they are learning all the life skills they will need as adults." The mother took a breath and smiled, thanking me for reminding her, not just of the importance of play but also that a momentary conflict or pause in the rhythm is a necessary part of the learning process. Those boys worked hard to keep the game going and ended up playing long after we finished our lunch.

Years ago, I took a workshop on play led by Deborah Meier, a pioneering educator. We were guided to meditate on how we played as children and to focus on a time before schooling when we were involved in games of our own creation. Then, we gathered in small groups to share our memories of childhood play and connect them to our current lives. Each person in my group easily connected their childhood games to their current profession, often in startling ways. In my own meditation, I recalled that while other children played "house" and vied to be the mommy or daddy, I wanted to play "school" and be the teacher. I marveled that this was my preferred game, created by me and not copied from the other kids, especially because it mirrored the profession that became my calling. Meier's workshop proved that the whims and nature of a young child reveal who they are and what they want to do, not just as a child but as a person and as an adult. The roots for our lives are found in early play. As we thrive and flourish, we may sprout many branches and leaves, yet we are forever drawing on the deep roots of our childhood, on our earliest games, wonders, and explorations from our days before school.

Through play, we discover what delights and engages us, find our pas-
sions, and discover our true selves. When we indulge in creative, unstructured,
self-created play, we eventually play in ways that help us to realize our life
purpose. We do not live with blinders, yet we wear them unknowingly, the result
of conformity and conditioning. When the blinders come off and the walls
disappear, we open ourselves to the universe. The sun doesn't just shine on our
face; it shines on our entire being.

"Once a child learns the 'spirit of play,' every new situation
turns up numberless new associations and abilities."

~Neva Boyd, Theory of Play[1]

---

1. See J – Resources on Listening, Giving and Taking, and Games

Chapter Fourteen

The Magic Formula

"Form a circle!" I call out to the class of youngsters ages 6-8, who jump out of their chairs and run to the center of the room. "You call that a circle?" I ask, laughing. Children adjust their position, changing the open-ended oval into a circle. I nod and pause then shout out, "Not it!" A chorus follows, "Not it! Not it! Not it!" The last to call out is a quiet, dark-skinned girl who walks to the center of the circle with a smile on her face. It's time for a favorite warm-up game, Pussy Wants a Corner.

In this course, all activities relate to animals. We make charts and graphs of animal measurements, comparing qualities like birth weight or adult height or maximum speed and we include humans. We read animal stories and poems and write our own. Each child becomes an expert on their chosen animal, teaches the class about it, and writes a fact-based fable or *pourquoi* tale. Imaginary animals are made using found objects. Science fiction tales or nonsense poems are penned about their lives. Animal-shaped books are fashioned from blank paper; animal masks painted and adorned. Yet, we always start with a game.

This is my Magic Formula in fast action. The Formula, honed over years of missteps, trials and errors, is simplicity itself, with three components making the ideal class.

1. Play a game
2. Learn something new.
3. Make something.

Because this animals course was for young children who often prefer short sessions in new settings, the parents requested a one-hour class. I wondered if I could fit all three components into a single hour and doubted my plan. Yet, the children accommodated me, eagerly moving to each new phase of the class and the course. Because of the wide variety of activities which include physical movement and creative expression, they could easily have gone for twice as long or longer.

I have applied this Magic Formula to every class, every course, every age. Students tackling a big project might add to their creations in stages throughout the course with a final presentation at the end. For young children, I plan simple crafts that can be finished in minutes, yet there might also be a larger project at the end of a series of classes such as a book or performance of collective work.

Experiencing this three-part structure in the same day, even in the same hour, results in a high degree of personal satisfaction. The body and mind are awakened with a game that promotes relaxation of self and connection with others. Our innate thirst for learning and sharing is quenched with the introduction and exchange of information and ideas. After a period of mental stimulation, it is calming and centering to work with your hands, creating something to keep, take home, and show off.

The order is less important than the variety. Each activity and each game appeals to a different learning style and personality. The combination of the Formula is greater than its parts. When we are attracted to one activity, we adapt more easily to what surrounds it. The learning process expands. Mind and body are fully engaged.

This is something I've experienced myself. Intensive periods of teaching and planning require contrasting activities to create balance. When I studied bookmaking for children, I found the act of making things out of paper calming. Creating things I liked gave me a feeling of delight, an unexpected personal bonus. There was a mixture of pleasure and satisfaction in the things I made. As adults, we tend to focus on work. As parents, we focus on our children. Too often we worry and forget to play and create, to make things just for ourselves. I was fortunate that the very nature of my work led me to experiences that were playful and creative. My own needs and experiences showed me the value of the Magic Formula.

In poetry classes, I begin with a game that includes words and images (part one). Then we read a poem or look at a poetic form (new information—part two). Together, we practice a brainstorming technique, followed by a short writing period and the option for sharing. Writing is creative expression and can fulfill part three (making something), but sharing is an exchange of new ideas and information, or part two. Children love to teach and learn from each other.

Even with only five minutes left in the class, there is enough time to focus on making something, perhaps a simple book, a pocket accordion or hotdog book, or one of many books that require a single sheet of paper or card stock. If any element of the Magic Formula is omitted, I promise the children that we will start with that in the next class. Sometimes starting with book arts is ideal. Children might want to fill a handmade book right away! Bookmaking inspires writing. Creativity inspires action.

In multicultural geography, I start with a traditional children's game that is played in the part of the world we are exploring. Then, we look at maps, cities, clothing, and art. We ask questions and listen to anyone who has been there. We read a folk or fairy tale from that place. Lastly, we do a hands-on cultural activity, exploring art, architecture, music, or poetry. During hands-on art activities, I play traditional music from that part of the world. The children giggle, dance, draw, and have so much fun they have no idea how much they are learning.

The Magic Formula can be applied to any subject. Even in math my kids played, drew and built objects for greater understanding. Playing games with cards or dice, my kids became comfortable counting and adding. They used manipulatives and tools to derive answers to problems hands-on, through building, drawing, measuring, and weighing. They applied math to art, science, stories, jokes, and riddles. My kids' math knowledge helped them to profit from a lemonade stand, plan and budget travel, make inventions, design and make costumes, theater sets and jewelry, and complete a spate of personal projects.

Of course, there isn't really a Magic Formula for anything. No wave of the wand or mysterious incantation will solve any problem. And yet, there are many

Magic Formulas. Whenever something complicated is put simply and it somehow works better, you've hit on one. The most powerful Magic Formula I know
was created by Viola Spolin and is evident throughout her book, *Improvisation
for the Theater*. In Spolin's comprehensive compilation of theater games, each
with a different focus, there is a common thread of three elements that remain
true for every game. The first element is the focus given to the players at the
start of each game. The second element is side-coaching, phrases spoken by the
teacher to help deepen and strengthen the players' focus. The third element
is non-judgmental evaluation, where questions explore the problem and the
experience but don't focus on the players. For example, in a Space Walk, the
focus is on feeling space with the whole body. Side-coached comments include,
"Feel the space around you. Feel the space against your back! Feel the space, and
let the space feel you!" In the evaluation, we ask questions such as, "Is there a
difference between feeling the space and letting the space feel you?" Students
share their experience in the game and learn from reflection without the usual
judgement or criticism that can halt learning and keep students nervous and
uncomfortable. In Spolin's evaluation process, there is no right or wrong.

My students probably play Spolin games for hours before I point out the
three elements common to every game. I explain to them that these three elements—focus, side-coaching and self-evaluation—are all you need to succeed at
anything! They are already deeply familiar with these elements, and now, they
can use them to accomplish anything in life! Once you know what you want to
accomplish, find the focus! Then, side-coach yourself through the process. The
side-coach is your mind, helping you to stay focused and to deepen the focus.
Periodically step back and ask yourself non-judgmental reflective questions.
How do I feel about the progress? Is something working in ways I didn't expect?
Is something not working as well as expected? These three elements in every
Spolin game—focus, side-coaching, and self-evaluation—are a Magic Formula
for Life!

Another simple way of explaining the path to success, simple enough to be
viewed as a Magic Formula, is the Four Steps to Success. This process was given
to me by actor and educator Kathy Hendrickson, who I believe got itfrom

George Morrison. When I share this path with my students, I draw it out as a four-step staircase, drawing each step as I label it. I often show this to a teen group working on a big project especially if some feel they have hurdles to overcome.

"Did you know that there are just four steps on the path to success?" Heads look up as I walk over to the white board and draw two sides of a rectangle, the bottom step of a staircase. Inside the bottom step, I write: I DUNNO. "This is the first step in learning, when you want to know or do something that you don't yet understand. I DUNNO is often the way you feel on the first day in a new course or a new school." Some kids are nodding.

While I draw the second step, I am remembering my own experiences with steps one and two. My black marker adds another rectangle to the stairs. Inside step two, I write: UH OH!

"The I DUNNO step leads to the next step which is the UH OH! step. This is where the learning feels hard." I know which kids are feeling that way, and I sympathize. "You don't understand what's going on, and it's frustrating. The Uh Oh! step can be dangerous because this is where most people bail. When it gets hard, we want to quit. But," I pause and gaze at the group, "if you persist and keep working at the Uh Oh! stage, sooner or later you will ascend to the third step." Now I add another half-rectangle, the third step up, and inside it I write: AHA! "And you get to the AHA! This is where you start to understand. You feel like you're starting to get it, learn it, maybe even do it."

The Aha! stage removes the acute frustration of the Uh Oh! stage. This third step is a level of success. Experiencing that Aha! feeling is a major turning point in any area of learning. But there is still one more step ahead. I draw the fourth step on the white board. "If you persist at the AHA! step, it will lead you to the fourth, top step, which is the TADA! This is where you can be recognized for your newly acquired knowledge and skill."

Whenever we learn anythingnew, we progress from the I DUNNO step to the UH OH! step to the AHA! step. If we continue, eventually we reach the TADA! Everyone who has tried to learn something new has faced a wall at the UH OH! step at one time or another. You only reach the AHA! step if you stick with that uncomfortable UH OH! step long enough to get through it and things start to make sense. As things make more and more sense, skills develop, confidence replaces frustration and confusion, and the TADA! is bound to happen.

My personal TADA! has appeared in many ways. One deeply gratifying indication of my success as a teacher is that my students often arrive early to class and stay late. I make a habit of arriving 15 minutes early, but sometimes students are already there, forming their own games and playing, starting class without me. Long after they are my students, I hear from them. Many are now adults, playing, creating, performing, teaching, writing, active in all sorts of professions, raising families, and putting down roots. They move through life with an awareness that they can learn anything. I have to pinch myself. It feels like magic. It's the same feeling that I get teaching a class that moves seamlessly from one activity to the next with children eager for every step. I knew I'd found a Magic Formula when my classes gave me that magical feeling. How did I fit it all in? How did we do so much? How could anything be so much fun?

Tada!

Aha!

Uh oh!

I dunno

Chapter Fifteen

Praising the Process

> In a culture where approval/disapproval has become the predominant regulator of effort and position, and often the substitute for love, our personal freedoms are dissipated. ...We must wander daily through the wish to be loved and the fear of rejection before we can be productive. ...We lose the ability to be organically involved in a problem ... self-identity is obscured ... learning is affected. ~Viola Spolin Improvisation for the Theater

Sabrina, a dark-eyed, eight-year-old girl, usually comes early to my writing class. She likes to borrow books and draw and often brings me a drawing as a gift. Sabrina hands me a sheet covered with rainbows, hearts, and flowers. As I take it, she asks me, "Do you like it?" These are the same hearts and rainbows she always draws, and I wish she would break away from what she's obviously received praise for in the past. I hesitate, not wanting to tell what she craves to hear, as I recall the cautionary story of Hugo, a boy I have known since he was born.

When Hugo was born, the first child and first grandchild in his family, everyone said, "He's so smart!" When he grabbed his grandmother's finger and cooed, she said, "See how clever he is!" When the baby was napping and she dropped her phone, he awoke with a sharp cry and she announced, "His hearing is perfect!" Hugo rolled over at age six weeks while his parents cheered. He spoke clearly at six months, and his parents said, "Listen to how smart he is!"

Hugo was still in the crawling stage when a musician friend called Hugo's mom to explain why Hugo was a genius. Playing on a keyboard together, whenever the friend switched to another key, the baby followed and moved into that same key. "And then he sang the notes. He has perfect pitch!" he exulted. "A musical genius!" Hugo's mom was delighted. After that, the friend always greeted Hugo with a grin, asking, "How's my little genius?"

Hugo loved numbers. By age five, he was playing card games with his Dad, figuring out how many wheels were on a tractor trailer and how many more Legos he needed to build a castle. When he won at cards or produced another sum, his parents praised him. At age six, Hugo showed his first grade teacher an error in the printed math workbook. "Your kid's a genius!" the teacher exclaimed to his dad at pick-up time.

Throughout his school years, the nickname "Genius" dogged Hugo. By the time he was a teenager, his parents realized it was doing more harm than good. Hugo's constant goal was to show off how smart he was and impress people with his intelligence. He adopted a sense of superiority to others. He selected and judged his friends according to how smart he thought they were. In music class, other students, who couldn't carry a tune and didn't understand their instrument, practiced hard and easily surpassed Hugo, who soon lost interest. Hugo tried another instrument and then another but didn't like how he sounded so he dropped each after a few months. Whenever serious effort was required, Hugo found an excuse to quit. He had grown up getting praise for easy results that looked and sounded smart, not for hard-won effort.

Carol S. Dweck, professor in psychology at Stanford University, did ground-breaking research on this topic in which she coined the terms *growth mindset* and *fixed mindset*. Students with a growth mindset believe that abilities can be developed so they are more likely to put in effort that leads to learning. Students with a fixed mindset approach a problem with the goal of looking good at the end. They shy away from hard work or challenging situations where they might not look smart. They believe mistakes indicate a lack of intelligence, so they don't try new things that are out of their comfort zone; they stick to what has always looked "smart."

Professor Dweck believes mindsets can be created and changed. She points out that we are each a mixture of fixed and growth mindsets that change as we grow. We can help to nurture a growth mindset in children by encouraging meaningful involvement and effort rather than rewarding model behavior or attractive results.

In my classroom, the sweet eight-year-old girl waits for approval as I hold the drawing of her hearts and rainbows. They are colorful, but there is a sameness to them that lacks energy. Sometimes a little scribble in the corner of the page looks more alive to me than all the hearts and rainbows. I wonder if she ever wants to draw a laughing hippo or a leaping turtle or if she would ever make something messy? If I tell her the hearts are lovely, will I be praising her for being stuck where she is? Will I be encouraging a lack of growth? I accept her drawing and thank her with a smile. She takes a blank page and draws a small cat surrounded with little hearts and rainbows. She hands it to me. "Do you like it?" Not approving of her work starts to feel like I'm expressing disapproval, and I feel my resolve weaken.

In her video talk, "The Flowering of Children's Creativity," art educator Michele Cassou speaks about the need for approval in her young students.

> [The children] repeat what they have been taught because they ... have not been put in a context where they know they can invent. So they will keep [repeating] and they will be bored. They say, "Do you like it?" And they are told yes, they like it.

The child wants to be creative and expressive but is stuck in a place where they are bored, repeating what has earned them the reward of praise. Praise can kill creativity! A performer or artist may try to duplicate again and again the thing that earned praise, putting aside the creative process.

When a student's primary goal is high marks and test scores, a fixed mindset easily dominates, leading to anxiety and lessening the desire and ability to explore new things and to creatively problem-solve from new directions. Creative, intuitive thinking, essential in all professions and fields of study but most especially in directing our own personal inner growth, is ignored. I adore the dark-eyed girl who likes to draw and wonder what might exist behind the hearts and rainbows. When will her creative voice emerge?

The distinction between encouragement and praise can be subtle. The distinction between approval and love can also be subtle. I love all of my students (I don't know how or why, but I do). I cheer them on, and I applaud their work and say, "Good job!" This can all feel like praise, but it's not empty praise, and it's not praising a predicted outcome. I have told an entire class, "You all created original characters that speak from the heart! I am blown away!" I have applauded classroom games, thanking the players for giving their all and playing full out. I have pointed out noteworthy moments in the work of individual students, telling them, "I love the vivid imagery and sensory writing that makes your story come to life. I can see it and feel it!" I highlight what I want to encourage. I praise the process.

> Attention is a moral act: it creates, brings aspects of things into being, but in doing so makes others recede. What a thing is depends on who is attending to it, and in what way.   ~Ian McGilchrist, The Master and His Emmisary

Playing children's games and improvisational theater games can open the doors of intuitive perception for an entire group. In a game, mistakes don't really feel like mistakes because it's all in fun. If it's a new game, then everyone makes mistakes together. In a large group, a game might require several teams to each take turns. We always thank the first team for teaching the rest of the group how to play the game; the audience applauds them and thanks them for showing the rest of us how. In the world of play, it's easier to take risks and explore something new. Improvisation builds a growth mindset in both teacher and student. In a Spolin Space Walk, we explore the space as if it's a new substance we are encountering for the first time. In mere moments, we have opened our minds to think in a new way and allow new ideas to emerge.

The games explore the unknown, and through that exploration we can find ourselves. Students who have been programmed to expect praise for attractive outcomes may feel uncomfortable at first when they don't receive the praise they have come to expect, but they will suspend this need in order to play a game. They willingly trade the goal of predictable praise for the excitement and adventure of creative exploration and self-discovery. There is no thrill like the thrill of discovering yourself.

I turn to my eight-year-old student and ask, "Do you want to play a game? Maybe Bananagrams or Stinky Pinky or a Word Ladder?" I suggest children's word games that she knows. "The others can join in when they arrive."

"Stinky Pinky!" She responds with confidence and a sparkle in her eye. She writes down some rhyming words and possible clues to describe them. Playing this game, she never asks me or the others if her riddles are good. She gives me a clue, "Boring Fun," adding, "it's a Stink Pink," meaning the answer is two one-syllable words that rhyme.

After a few weak guesses, I think I have it. "Lame Game!" She laughs, nodding, and then it's my turn to stump her. She is actively learning, fully in the game without any apparent need for approval.

The others arrive and join the game. Then, we discuss Kipling's *Just So Stories* and the *pourquoi* tales the children are writing. Sabrina has decided to write about how the panda got his mask. While we talk, she draws, moving her pencil across a pad of lined paper, ignoring the lines. A strong central figure appears on the page. It's a masked panda in a power stance, with a big grin and glowing eyes. Behind the panda is its friend, an ape that seems to be cheering the panda on. In the background is the entrance to the zoo with a zookeeper in the distance; an entire field lies between the zookeeper and the happy panda. Molly the Panda is on an adventure, ready to take on the world. The entire picture is alive! I ask Sabrina if I can put her picture up on the wall, and she hands it to me. I look at my class of active writers and artists, all taking chances and being creative without fear of disapproval. At the end of the day, their work will adorn the walls (hearts and rainbows, too), and later, they will send me their stories and illustrations, and I will be moved to tears by their beauty and originality and aliveness.

Chapter Sixteen

Seven Ingredients for a Child-Led Classroom

1. Kids' Questions and Topics

Teachers and students can write down questions and requested topics, perhaps on a large blank pad or whiteboard or stack of blank post-its by an empty wall with the words "I Want to Learn" at the top and space for any child to write down anything they want to learn. Topics and notes on the wall can be explored at any time.

2. "Corners" on Different Topics or Themes

A corner can be an actual corner or nook, or it can be a bookcase, bureau, box, bin or table. Examples: a reading corner mini-library with cushions on the floor; a poetry corner with poetry games, writing materials, and post-its for poetry to stick on the wall; a science corner with live animals (maybe fish or a gerbil), magnifying glasses, magnets, rocks and minerals, plants (changing exhibits); a math corner with Cuisenaire rods, tangrams, geo-boards and rubber bands, measuring tape, rulers, scales, graph paper, math puzzles; a history corner on a time period such as the Middle Ages with books, maps, a box of costumes, etc. Ideas for corners can come from the students. One classroom created a Blue Corner, filled with various blue-colored objects brought in by students.

3. Questions that Students can Think About and Respond to in Any Way They Like

Questions or thoughtful statements can be posted on a board or wall with space for responses and additional questions. Questions can be taken from Ingredient #1 (above) or from any topic or discussion. Examples:

- 1. How is chewing gum made?

- 2. Why do birds have feathers?

- 3. What Native American words do we use in English?

- 4. When and where was money invented?

These questions can lead to discussion, research, and more questions!

4. Empty Space

The ability to clear the space to make room for artwork, projects, game playing, dancing. Make sure chairs, desks and/or tables can be moved

5. The Freedom to Explore, Ask Questions, Move Around, Create. The Freedom to Not Do.

6. Students who want to be there!

7. Teachers who want to be there!

Chapter Seventeen

Ten Principles of a Child-Led Classroom

1. Learning happens on a voluntary, consensual basis.

Students reaching for what they are ready and eager to learn have a greater learning experience.

2. Students and teachers make the rules together.

Rules are never imposed as an act of authority but arrived at by mutual agreement. Students and teachers are working partners.

3. Teachers and students work and play side-by-side as a team.

The traditional authoritarian view of the teacher is absent. The teacher serves as guide, companion, and co-player. Players bond as a team.

4. Students influence or choose the subject matter and approach.

This principle is achieved by honoring student questions and requests, responding to student interests, and utilizing individual students and the environment and community as valued resources. Plans are changed or adapted to suit needs, preferences, learning styles, and to satisfy a student's curiosity. Different students will learn differently and do different things in the same class (an inevitable result regardless of approach).

5. No enforced curriculum or mandatory homework!

6. No student is expected (or coerced) to comply or do something they do not want to do.

All assignments are Suggested Assignments. Ideally, homework is an extension of a project originated and created by the student. Ask students what they want (or think they need) to work on before the next class, and they will come up with their own Suggested Assignments.

7. Choices are offered constantly!

These choices are not just in subject matter but also in types of resources, techniques, approach, method, learning style, and environment.

8. Tests, grades, marks, or scores are not used for evaluations or set as goals. Instead, the primary goal is full engagement and the enjoyment of learning.

9. Goals include a growing sense of self-awareness and self-esteem. Intuitive learning and creative expression are a core part of the process.

10. Students are encouraged to learn what they want to learn and to express themselves in ways that suit each student.

Individuality is the norm. No finished work or projects are alike.

Work and Play are not separate. Kids are encouraged to be themselves!

Planning To Be
Surprised

Chapter Eighteen

Basement Games

"One! Two! Three! Four!"

Each number was shouted out when a child touched another wall, jumping and yelling as they slapped the wall, running nonstop around the room.

"Five! Six! Seven!"

Collapsing in a pile on the floor, momentarily resting in a heap, they jumped up and did it again.

"No!"

"Yes!"

"Not that way — this way! You got it!"

"Three!" (*pant, pant*)

"Four!"

Two boys high-fived as they passed each other. One seemed to forget his count, screwed up his face in distress, and ran out of the room. The others continued to run.

I sat on a low, brown couch. Another mother sat off to the side, working on a laptop perched on her knees.

The boys fell on the floor, wrestled, grabbed, and released. "Let's play a new game!" shouted the boy who lived there. He instructed the others to run, this time back and forth between two walls as if they were bouncing from wall to wall. I watched the game transform as they mirrored each other's changes. Now, they were jumping in place, now hopping on the same foot, now jumping like pogo sticks across the floor.

"I win!"

"We all win!"

"I didn't win. I hate this game."

When parents hired me to teach a class to homeschoolers ages 7-9, one afternoon a week, I thought I had hit the jackpot; it was a five-minute drive from my apartment and I could park in a private driveway, eliminating my typically lengthy, costly commute. The host parent had a small house with a basement for classroom use, which I visited first. It was a large open space with a bathroom, decent lighting, and lots of outdoor equipment that the parent promised to store behind a barricade. I already knew and liked the children. Little did I know that my patience would be tested in more ways than I could imagine.

I had taught a board game class the previous season to the same group but with a few more students. The girls hadn't signed up this time, leaving a smaller group that was all boys. A group of boys was not unusual. What was rare was the range of learning and behavioral issues that arose, in conflict, during every class.

One kid was verbal, extroverted, and liked to lead. Another was overwhelmingly shy and often left the room without saying why. A moon-faced boy loved to touch, hug, and playfully punch. When his hugs were too tight or the punches hurt, he was yelled at by the others. Another child hated being touched and ran whenever he saw this boy getting close. A slim, graceful boy could not sit still; he had to fidget or run, jump, or skip all the time. He rarely spoke and always seemed distracted, but if I asked him a question, he was ready with an answer. No matter how distracted this overactive child appeared to be, he paid attention. The tallest child sat quietly, looking into my eyes with a gentle, affectionate attitude. Yet, when I asked him a question he was confused or unable to answer; his mind was elsewhere while his body was present.

Theater games are among my favorite warm-ups because they increase awareness and develop skills. My plan was to coach Story Theater using games to rehearse, leading up to a performance of a fairytale. Preparing for this class, I read several tales and selected Rumpelstiltskin for the number of students, arriving the first day with copies for everyone.

The verbally gifted child wanted to read the entire story out loud by himself. The over-active child didn't glance at the pages, appeared aloof, fidgeted but listened. The shy boy fled the room to find his mother upstairs. The child who liked to hug gave his copy to his mother and went back to playing. Before we had finished reading it, each kid told me he would not perform the story. Rumpelstiltskin was abandoned on day one.

I wrote to my mentor in Story Theater, Carol Sills, who wisely advised lots of circle games to bring the group together. She also suggested a new story. "Try Bremen Town Musicians. They can sing 'Goin' Down the Road Feelin' Bad' (Woody Guthrie) in the traveling sequences between dialogue. There are good parts for five players with others on sound and lights or costumes. No stress!" A brilliant idea! They can all be animals! I was grateful to Carol. I would never have come up with this combination of song and story on my own. I armed myself with copies of Bremen Town and the song lyrics.

Days later a parent sent me an email that their child (the one who was outspoken) and his best friend (the one who couldn't sit still) both refused to perform. These kids were natural performers and could have set the tone for the group. On-the-other-hand, I can relate to feeling insecure about a new project or course. I've had many students who refrained from participating on the first day of class. I always gave them a choice. Do you want to play? Or watch? They started by observing, and before I knew it, they joined in and played. Insecurities pass in time, often more quickly when there is no pressure. I decided to cancel the planned evening performance for working parents and also the Bremen Town story. There would be no show, no rehearsals, and also no sense of urgency.

Taking an adaptable approach to the course, I encouraged the children to play their own games and invent new ones. When I showed up early for class, children were already playing. They called out to me, "Look at the games we made up!" Watching their endless running games from my seat on the couch made me feel winded. This became the warm-up period for every class. The parent of the hugging child (the boy who seemed to cause the most upsets) sat in the room with me. I was grateful for her presence since she was there whenever her child needed her. The other moms gathered upstairs.

When the kids tired of their made-up games, I introduced theater games designed to build communication and performance skills, a new game every time with no repeats. As soon as a game was underway, the children became focused, sometimes for as long as a half hour or more in a single game. Using *Improvisation for the Classroom* by Viola Spolin and *Handbook of Recreational Games* by Neva Boyd, I found games to help them speak more directly, listen more closely, develop observational skills, combine fluid movement with imagination, connect players with each other, and help players access their intuition. These games opened doors within the children themselves. Once the kids started playing, they wanted more.

As the children learned and played, problems persisted. One of the worst was fighting over the bathroom light. When a child needed to use the bathroom, located under the basement stairs, they had to flip the light switch on the outside wall before they went in. Moments after they closed the door, the child who loved to touch would run to the switch and flip it, causing the child sitting on the toilet to cry out in the dark. His mom and I would see it coming as he raced to the switch, but saying, "No!" had no effect. All we could do was turn the light back on. The child coming out of the room was always angry, and the culprit's response was always, "I didn't mean to," which resulted in the boy who shut out the light getting yelled at by the boy who'd been in the darkened bathroom. Everyone was frustrated. How could he not mean to do it when he willfully did it again and again? After these episodes, the moon-faced child ended up in his mother's lap, and sometimes the pair left the room for a brief decompression and so the others could calm down. Other problems included lack of continuity and togetherness. It was rare for all the players to share the same focus or to experience any sense of unity.

I let the parents know that, since there was no planned performance, the final hour of class was open for observation. We would play some new games, and there might be an unplanned, spontaneous surprise performance.

The final class was devoted to Gibberish games. We warmed up by creating made-up words, first using long vowel sounds then using sharp consonant sounds. They played Gibberish English, speaking intermittent Gibberish and English as I side-coached players to switch back and forth between the two languages. Next was Gibberish Teacher, where a student taught the class something in Gibberish while another student translated in English. Then came one of my personal favorite games, Gibberish Translator, which always makes the audience laugh, where everyone takes turns at playing a translator or a speaker of Gibberish.

When we took our snack break, the bathroom fiasco repeated, with the light suddenly extinguished by our round-faced troublemaker, leaving another child in the dark. But this time there was a difference.

The child inside the darkened room shrieked and came out angry. The one guilty of shutting the light responded as he always had. "I didn't mean to...." Only this time he said more. "I didn't mean to ... scare you. I didn't mean to ... get you upset."

All season long we had been frustrated, even angry, at this child for repeatedly upsetting his class-mates and then saying that he didn't mean to. Now, in our last class, I realized for the first time that he had never finished his sentences! "I didn't mean to" was just the first part! Hearing only that part had made it sound like a thoughtless denial that just made the others angrier. But this time we all heard more. "I didn't mean *to scare you!* I didn't mean *to upset you!*" You could see and hear this child's earnest sincerity. He may have intended to shut the light but as a game, not to be mean! He was upset on the verge of tears. The rest of the group, who every other week had shouted at him, surrounded him with words of comfort.

"That's okay. I'm not scared now."

"We're not upset any more. It's okay."

They gave him a group hug!

I have never had a teaching experience with such extreme and divergent types in such close quarters, not before or since. I was ready more than once to tear my hair out or to pack it in. But in the end, the children proved me and my impatience wrong. Each class they were learning and growing even if I failed to notice. I will never again underestimate the power of Gibberish! Speaking with made-up words and sounds pushed the children's communication skills to new levels. This boy was finally able to express how he felt more fully with the result that the group came together for the first time. Instead of feeling frustrated and pushed apart, they were unified!

If I had stuck with my first plan or my second plan and hadn't stepped back to let them play their own made-up games, perhaps this unforgettable turning point would have never happened. I needed to let the children show me what they were ready for, and I needed to let them grow and mature in their own way.

In the final hour of class, I handed each child a page of Mother Goose nursery rhymes. We played a quick game of Give and Take, and they were off. Children selected the rhymes and improvised roles on the spot. Hot Cross Buns was performed by the entire group, some speaking, some singing, some silent, all while they bought or sold or ate invisible buns. Little Miss Muffet met several spiders. Pussycat Pussycat frightened away more than one mouse. Hey Diddle Diddle had everyone jumping over the moon! The spontaneous group performance, completely unplanned and unrehearsed, was a hit.

When the course was over, I received an email from the mom who sat next to me during every class. It's a good thing that I had no clue she was an educational evaluator! Here's what she wrote:

> Dear Laurie,
>
> I want to thank you for all that you have brought to our children over the past few months. For a number of years (until I had my son and resigned from my tenured senior faculty position at CUNY [City University of New York], I evaluated teachers professionally and also taught them how to teach. I have observed every session of the class and I have never seen anyone bring more intelligence, passion, sensitivity, and joy to a class. I actually think it would be hard for anyone to maintain

"full-time" the energy level you have. As homeschoolers, we are blessed to have you.

Thank goodness I didn't know she was an evaluator while I sat there letting children go wild playing their own games, running around the room slapping the walls. In those moments, I reminded myself to stay calm, so I wouldn't go bonkers! Yet in the end, I loved every moment and every game, no matter how wild. And I loved every one of those boys and their moms too, even more than when we started. I think of Gibberish Day as Breakthrough Day and still get choked up every time I think about it. As challenging as this class was, it was all wonderful.

1

---

1. Find J – Resources on Listening, Giving and Taking, and Games

Chapter Nineteen

Geography by Culture

E ight children sit or stand around a large table covered in bright oilcloth
with paint stains and marker scribbles. On sheets of clear acetate laid over
circle templates, busy hands create stained glass windows inspired by the rose
windows of Notre Dame. One boy suddenly shouts, "Whoever's having fun
raise their hands!" and every kid in the room shoots up one hand while the other
hand continues to draw. A child takes her drawing to the window and tapes it
on the glass, steps back to see how the light filters through, and then adds more
color to it while standing at the window. The room is abuzz.

It all started when I met eight-year-old Wesley, with his tousled hair and
earnest eyes, who told me geography was his favorite subject. No wonder since
he had just moved to New York City from Australia after visiting other countries along the way. When I asked him if he wanted me to teach a geography class
with other kids, his face lit up. "Yes, please!" Multicultural Geography began as a
spark between teacher and child, igniting a series that would become curriculum
candy, the kind children want to eat all day long.

Students choose the places, maybe a country, city, or island. To start the
process, we play a game of Geography, using random place names to create a
chain by taking the last letter of the previous place as the initial of the next. If
a child gets stuck, they can ask for a clue and call on any student whose hand

is raised. That child can suggest a food or landmark or utter a foreign word, anything they can think of to help the player come up with an appropriate place name. The games puts all sorts of place names into the space. Then, we explore where students' families are from, the places they've visited and want to return to, or places they've heard of or read about or yearn to see. Throughout the discussion, a list forms on the board. Every child will select a first choice and maybe a second or third. I will write down their selections and try to schedule enough classes so each child gets their first choice.

Responses to "What do you want to know about each place?" vary with every group. How do you say hello in that language? How do they celebrate New Year's? What do they believe there? What are their symbols (the flag, national bird, etc.)? What do they eat and what do their clothes and houses look like? What kinds of animals live there? Normally politics doesn't come up in an elementary-aged group, but once, a nine-year-old asked about government: "Is a group of people in charge, or does one person decide everything?" I applied this question, and the others, to each place, but normally I avoid politics and news, suggesting they ask their parents. Besides answers to their questions I also supply images, a game played by children who live there ("Yes!" some children jump out of their seats when they hear this), a folktale or fairy tale from that place (big smiles and thumbs up), and a hands-on activity on art, music, or dance (sometimes they jump up or start dancing in their seats with arms and legs moving wildly about while the child is in a chair). At the end of each class, I remind them which place comes next and take down any specific questions such as, for Paris, France, "How high is the Eiffel Tower?"; for Italy, "Do they eat meatballs on spaghetti?" (They do not.); for Hawaii, "Does everybody swim?"

We spend one or two classes on each place with a game, maps, fun facts, symbols, a folktale read together, and a hands-on activity relating to the culture. The range of topics included in questions, story, and activity makes this an interdisciplinary course where all academic subjects meet. This is not just geography! Games, maps, and architecture include math; animals are part of science; religion and art contain history; children read and discuss stories, and sometimes write stories or poetry.

World maps are used in the selection process on the first day, establishing map-reading skills at the outset. Looking at a map, what can we tell about the people who live there? Regarding the coastline of Portugal, one child said, "I bet they eat a lot of fish!" That led to mentions of boat-building and then to world exploration. We consider the environment, mountains, ocean, or desert and consider what kinds of animals might live there and what kinds of activities people might do. Early maps can be amusing such as one that showed California as an island or another that revealed as the tiny walled city of Paris. Careful examination of a map leads to more questions, and each map becomes a story that can be read.

In our first class, I explain and demonstrate map distortion. We live on a curved planet that is three-dimensional, but maps are flat and two-dimensional, resulting in inevitable flaws. For our first hands-on activity, each student needs an orange (preferably a large naval orange rather than a small mandarin) and a permanent marker in a dark color. I tell them to, first, color the continents on the orange, turning it into a world map, an orange globe. Then peel the orange carefully, keeping the peel as intact as possible while trying not to erase the map. Finally, spread the peel out on a flat surface. The peel will have to tear in some places in order to come away from the orange and even more in order to flatten, but try to keep it in one piece. Does it look like a map of the world? What's wrong with it? How would you fix it to make it a flat map? Then, we look at different versions of flat world maps and compare how the distortions vary from map to map. Comparing common versions such as the Robinson projection to the Peters projection (showing equal mass land values) is enlightening and can lead to discussion. Shapes and sizes of countries and continents change with every map often creating very different perspectives.

For elementary students, I introduce Cinderella tales from around the world with various differences in the classic tale depending on where it's from. Does she wear a kimono or a cloak of feathers? Does she eat honey or figs or rice? Does she lose a glass slipper or a golden sandal? Several versions are depicted in one book, *Glass Slipper Gold Sandal: A Worldwide Cinderella* by Paul Fleischman with illustrations and content reflecting different countries.

Our collective virtual journeys always highlight the heritage and cultures of students. A boy from Turkey, proud of his Islamic heritage, visits his grandparents every summer in the town where Rumi wrote his famous poems. In that class, we read Rumi poems as well as a Turkish folktale. After looking at beautiful tiles and wall designs in Turkey, we drew geometric patterns found in Islamic art (from the *Islamic Art and Geometric Design Activity Book*, free from the Metropolitan Museum of Art). The student from Turkey taught us how to say hello in Turkish and shared his favorite recipes, licking his lips over how yummy food is in Turkey.

A girl from India said she wanted to hear *all* the stories about *all* the gods. I laughed, and she admitted that a single story can take two weeks. We read a short tale that introduced a few Hindu gods. Looking at images of traditional Indian clothing, the student was excited to tell us that her grandmother wears a traditional sari and a bindi (marking the third eye) on her forehead. She also told us about celebrating Holi (the Festival of Color) in New Jersey with friends and family. As an art project, we drew mandalas in bright colors.

A student with Mexican heritage taught us how to pronounce the words for images in Loteria (Mexican Bingo), which she plays with her grandmother. The others enjoyed learning Spanish nouns while playing this game. We played long enough for each child to become a winner and call out *Loteria*! The folktale we read was "The Day It Snowed Tortillas," which made the children laugh (there's a spoken version on YouTube by author Joe Hayes). We decorated Jaguar Masks and Day of the Dead masks (online templates can be printed). We looked at the work of Diego Rivera and Frida Kahlo, and used Frida Kahlo's paintings for inspiration to draw a self-portrait or a still life with fruit and animal. I suggested fruit with a stuffed animal. This was a Zoom class, and I watched each child run to the kitchen and their bedroom and return to set up a still life with fruit and stuffed animal, which they drew while listening to mariachi music.

Games have included clapping games from South Africa, red-light-green-light in French (un, deux, trois, soleil!), rock/paper/scissors in Japanese (where it may have originated), saying tongue twisters (popular in

Turkey), and Grandma's Bloomers, which was as huge a hit here as it is in Russia.

For each place, we read a folktale that reflects the culture, perhaps mentioning the geography, foods, animals, customs, and beliefs. Examples include how the trickster God Maui fished up the Hawaiian Islands and how ancient Egyptians looked forward to life after death. Copies are passed out or text is shared via Zoom, and readers take turns (reading aloud is voluntary), sometimes joining together for a chorus or phrase, sometimes standing to act out a part. If there is a food or herb in the story, I might have it on the table to look at or smell, or I'll send a recipe in advance. After reading the story, we talk about what it reveals about the place. Does it confirm or change our impressions? What surprised us? If it was funny, what does that tell us about their sense of humor? What else can we learn from the story? Each story is a portal into another culture.

Hands-on activities deepen our understanding because the senses and physical body are activated. We danced the hula and sang the Hukilau song (Hawaii), made stained glass windows (France), designed kimono art with haiku (Japan), wrote our names in hieroglyphs on papyrus scrolls (ancient Egypt), drew imaginary upside-down landscapes inspired by Chagall (Russia), and more.

Whenever possible, parents supply food. One year at in-person classes parents donated platters of food, and we feasted our way around the world. The child who chose the place was usually responsible for supplying food, and often a mom or grandparent contributed traditional dishes. We ate homemade mochi (Japan), pizza (Italy), dolmas (stuffed grape leaves), and even squid, which most refused to taste (Greece). The student from Greece taught the class the proper way to eat Greek sugar cookies so they wouldn't choke on the sugar. The secret— exhale first!

Sometimes children change their minds about the place they chose. If they're not sure of their choice, I move them down the list to give them extra time. One year, a girl who had chosen New Zealand changed it to Mexico because she wanted to know more about where her grandparents lived. Another girl swapped her choice of China for Portugal since her grandmother had just come back from a trip there. Another student traded Iceland for Florida after moving there because she wanted to learn about her new home. For the Florida class, we read two stories, a traditional Seminole tale and a children's biography about Marjorie Stoneman Douglas, who saved the Everglades. They were just as engaged with the biography as they were with the native tale.

Days, maybe weeks before each class, I find myself perusing lists of children's games, photos of landmarks and holiday celebrations, history books and works by great artists. I browse folktales and search YouTube for traditional music and e-mail recipes so children can plan international dishes at home, extending their virtual travel beyond class to their next meal. I experiment with art projects, and my study becomes littered with origami, mask templates, examples of foreign architecture, books on artists from around the world. It can be a lot of work to create a fresh class every week, but it's a thrill to experience world travel through the eyes of children taking a multi-sensory, hands-on approach to places that hold personal meaning. And we don't have to leave home. Pull up a chair to your computer, and join us as we Zoom ourselves far away, roaming the world, playing, exploring, discovering, eating, and creating as we go.

My love of travel is contagious. I was raised traveling with parents who spoke several languages. They often taught in other countries, taking us with them for the summer. The first memory I have of being immersed in another culture included a sense of separation, as if I were trapped in a bubble with my family, the only ones I could freely communicate with. And then suddenly, the bubble burst as I experienced communication without spoken language. And then when I started to learn a few words, I felt less afraid, more at home in a strange place. The learning experience of travel is transformational. Experiencing a place other than my homeland while still a child, I began to see the whole world differently. I learned there's something new and interesting around every corner. These classes were a way for me to share the thrill of travel. Even if a true immersive travel experience isn't possible, the constant variety of activities makes it feel like a whirlwind vacation.

Travel is a learning experience like no other. It is not just knowledge about other places. When we experience another culture, we grow towards greater understanding and tolerance, appreciating each other and our own heritage better. We start to see our own culture and ourselves differently. We learn to embraces our own culture as we embrace others.

Endless journeys are possible. There are a limitless number of places to explore and a limitless number of things to learn and do in each place. One or two classes on a single location only scratches the surface. We could spend an entire year on any one place and not get bored. Our appetite increases, and we become curious about the entire world.[1]

---

1. See A – Multicultural Geography Syllabus

Chapter Twenty

Puppets in the Snow

O n a mountain in Maine sits a red one-room schoolhouse, recently built, with large windows, a loft, a performance space, and a cozy feel. It has an old school bell that I've had the privilege of ringing, beckoning children from all directions beyond the horse barn and the greenhouses. They run barefoot through cooperative gardens, past a circle of apple trees planted so closely together they are called the Apple House. In this Wild Mountain community, I have taught mapmaking, poetry and bookmaking, and children's games outdoors in summer. This time, I was invited in mid-January, with the ground covered in snow, to teach puppetry.

A group of women had rented the schoolhouse for a weekend business retreat and needed an activity to occupy their children while they worked. I had a month's advance notice, barely enough time to plan a workshop that I had never taught before. My goals were lofty: for each child to create one or two original puppets and develop the skills needed to improvise puppet plays with each other. I drew up a list of games and activities that I believed would achieve this goal. Counting the hours, I realized I would need five to ten days of play and development instead of just two. Did I need to reassess my goal and aim for less? Or was it possible for me to give them what I wanted in so little time?

My ideal list relied heavily on Mervyn Millar's book *Puppetry: How to Do It*, a classic with everything needed to teach this art. For Millar's stick activity, I foraged the forest floor for a bag full of twigs as potential first puppets, seeing in each a unique, expressive figure that could move in a myriad of ways. I practiced the activity alone and was enchanted that a mere twig, typically ignored and trod upon, could come to life without any adornment and behave like a puppet. Once you can turn a stick into a puppet, any object can become a puppet! Yet, I knew this exercise could take an entire morning, one fourth of the workshop. With a pang of regret, I deleted the activity.

I pruned the list further, skipping some of the warm-up games, trying to get to the heart of the experience. How quickly could I introduce basic skills? How fast could we get to the core of the work? I stared at a page in Spolin's book, *Improvisation for the Theater*, considering a game called Hands Alone. It was similar to a game called Backs Alone, which I had played near the end of my first week of intensive Spolin training many years earlier. Backs Alone had terrified me. Each player silently selected an emotion or feeling to express and then sat on a stool with their back to the audience while playing an invisible piano. I couldn't imagine that I would be able to express emotion through my back or that I would be able to detect it in someone else's. I postponed my turn until I was last. By then, I had already surprised myself by noticing emotions and feelings expressed in the backs of other players' bodies as they swayed back and forth over a keyboard in space. Now it was my turn. Hunched down, my face unseen by the audience, I pounded imaginary piano keys and focused on the feeling. Aretha Sills side-coached me, as she had others, to deepen my focus, to feel the emotion in the back of my legs, in my elbows, the back of my head as I played the piano some more. Afterwards, group feedback named the feeling I was trying to express, surprising me yet again.

Hands Alone was the same game but with hands instead of backs. As a middle-aged adult I had been scared to play this game at the end of a five-day workshop. How could I ask young children to play it on day one? Was it crazy for me to consider playing it the *morning* of day one?

For weeks, I amended my plan, searching again and again for the quickest route to essential skills. I doubt if I ever worked longer on a curriculum for a short-term workshop. I arrived on a cold morning, clouds of breath coming from my mouth as I walked to the Common House. Inside, it was warm with the sound of children's laughter coming from above. I climbed the stairs, where my friend and co-teacher had finished a morning circle meditation with eleven children, ages 4-12, who were now discussing Common House rules and good behavior.

Introductions included name tagging and portrait photos taken on my phone. I would use the photos later that day to memorize their names. A warm-up game of Pussy Wants a Corner had the kids running, laughing, and looking each other in the eye. This was followed with body stretches. "Make yourself as big as you can! Stretch to the ceiling as if you could reach the sky! Puff up yourself! Get bigger! Now make the biggest sound you can!" Deep whooshes of noise entered the room. Then I coached them to become small, tiny, hidden, to make the smallest noise they could, which emerged as squeaky peeps. Next, everyone donned facial and body expressions for major emotions. What does tiredness (or anger or joy or confusion) look like in your face? In your body? Physical stretches were accompanied by creative emotional stretches. We all did a Space Walk with the focus to See and Be Seen, including and occluding fellow players. These exercises connected the group and laid a foundation for intuitive play and performance.

We pulled the couch away from the wall to create a stage for Hands Alone. Each child silently chose an emotion. One at a time, they crouched behind the stage and let just their hand be seen to express the feeling. One hand strutted or marched, fingers held high; another cowered and shook, jumping at every sound; another danced a jig; another kept changing direction, going in circles; another kept making a fist. Group feedback following each mini-performance spontaneously named the emotion expressed. I could see it too, clearly defined in the behavior of each hand. Afterwards, I asked the kids if they had thought they'd be able to do this, to see and express an emotion in only one hand, and they all shook their heads solemnly, "No." My teacher-friend leaned over and whispered in my ear, "Neither did I." My elation at that moment was so great I felt like I could reach the sky. I'd thrown the entire group into the deep end of the pool, and they all swam! Everyone had, individually and collectively, experienced something they didn't think was possible. To start off a workshop with a revelatory, life-changing experience took my breath away. From that moment on, the children saw themselves differently. The workshop was alive!

I handed out their first puppets, two pairs of Oobie Eyes for each student. These are just a pair of googly eyes with a plastic bridge that can slip over a child's fingers, turning a hand instantly into a puppet. The children needed no additional instruction. Puppet plays were already happening.

After lunch, I walked alone in the snow, calm and alert from the morning's brilliance. I stumbled on a snowman the children had just finished. Larger than adult size, it looked happy in a rakish straw hat and Oobi eyes set into its face: a giant puppet snowman!

The afternoon was an explosion of energy as materials were spread out on tables and children eagerly made puppets. There were colorful tube socks and blank canvas hand puppet forms, which they could choose as the puppet base. Boxes of fabric pens, jars of buttons, bags of puff balls, curly yarn, pipe cleaners, wiggly eyes in all shapes and colors offered an endless assortment of goodies. As characters appeared, I asked each maker, "Does your puppet have a name?"

"Yoooshie," whispered the youngest member of the group, scrunching his sock puppet as he scrunched his face.

"Side-eye," mused one of the older kids regarding his puppet. "He's an alien with two faces." He flipped his hand around to show the second character drawn on the back (or front?) of the canvas form. Literally a two-faced character!

"Neat!" commented an admiring fellow student as she put a mustache on her puppet and gave him an Italian name.

"Slither," a young puppet-maker held out his arm with a dark puppet on his hand. "He's an alien snake."

Two girls were flopped down on their stomachs on the floor, sharing ideas with a pile of decorating material between them, hard at work designing their puppets. The room hummed with creativity, an organized mayhem.

That day, children took home two sets of Oobi eyes, handmade original puppets-in-progress, and blank character sheets to complete for a game the following day. They were invited to practice their new-found puppetry skills, play Hands Alone, play with Oobi eyes, finish their puppets, and complete as much possible on the character sheets. I told them not to worry if they didn't have enough time at home because we could finish the next morning.

The ideal kind of "homework" is not an imposed assignment or (worse yet) boring rote practice, but the extension of a project created by the child that they are already motivated to finish. The child's enthusiasm adds to the work and has them aspire to new heights, while the threat of a low grade or a teacher's disapproval adds stress, impedes the creative process, and lessens the learning experience. The next morning, the children brought their enthusiasm with them. I, too, showed up eager for more. There was no slowing our momentum.

Warm-up games were Who games, laying groundwork for character development. Who Started the Motion is a traditional children's game that increases awareness. Red Light Green Light is a universal children's game with endless variations. We played as animals with each player at the front assigning the animal every child would be. To slow the game down, they might choose a sloth or turtle, but there are never instructions as to how an animal moves. Each player makes that interpretation in the moment. Having played this game myself, I know the delight of seeing a row of human ducks or hummingbirds race towards me. Then we did a second Space Walk, this time with a focus on support.

Now, it was time to wake up the puppets. Each handmade puppet was invited to wake up slowly, in the way a character might naturally awaken, and then to explore the room. Where did they want to go? What obstacles were in their way? Were they scared? Excited? Rebellious? Confused? What were their interests and their fears? We watched puppets explore, react, and explore some more. This led to the completion of character sheets with both teachers and a parent volunteer available to help if the younger children needed scribes.

In puppetry, as in playwriting, when character sheets are completed, we play the Interview Game where each puppet finds its voice. First, the maker of the puppet reads the character sheet out loud or has it read by an adult or older child. Then the puppet, moved by the maker's hand, enters the performance space. Once in this space, the puppet stays in character vocally and physically. I welcome each character by name and thank it for consenting to be interviewed at the start and again at the end when the group applauds their thanks. During the interview, audience members are invited to ask questions. The character is invited to call on anyone whose hand is raised. The character sheet info, read aloud before the interview, always inspires questions such as, "Why are you afraid of dogs (What happened?)," or "What act would you perform if you actually joined the circus?" or "Why are you angry at your brother? What did he do?" Characters answer impromptu as part of the game. Answers spark new questions; interviews keep going to make sure everyone gets a turn. At some point, I will say, "That's all we have time for," perhaps allowing for one last question. Reluctant students usually lose their hesitancy at taking the interview seat after hearing the first player's feedback. Everyone who experiences this game is grateful for the additional insights into their character. Stories can be developed from a character sheet, but they are born naturally in the interview process.

Lunch interrupted the interviews, which continued after the break. In another course with a different time frame, I would have stretched the interviews out over several sessions doing a few in any given day. But it was essential now, in the middle of our last day, to meet every puppet and hear them speak.

Then we played Puppet Encounters[1], which is the start of improvised scenes between players. Previously the puppets had explored the room. Now they explored each other. Puppets realized they were not alone and became curious or nervous, scared, aggressive, sneaky, talkative, or even silly when they saw their fellow puppets. They hid or approached, laughed or shouted, argued or whispered, battled or befriended. All around the room puppet relationships had commenced.

Yet, there was still an important missing ingredient. We had focused on the Who with character development but had, up to this moment, neglected the Where. In order to perform a scene, a setting must be present, a place where the characters can interact with each other and with the setting itself. In other classes, I've spent hours developing settings with students sometimes beginning with the setting rather than the character. We had less than an hour until performance time. There are many Spolin "Where" games to choose from, and I selected a simple weather exercise. Players were split into three groups. Each quietly chose a specific type of weather with a location. They were instructed to show us the weather, not tell us. As each group entered the performance space, I side-coached them to react to the weather, to feel it in their body, to see it, hear it, smell it. Audience members gave feedback indicating they saw the weather and sometimes a setting as well. We all saw flashes of lightening in a thunder storm lighting up the night sky. And we all saw a hot summer day on a beach as players sweltered in the sun. This brief game was just enough to give children the skill they needed to establish a setting.

The couch was moved away from the wall for final performances. Parents who were available trickled into the room to watch. Scenes with fully-formed characters emerged in play after play. There was combat! We watched a puppet do martial arts moves that had him flying across the stage! There was humor! The mustachioed Italian gentleman had a pet who purposely did the opposite of whatever it was told to do. The audience roared! Knowing the character would rebel each time it was spoken to only increased our delight. Characters rebelled against each other, tricked each other, fought with each other, got into mischief together, and became friends. We laughed and laughed. Then suddenly in the waning light of a winter Sunday, I had to leave.

On my long ride home, I was alternately elated and concerned. The improvised puppet performances were thrilling, and the energy in the room was high. Even so, I knew my plan was risky. We could have done more, starting with games like Dog and Bone (increasing listening skills and awareness), Give and Take (working in groups seamlessly), and Space Shaping (creating something out of nothing). Warm-ups for performance could have included the hand puppets waking up, starting their day in the setting, exploring feelings and relationships that could start a scene. Going straight from the weather game to performance was not ideal even if it worked. Puppets need time to breathe! So do players! Performing other stories first such as fairy tales or fables would have given students a foundation of puppetry and performance skills. Children went home with copies of Aesop tales that we didn't perform, just as I went home with a list of games we didn't play. There is never enough time to do everything, but this time the choices were a tight squeeze. I wished this ten-hour workshop could have been 20 or 30 hours. Yet in the world of creative intuition where puppets come to life, time and space seemed to melt away.

It is amazing that in two short days the children created and built fully-developed puppet characters and learned the skills needed to improvise plays together. Later that week, my co-teacher emailed feedback. The children had agreed that Tuesdays would now be called Puppet Tuesdays! They would gather every Tuesday evening to perform puppet shows for family and friends! My residual doubts melted away. There is no greater response to a course of study than continued enthusiasm and sustained involvement. I knew that in just two short days the lives of children, families and, yes, puppets, had transformed. [2]

---

1. * from Mervyn Melvil's *Puppetry: How to Do It*

2. See B – Puppetry Activities and Syllabus

Chapter Twenty-One

Board Game Land

Was I really flying to the other side of the world? As I stretched my legs and tipped back my seat, I mentally tipped the globe, placing the North Pole at the bottom, and imagined the giant silver bird that carried me arcing towards the top of the world. It had taken years of effort after being invited to make this trip happen. The 22-hour flight was, comparatively, a mere moment, whisking me away to a mysterious kingdom. There, I would reunite with my dear friend and mentor, Jim Hooson, an educational wizard who spoke the language of all children and the person instrumental in organizing my workshops. I had planned two four-day workshops, How to Make Your Own Board Game for ages 8-12 and Playwriting for Teens, with additional lectures and half-day workshops for parents and teachers on the weekends. I quieted my usual nervousness before the start of every new class and focused on what I wanted the most, to see Jim's smiling face with that twinkle in his eyes and wrap my arms around his broad chest to give him a bear hug.

My husband had shopped around for tickets and got us free stopovers to and from our destination in Sydney, Australia. Our first stop was for two days in New Zealand, a place we longed to explore, but we woke to a raging blizzard, closed roads, and halted flights. Snow is rare in Auckland, and people ran outside in T-shirts to taste the snowflakes and catch them in their hands. We abandoned fantasies of wild beaches and winding mountain roads and walked, shivering, to a museum.

That evening, I got a call. Jim had died. The magic carpet of my journey gave way, and I felt a nothingness beneath me, a complete loss of support. His son had called me right away with the news and to ask one question: Would I continue, or would I cancel the events that had been planned?

Every fairy tale adventure is fraught with obstacles, villains, and danger. Jim and I had dealt with many obstacles, separately and together. Although he had been ill for some time, I never thought that the villain would be Death. In this call, Death greeted me like a threatening ambassador, daring me to arrive in Sydney the next day wearing a shadow. Believing I was equal to the challenge, I met the situation head on. Every detail of Jim's plans would be honored, and in this way, I would celebrate his spirit.

I looked down from the sky as silver clouds parted to reveal a golden city with sparkling beaches. We circled over the Sydney Opera House that looked like an origami bird about to open its wings and passed more crescent beaches. How could this be winter? I had left New York City in late August; the last food I had eaten was a ripe peach with juice dripping down my chin. I had just wintered for two days in Auckland in a snowstorm we were unprepared for. Now, I saw a sun-splashed city with people surfing and bobbing in the waves. Surely this was another world.

We were met at the airport by the father of students I had taught in New York, who drove us to a great house on a hill. Friends of Jim, they had invited us to stay in their home. We cooked in a spacious modern kitchen and dined with a view of the bay. It felt unreal, as if I were in a dream.

The next day, I visited Jim's workplace for the first time to give a lecture to parents and educators on child-led learning. I had always imagined Jim's office to be large and busy with room for a staff to work with several children, so I was surprised to find three small rooms full of books and toys. We made a large circle of chairs, and I got out my notes. As people arrived, they learned of Jim's death, and grief grabbed them without warning. I hadn't expected Death to make it so difficult for me. Questions and comments were interrupted by uncontrollable sobbing. We sat and waited quietly, patiently, for the person to weep so they could finish their question. And then it would happen again, the uncontrollable weeping. Each time I breathed deeply, focusing on my breath rather than on the grief. I imagined energy rising through my feet and felt rooted and strong. I was aware and connected but also carefully distanced so that I wouldn't cry too.

Jim had rescued children from punitive schools, helped parents to home-school, and guided children to overcome learning difficulties using his unique creative approaches. A pioneer in special education, Jim invented techniques that empowered children. Parents and kids of all ages adored him. All the years I knew Jim, I had yearned to see him in his workspace and home. Now, perversely, I felt fortunate I hadn't because the place I was visiting didn't trigger personal memories and fresh grief. I was able to put aside my own sense of shock and loss and be not just a teacher for this community but also an unwitting grief counselor, allowing others to express their emotions openly in a safe and understanding environment. It wasn't until years after this trip that I realized I had still not allowed myself to grieve.

After the lecture, I asked volunteers to inform class parents of Jim's passing so the news would not be shared around young children on the first day of Make Your Own Board Game. I needed to avoid shock and emotional outbursts and create a playful, gentle atmosphere. Before we made games, we would play.

The first day, my driver, a volunteer parent, parked the car alongside a suburban park by the sea. As if I were wearing magic slippers out of Arabian Nights, I looked at my feet, charmed to see them strolling down a twisty tree-lined path that curved towards a small beach. Straight ahead was the classroom space, a one-room, low-roofed building with large windows and double doors facing the ocean. Entering, I looked up at the expansive white ceiling with delicate crystal chandeliers that cast little rainbows on the walls. This place must get rented for weddings, I thought. I knew Jim had found the best place to work for the best price. People have been known to bend the rules when it comes to providing rare learning experiences for children. I've had the pleasure of teaching in many beautiful places, but none compared with this.

An ocean breeze wafted through the classroom space, the water peeking out from a distance. The park was part wild, part landscaped garden, part old-growth forest, part beach. At lunchtime, kids climbed trees and rocks, picnicked on grass or sand, swam in the ocean and returned refreshed, laughing with new friends, shaking the water out of their wet hair. From 10am to 4pm, we played games and made games.

Parents stayed to observe and assist. About half were homeschooling families and the rest had taken their kids out of school for the week. On the first day at mid-morning break, an 8-year-old girl accused her father.

"You lied to me!" Her voice was shrill. He looked as surprised as I felt.

"What do you mean?" he asked.

"You lied to me! She can't be a teacher! She's too much fun!" She was referring to me, of course, but she was dead serious. Her father laughed and said, no, I was really a teacher. "But she can't be!" insisted his daughter. I had heard that Australia had cold, regimented schools, but her accusation made me shudder.

Break was over; we played another game. Each time, it was like waving a magic wand again. If children felt shy, perhaps because they didn't know anyone and they weren't speaking, we played Extended Sound, a circle game where players physically and vocally throw and catch sounds to each other. Afterwards, talk and communication flowed. If they couldn't stop talking and weren't listening, we played a different circle game called Dog and Bone, where even the antsiest, most talkative kids don't move a muscle and strain to hear every sound. After a group of students have played that game, I never need to call for quiet or ask for attention because everyone is already listening. Perhaps the most popular game in this workshop is Stump the Class, a game that came out of the board game course organically.

On the first day, I ask the students to each choose a topic they are already interested in and want to learn more about. Students have chosen topics such as the solar system, soccer, the city of London, cats, horses, pigs, money, chocolate, Greek mythology, the Civil War, horror movies, music of the 1980's, orchids of Puerto Rico — there is no end to the topics that children might choose.

Once a student couldn't decide whether to focus his game on diseases or the history of hospitals. We had a zany question session where students asked as many questions as they possibly could in a five-minute period without changing or correcting any of the questions while I wrote them down at madcap speed. Then we discussed the questions. We changed any statements into questions. We placed a C next to closed questions that had simple, finite answers, and an O next to open questions that had long, variable answers. We changed at least one open question to a closed and vice versa. We broke up some questions into smaller questions and added questions that seemed to be implied within others. During this process, we looked for categories to emerge. Were the questions all on one subject or on several subtopics? Examining the board filled with questions on hospitals and diseases, it became clear to the student that his topic was Diseases and Cures. Immediately all of the other students' hands rose into the air. "Can we do my topic now?" "Can we do mine too?" They all wanted a question-storming session!

My mother, a professor specializing in art history, asked her grandson when he was about four or five if he knew what research was. "That's when you look something up on the Internet to find out what it is," he answered.

"Well, that's what most people think it is," my mother gave him a sharp glance.

"What do you think it is?" he honestly wanted to know.

"To me, research is about discovering something new! And there are so many new things to discover!" My mother's enthusiasm knew no bounds. Every day she could open a book, visit a museum, or go to a library with a certainty she would discover something new.

When research is question-based and driven by innate curiosity— wanting to learn more about something already interesting— it is a constant flow of discovery. We discover more than information. We discover how to obtain the information and how to learn about it. We acquire the skill of learning how to learn. And we discover how we feel about the information. The final result of our research is the most fulfilling— we discover ourselves!

After game topics are chosen, I ask them what they think research is and where they might find information about their topic. They answer just as my son did and say the Internet. Then they add books. Together, we list at least seven different types of research, seven different kinds of resources that I hope they will use: (1) the Internet (I require reliable sources. I explain why Wikipedia can be used as a stepping stone to find an official site but not as a factual resource.), (2) books, (3) periodicals (newspapers, magazines, and newsletters), (4) interviews with experts, (5) personal observation (such as observing animals in a zoo or in the wild), (6) museums and historic sites and (7) specialized libraries, collections, and archives (examples include the picture collection at the main New York Public Library, the Black history archives in the Schomburg Collection, and the natural history library in the American Museum of Natural History).

Stump the Class lets students test their questions or fact cards on the class. If parents are present, after the students are stumped, we might toss the question to the parents. In this game, each student becomes the teacher. By researching their game and playing Stump the Class, they unknowingly make a curriculum and teach it. Students rapidly develop expertise in their topic and learn facts we couldn't possibly know. Every morning when I ask, "Who wants to stump the class?" hands shoot up across the room. Questions have included: "When was the helicopter invented?" "How much does a baby owl weigh?" "What is the average lifespan of an isopod?" "What is the world's largest bear?" Students raise their hands to be called on by the Stumper and usually guess wrong. Before the correct answer is given, parents might be given a chance to answer. When we all give up, the student announces the answer with pride, standing taller before our eyes. And then they pose another question and stump us again!

One parent came to me midweek, perplexed and smiling, to tell me this was the first time he didn't have to make his kid do the homework. Odder still, he couldn't *stop* his kid from doing it! Long past bedtime, bleary-eyed, the child begged, "Please Dad, let me write down just one more fact so I can stump the class tomorrow!" The father shook his head in disbelief. He didn't understand the magic formula to make a kid want to do homework. Motivation ignites the moment a project is chosen by the child and the flames are fanned by audience enthusiasm. Stumping an entire class is a confidence-building experience, fun for all because everyone knows they will get a turn.

I have taught hundreds of students How to Make Your Own Board Game, yet in every class, I am surprised. A child once asked me if he had to use the board. I told him that the choice of game design was up to him, but since he was given a blank board, he might as well see if there was a way he could incorporate it into his game. Not long before Game Day he showed me the result. The blank square board was diagonally striped in various colors, a stunning rainbow from corner to corner. His board timed the length of play with all pawns starting on the stripe at one corner, each moving one at a time to the next stripe with the game ending when they all reached the final stripe in the opposite corner. I have never seen a board like that before or since nor have I seen a game timed in that manner. I explained to the student that this was an example of creativity resulting from limitations. He didn't want to use the board and felt limited by it yet came up with an original use and created something truly beautiful. He was quite proud of the item he hadn't wanted!

Another student, the one who created a game on diseases and cures, wanted to make a 3-D board. The square boards fold up, and he used that folding feature along with some well-placed velcro to turn his board into a cube. Pawns could travel on all sides. This is another original use of a flat game board that I have not seen before or since.

In Board Game class in Australia, one child invented his own spinner. First, he pushed his paper needle straight across the floor as if he was playing shuffleboard but overshot the ladder-like row of numbers. So he placed the numbers in a circle and spun a shorter paper dial with his finger until it stopped, pointing at a number. He also invented a complicated grid where the pawns, shaped like boats, moved. His game was called The First Fleet, based on the first arrival of European settlers to Australia, and his complicated grid represented trade winds where ships easily get lost.

An older student invented a generic board game called What Do You Want to Know? The board itself could be used for any subject: you only had to swap out the fact cards for a different set. This way she could use the game whenever she wanted to study a specific subject by making a set of cards and playing the game. A multiple-use board game, another brilliant invention!

The youngest child in board game class was seven, a year younger than the suggested age range. She was there with her older sister, eager to make a game. Her topic was baby monkeys in the rainforest, and her board design was ambitious. She wanted a pop-up rain forest with baby monkeys traveling across the treetops. I suggested, "You could draw the tops of trees on the board, and monkeys can walk across." But she shook her head no to this and all other suggestions. Several adults, including me, tried to dissuade her from her vision of a pop-up rainforest with baby monkeys walking along the treetops! But she had her heart set on it and went straight to work, starting by measuring and folding paper supports for pop-up trees. With her sister's help, she drew and cut out trees and attached them to the folding supports so the trees would fold when the board was closed and pop up when it opened. Her mother and other students, new-found friends, assisted too. She drew and cut out paper baby monkeys and created a paper path that snaked through the treetops. You could slide a baby monkey pawn along the path any number of spaces and park it at a slit in the side of the paper strip so the little monkey rested upright on the path. She not only created a pop-up forest but also a new way of moving pieces along a path and affixing them in place. The youngest child in the class succeeded in making the most complicated board! As in every board game class, I was astonished.

On Game Day, everyone, children and adults, played game after game on the floor, across the tables, on grass outside. The Perilous Pirates! game board included lyrics to "Fifteen Men on a Dead Man's Chest." The game taught the history of piracy on the high seas with a cheeky sense of humor. Time Travel Through British History had a board like a wheel with several paths reaching from the circumference to the center and stacks of cards labeled Tudors, Stuarts, Normans, Victorians, and more— British time travel in a board game! World Cup Soccer was all in green with fact cards covering every World Cup event. Heliport had a bright blue helicopter flying across the board. Mr. Zebra was decorated in black and white stripes with the game pathway in the shape of a giant Z going from corner to corner.

Some games had different takes on the same topic. Greek Mythology had a wandering path surrounded by graceful goddesses while "Labyrinth" was an ominous maze of dark squares and stacks of cards with images of statues of fierce Greek gods. Ancient Egypt looked like a map of an Egyptian tomb; Pharaohs used the symbols of the crook and flail and the ankh on the board pathway. Solar System had a spiral pathway filled with stars and planets. There were more! Bees and Butterflies, Dolphins, Railroads, Horses, World War I, Owls, and Mythical Creatures! Twenty games[1] had been made, and students played as many as they could. We were drunk on games!

This event is always magical for me. On Game Day, I don't do anything except watch the children play. Normally an active leader and guide, I am now a passive audience witnessing their success. No one needs to explain their game or entice others to play it. The students have been educated in each game by playing Stump the Class and are eager to compete. Game instructions were peer edited by the responses of fellow students who experimented with each game during the development process. The magical motivator is group play!

Throughout the course, I heard children during breaks and lunchtime roaring with laughter as they ran towards the woods or the beach. Four boys, including the makers of Perilous Pirates and Heliport, built a fort. Children leaped off of boulders onto a grassy field with wide open smiles jubilant in flight. In the ocean, groups held hands, wading back to shore in a connected line when it was time, laughing with the sound of birds and waves. One child claimed, "I made more friends here in a single week than I did in all my years at school!"

The final weekend after all workshops and events were over, a quiet memorial for Jim was held in the same space that served as my classroom. People brought fairy-colored cupcakes and other favorite foods of Jim's and shared laugh-out-loud memories. Telegrams were read. People cried. Everyone gently hugged Jim's frail mother and his silent, brooding son. On the beach, teen students had written Jim's name in beach pebbles next to hand prints, hearts, and smiles drawn in the sand destined to wash away with the tide.

So many plans that Jim and I had made together remain undone. Yet, Jim's work and his spirit live on. Former assistants and co-workers continue to apply his groundbreaking work to help struggling students become strong individuals. Friendships I made on this trip proved to be lasting ones. Families I met in Sydney years ago are still my friends today. The sudden awfulness of Death cannot stop the flow of Love or end the work of a mighty wizard.

The power of games and the spirit of play are kin to the magical power of storytelling. All knowledge is secretly contained in stories, all skill secretly hidden in play. It is the most artful way of learning, unaware that we are gaining wisdom or developing ideas because we're having so much fun, taking a lighthearted, low-pressure, non-judgmental approach that allows our spirits to soar. Yet, we think it's just a story or just a game.

A friend told me about a conversation she had with a parent whose child attended a board game class. The mother listed the courses her homeschooled son took that year and added at the end, "and then there was a fluff course with Laurie."

"A fluff course?" my friend raised her eyebrows.

"Yeah, it was a board game class where he made a game on dinosaurs. And you wouldn't believe how much he learned in that course!"

I laughed when my friend told me about the "fluff" comment. It's easy for me to comprehend the vast amount of knowledge and skill acquired in developing a game and to recognize that the process builds confidence, increases self-awareness, and even confirms future direction. That dinosaur game-maker, years later, pursued a career in paleontology!

Is there magic in a game? Is there magic in the playing of traditional games? Are the inventions of new games like Stump the Class and new board game designs made by children part of a magical process? Yes! Real magic exists in these things! It is in the playfulness with which we approach ideas and projects, in the camaraderie that develops, in a learning process that practically unfolds by itself, in a constant state of play. We become collaborators, a community, even a family. Magic is in the expanding horizons of children as they acquire skills and techniques that are lifelong, in the transformation of ideas from the imagined to the real, where curiosity — about helicopters or horses or Greek myths — becomes an actual hands-on game full of fun and learning that will be played again and again. Perhaps the magic wand is invisible or appears as only a bit of fluff waving about in the air. This wand needs no fairy godmother. Each child, each game, each class makes its own magic.[2]

---

1. *Images of Board Game class in Australia: http://homeschoolnyc.com/images/gallery-australia.html

2. See C – Board Game Course Syllabus

Chapter Twenty-Two

Interviewing: The Lives We Live

YOU NEVER KNOW WHO WILL SHOW UP IN THE CLASSROOM
DURING AN INTERVIEW CLASS

STORIES FROM AROUND THE WORLD

Students interviewed a psychologies who, as a boy, met Martin Luther King, Jr. They interviewed a People Magazine interviewer and a man living on an island in Greece.

HIDDEN MEMORIES

One family never knew about their Russian grandfather's involvement in World War II. He had just never talked about it, but now that he was being interviewed, lots of questions and all sorts of stories came out.

~ad written by a parent for one of my interview classes

One family never knew about their Russian grandfather's involvement in World War II. He had just never talked about it, but now that he was being interviewed, lots of questions and all sorts of stories came out.

"We call it Trinterview. You know, Trio and Interview combined," the girl in the plaid dress grinned. Three middle schoolers sat in a triangle and demonstrated the game they had just invented. Students had paired off to play a warm-up game and then interview each other. There was an odd number of students and a trio was left taking turns to play, so they invented a game that all three could play together. When the other kids saw it, they wanted to join, and the triangle expanded to a circle as rules were explained. One player starts by asking a simple, closed-ended yes/no question. Each player answers without repeating a previous answer. Nonsense questions and answers are A freckle-faced boy asked the group, "Are you a box?" They each answered in turn, quickly getting the 'yes' and 'no' options out of the way.

"Yes, I am."

"No!"

"I prefer *cube*," a long-faced boy smiled slyly.

"Well, I've been trying to get out of it." The student squirmed as if trapped in a box.

"I am human, made of flesh and blood!" He sat up bold and tall.

"A real square," a girl traced a square in the air.

"Just 'cause I had trouble rolling down the hill? Really?" a tall girl giggled.

"I *have* been a little *edgy* lately," a child spoke stiffly, elbows poked out.

"All tied up with ribbon!" a girl pantomimed tying a bow on her head.

"Can't you see that I'm actually a sphere?" a boy philosophized, encircling his arms.

The circle is laughing so hard that some of us have a hard time not sliding out of our folding chairs onto the floor. It's true that you never know what will happen in an interview class!

When I started using the interview as a teaching and learning device, I had no idea that it would be so much fun. I saw it as a way to keep my kids engaged and to use writing standards that exist in the professional world. Interviews are published in every magazine and newspaper, so great examples are readily available. But most school programs ignore interview writing and research, instead perpetuating the standard assignment of the five-paragraph essay, which elementary school students are tasked to write year after year. Yet, I have never seen a single five-paragraph essay in any professional publication, and I have yet to read a good one! An interview, like any magazine article, is a form of essay, and a good essay should be hard to put down!

Each year I homeschooled my sons, I asked them who they were going to interview. When my older son announced he wanted to become a costume designer, we put out a request to the New York City homeschooling community, and he met a costume designer who worked in film and the costume master for a Broadway show. I felt a twinge of jealousy when we dropped off our son, age 11, at the backstage door of *Annie Get Your Gun*, where he received a personal tour of each costume and interviewed the costume master. When we picked him up about an hour later, his face was pink with excitement! He couldn't stop describing the costumes!

When my younger, ocean-loving son was eight, he interviewed a whale scientist. We were at a children's museum in St. John, Canada, when he grabbed my arm and pointed up the stairs to another floor where an enormous whale skeleton hung suspended from the ceiling. We left his older brother and dad on the children's floor and went up to the whale exhibit. Below the skeleton was a video, filmed on Grand Manan Island, of the man who found it. My son watched it again and again, looking back and forth from video to skeleton. I asked if he'd like to visit Grand Manan Island to see if he could interview the scientist, and he nodded yes, still staring at the video and skeleton.

Our route back home would pass near Grand Manan Island in about a week, so I checked the hours of the marine bird and whale research station and the ferry schedule. That week, as we drove through Atlantic Canada, my son filled pages in his notebook with questions, some resulting from backseat arguments such as, "My brother says a sperm whale's head is full of gunk. Is this true?"

Arriving at Grand Manan, we spotted the research station across the street from the ferry dock. The door opened to our knock, and a slightly sunburned young woman said, "Sorry, we're closed. Today's our last day, and we're packing everything up."

We were crushed. Why hadn't I called ahead? "But we came all this way," I explained taking my son's hand. "He wants to interview a whale researcher, and he has questions." She looked at me and then looked at the little boy with an unwavering expression in his blue-gray eyes. The next thing I knew, she yelled over her shoulder to the crew, "Guys, I'm going to be busy for the next hour. I'm being interviewed!"

We followed her into the education room, where pictures and facts covered the walls from floor to ceiling, corner to corner. My son could have stared at these walls for days, but instead, he sat in a low child's chair, took out his notebook and pencil, and focused respectfully on the scientist as he read his carefully-worded questions. When he came to the question about 'gunk,' she grinned. "Well, I wouldn't call it 'gunk,' but there is a gelatinous substance in a sperm whale's head." He jotted down the answers.

He asked how scientists learn about whales. "Can they follow them in the ocean?" She showed him tags used as tracking devices, explaining how they are attached. He held one and looked at a photo on the wall of a tagged whale.

"Does it hurt?" he asked.

"Well, we don't really know what the whales feel, but we don't think it bothers them much." She mentioned the information gained by tracking and that anyone can follow creatures like Humpbacks and Right Whales on sites like NOAA and Whalemap. As we left, she urged us to walk the dock at the north of the island, where we saw long fin whales swimming slowly past us in the sunset. Grand Manan Island and this interview left us with a lasting glow.

The interview process is a unique learning experience that happens before, during, and after. Before, as we research the person and topic in order to ask appropriate and probing questions. During, as we listen carefully, ask questions, receive responses and spontaneously ask new, unplanned questions. And after, as we write it down and reflect, come up with follow-up questions, make new connections, and draw conclusions.

It is an illusion that an interviewer's job is all about asking questions. It is more about listening than about speaking. To put the person being interviewed at ease, draw them out, and ask better questions, we must listen deeply to more than just words. We listen to what isn't said. We listen to our inner thoughts and questions. We listen not just with our ears but also with our eyes, detecting body language. Most important, we listen with our hearts, sensing feelings behind the words. What do we want to know more about? What gives us the feeling there is more? Which questions do we think are important, and how do we feel about those questions and the answers? An interview tells us about the interviewee, but it also reveals the interviewer. As we learn about the other person's world, we learn about ourselves.

In each interview class, we begin with a circle game that builds communication skills, verbal and listening skills. We might play Extended Sound or Dog and Bone or Playing Catch. Then we pair off and play games in twos, perhaps Mirror followed by Three Changes (which become six and then nine changes), games that sharpen observational skills and increase awareness and collaboration.

Games might also close a class or happen mid-class. One popular comedic game is Good, Bad, and Ugly Advice. Three chairs are placed at the front of the room for the Advice Panel that is introduced as all-knowing and all-wise; there is no question this panel cannot answer! The first chair becomes the seat for Good Advice. The second chair delivers Bad Advice. The third chair must deliver worse advice than the second chair, truly Ugly Advice. Every student gets a chance in each seat; everyone in the audience gets a chance to ask a question. Questions have included: How do I cure my cold? What do I serve my new mother-in-law for dinner? How do I ask someone out on a date? How should I tell my brother that he smells? After each question is answered by the three chairs, we hum the theme music from TV's Jeopardy while everyone moves down one chair with a new audience member taking the Good Advice seat and the Ugly Advice player returning to the audience.

Before we start the game, I give an example that happened when my husband and I were driving in a car with my son and his friend. My husband, who was driving, asked a humorous question. "Sometimes my pants start slipping. How can I keep my pants up?"

I gave good advice. "Try a belt or suspenders, but a belt should do the trick."

My son's friend gave bad advice. "Glue! Lots and lots of glue! Just smear it all over."

My son gave the ugly advice. "Who needs pants?"

Roaring with laughter, the class plays with speed as each player looks forward to the moment when they can deliver awfully ugly advice.

At the start of every course, I define the topic or focus and start to unpeel its layers. Together, the class defines an interview and shares personal experiences. Have you ever interviewed anyone or been interviewed? Have you seen an interview? What kinds of interviews have you heard about? Students often mention college interviews and job interviews, especially if they have older siblings. These are worth bringing up because they will likely experience these kinds of interviews several times in their lives.

How does an interviewer prepare? We talk about three stages of the process:

- preparation and organization (including locating an interview subject [person] and arranging to meet or communicate)

- the actual interview (greeting, asking questions, taking notes, being spontaneous, courteous, and thankful)

- writing up the interview (reflection, post-research, and revision).

I ask them how they might interview three different people: a children's author, a scientist, and a relative. How would you prepare? What sort of questions would you ask? How would these three preparations and sets of questions be different? I write their questions on the board, and we make our first list of brainstormed interview questions.

Before or during class, I ask a parent or other volunteer to be interviewed. If no one is available, we begin with peer interviews. Once, I invited a mother to volunteer, knowing she usually waited nearby during class. She was an immigrant and spoke softly with an accent. "I am just a mother. You don't want to interview me." But I insisted we did and told her she would be helping the class. When I brought her in, she sat down nervously. Her daughter warmly introduced her, and questions began. Students raised their hands, and the mother pointed to each. As they asked about her interests, we learned she was an amateur photographer who liked to take pictures of street scenes and close-ups of contrasting textures. Asking about her childhood, she reminisced about learning to cook Latin food from her grandmother. The more she spoke, the more interesting she became. Her nervousness disappeared, and her smile grew. An interview begins with mutual respect, which grows as the person reveals their story, the story they want to tell. At the request of the students, she later returned to show us some of her photographs. This woman thought she had nothing to say, and yet she was asked to return because they wanted more.

The process of interviewing requires respect from the interviewer and the audience towards the interviewee. The result of feeling respected is a relaxed, confident person willing to open up. By interviewing parents, local workers, even passers-by, students learn not to dismiss someone who may appear ordinary on the surface. We read and discuss the poem *A Worker Reads History* by Bertolt Brecht. I ask the students questions such as, "Would you rather interview the President or CEO of a big company or the secretary?" If you think that the CEO knows what's going on in the company, you might be surprised at how much more detail the secretary knows! The "ordinary" worker might have the real story while the head honcho might be living in a bubble. I have a saying that everyone is a novel. Everyone has a story worth telling.

The next class, we might have a follow-up interview with the same volunteer or someone else drops by. Students also practice by interviewing each other. Discussing different kinds of questions, we define open and closed questions and list questions that could be posed to anyone. One child might suggest asking, "What's your favorite music?" I then ask what that could tell you about a person. Where could that question lead? If it's a short, finite, one-word answer, then it's a closed question. I ask if they can think of a follow-up that's an open-ended question that might leading to a longer more interesting answer. They might offer, "Why is it your favorite?" or, "When do you like to listen to it and how does it make you feel?" We brainstorm questions on family, travel, hobbies, friends, pet peeves, personal likes, and ambitions.

For peer interviews, children pair off and take a few moments to write down questions they want to ask each other, leaving space for answers. They decide who goes first and complete two short interviews. Afterwards, we talk about the process while practicing non-judgmental feedback. I focus on the task not the students, avoiding statements of good or bad. How did it feel to be the interviewer? The interviewee? Which was easier? When did it feel hard or uncomfortable? What changes do you suggest? We share the interviews. Are there any questions you would change? Are there other questions you wanted to ask or be asked?

After conducting peer and group interviews in the classroom, students are ready to go out on their own, armed with dictation notebooks (I prefer steno pads, but any notebook will do) and pencils, an optional recording device (usually their phone), and lists of questions with room for more. We play a game based on World's Worst from TV's *Whose Line Is It Anyway?* In this game, anyone can take the "stage" (front of the classroom) as the world's worst interviewer and treat the audience as if they're being interviewed. What's the worst behavior for an interviewer? What's an awful question? Show us! If they don't know how to begin, I might jump in myself and ask a rude or leading question such as, "You really hate your brother, don't you?" Or I might be a grouchy, selfish interviewer. "I really don't want to interview you, but my parents are making me do this." Or I could insult them. "Why did you wear *that*?" Or I could yawn in their face and not ask anything. After a single demonstration, kids are usually eager to show their idea of the world's worst interviewer. This game often speeds up as the kids relax and return to the stage to display more "awful" moments. The freedom to do the wrong thing in an environment full of humor and support is a big release. Having fun behaving in the opposite extreme amplifies the good choices we can make. The game puts us at ease as we laugh our way into the role of a generous, attentive, caring interviewer.

The first independent interview assignment is with a grandparent or elderly relative. Often, this interview includes an immigration story. When we prepare questions for an elderly relative, we include some about who came to this country first and from where. I ask what they want to know about their relatives. Do they want know about their childhoods? What games they used to play? Their favorite foods? If they ever got into trouble or fought with their siblings? Ideas start flowing as students think of questions that relate to their own lives. They ask about school, lunch, chores, religion, holidays, travel. We sort questions into three categories: immigration history, childhood, and work or professional life. Other topics may come up such as aspects about where they live or the story of how they met their spouse. I encourage students to choose interesting and appropriate questions and to add questions tailored to the experience or profession of the person.

One interview was conducted by a student over the phone to his Russian grandparent. The conversation became so lengthy that the interview was completed over three calls. The parents accompanied their child to the next class to share the revelations they had listening to the dad's father talk about his experience in World War II, which he had never spoken of before. The entire class was moved by his story, which told of heavy sacrifices made by Russian people to halt Hitler's attempt to rule the world. This primary source experience gave us a history lesson we'll never forget!

After interviewing a relative, I encourage them to choose a neighbor or family friend. This is a chance to ask someone you might only know on the surface about their personal history and life. The clerk at the corner store who calls you by name, the doorman in your apartment building who jokes with you every day, the babysitter or person who cares for your cat when you're away, they each have a unique story to tell. You never know who marched in the Civil Rights Movement or escaped from a war as a child with their family or once performed in a rock and roll band.

The third and last independent assignment is to interview someone they have never met, perhaps someone in a profession they are curious about. I share this list with parents and the homeschooling community at large, putting out a call for interview subjects in these professions. Students can also go online to "ask an expert" or to universities for e-mail contacts for faculty members or ask everyone they know, what I call "shake every tree." My students have met and interviewed many professionals including musicians, actors, teachers, artists, authors, scientists, dog trainer, doll maker, camp counselor, tattoo artist, doorman, nanny, biological psychologist, blacksmith, boxer, nurse, and even a reporter from *People Magazine*.

For a final group presentation, we create a magazine of interviews with portrait photographs of people, usually taken by the students, and essays written by student interviewers. Titles are nominated and the class votes. Past titles have included "Interesting People, Interesting Lives," "Their Lives in the Raw," and "People and Their Shenanigans." Essay styles vary: some might have a Q and A format with questions in bold; others might be paragraphs of prose peppered with the author's internal thoughts and observations. Each interview is engaging from beginning to end. We invite family, friends, and interviewees to attend a "publishing party." Issues are handed or e-mailed to participants, excerpts are read, people are thanked.

Afterwards, I get responses from interviewees, often surprised at the effectiveness of young, first-time interviewers. When one student asked to interview a published author, I connected her with someone who wrote children's books and who I had met years earlier at a writers' workshop. When the author read the finished interview, she was impressed, saying, "I enjoyed the process. Things came up that I hadn't expected!"

This is the result of being prepared, listening with open ears, and being spontaneous, present in the moment. History is not limited to the dusty and dead; history is alive and happening now! Through interviews students actively participate in history, research, and writing. Far from being dull, there is an ongoing sense of discovery as they learn about other people's lives and also about what matters to them, what they want to ask. Yet, there is also a bigger feeling: the knowledge that they are chronicling a moment in history. Something that happened in a person's life is somehow anchored in the present. As it's told and recorded, it feels like it's happening now. Writing about it and sharing the information enlarges the experience so the story continues. Interviewer and interviewee share something special, yet the experience is bigger than both. Putting a magnifying glass on life enlarges that life and reflects other lives. In interviews, we can all shine a light. [1]

---

1. See D – Interview Course Syllabus

Chapter Twenty-Three

Time Travel in the Classroom

My homeschooled son, at his request, returned to middle school for two years before deciding to homeschool through high school. Halfway through 6th grade, a class assignment triggered a storm of creativity. The result was two handmade books on history: a biographical comic book on the builder of the Brooklyn Bridge and a historical fiction with the setting of NASA's Apollo 11 spaceflight mission.

Each student in a class of more than thirty chose a topic from 20th-century history. The teacher made sure the focus was specific enough for a children's book. Then students had to come up with a fictional point of view to tell the story. The children's enthusiasm was evident in the final projects, where imagination merged with history and an actual event became the fabric of a fictional story.

My son first wanted to write about the Race for Space between Russia and the U.S. The teacher said no, the topic was too broad. So he asked to do the Apollo 11 mission that put a man on the moon. Still too broad. When he focused on the training for that mission, she said yes.

Now he had to find a fictional point of view. As he learned about the astronauts and their training techniques, he suddenly got the idea of seeing it through the eyes of a mouse. An escaped lab mouse! Hiding on the spaceship! The result was *The First Mouse in Space.*

Students had to include at least one researched fact per page. This was his opening:

I watched alone as the ship took off. Guzzling 15 tons of fuel a second, the rocket carried my father towards the moon. This bright and sunny day would be a day to remember. At 8:32 pm July 16th 1969, he became the first mouse in space, and I had in my paws the diary of his space training.

After the space shuttle disappeared into the sky, I scurried home to read my dad's journal, and find out how he had become an astro-mouse.

Opposite each page of text was a hand-drawn illustration. A wordless two-page drawing occupied the center of the book, showing a landscape of the astro-mouse in a hot air balloon floating above wilderness as part of survival training. Later, the mouse stumbled on an open survival manual and read a page.

"Anything that flies, crawls, or swims can be eaten. Trout, squirrels, mice, etc." MICE?! I began to shiver as I read on. "Above all else do not eat toads!" I began to wish that I were an amphibian.

This wasn't just history. It was funny, strangely relatable, and full of adventure.

At the final class presentation, a huge range of projects were revealed on biographies and major events in a range of styles. I browsed through a brightly-colored comic book, a pop-up book thick with extra pages, a book covered in black and white pen and ink line drawings and more. Students each read a page out loud. Parents were given an entertaining peek into more than 30 turning points in 20th-century U.S. history.

I admired that teacher's project that succeeded so well in a crowded classroom. I offered a similar course for homeschoolers, using affordable blank hardcover books from . The best results happened when a parent hired an art teacher who taught drawing to the same group in the afternoon after my morning writing class. Students were guided to draw in perspective and to create portraits as they selected scenes from their stories to illustrate.

Historical fiction is an ideal opportunity to use primary sources and research like a historian. Each student chooses a period of history, a specific event, perhaps the building of a monument or structure or a major historical figure. There are no restrictions to time or place since we don't have to comply with a specific curriculum that focuses on a single country or century. Research and writing skills acquired are the same regardless of subject, time period, and location. I approve each topic to make sure it isn't too broad.

As they start their research, they begin to imagine a point of view and create the fictional aspect of the project. In a group of six girls, the following topics were chosen:

- Ancient Egypt at the end of Akhenaten's reign from the point of view of Nefertiti.

- London, 1665 during the Plague told by a young girl.

- Pioneer America in a small town in Wisconsin from a young girl's point of view.

- England 1829, Edgar Allen Poe's boyhood, a mystery lived and told by Poe as a boy.

- Civil War Battle of Gettysburg told by a war horse.

- Queen Victoria's Jubilee in London, 1897, told by a cat.

Inspiration came from many sources. One student had recently read about the Victorian era; another was reading about the plague in London. Another student's brother was studying the Civil War, and she wanted to do a different take on it. The interest in pioneer Wisconsin was personal: the girl in the story was based on the student's actual great-great-grandmother, who was the first white baby born in a small town in Wisconsin. Most of her relatives still lived in Wisconsin, and one, a librarian and the unofficial family historian, was able to supply the young author with detailed information including a map of the town, a list of students who attended the one-room schoolhouse, and a list of items sold in the general store. A research treasure trove of primary sources! The names in her story were taken from actual names, and the drawings of the town were based on the actual town. On her book's last page, she included her family tree with her name at the bottom, traced back to her great-great-grandmother who was the girl in the story.

Other projects were less personal. The story set in ancient Egypt was written in the form of Nefertiti's diary with entries honoring the new religion of Ra and talking about the limited life of a queen. An imaginary mystery in Poe's childhood that inspired him to write mysteries was created by the author. That mystery remained unsolved in the book, which made it even spookier! When she read her story out loud, in progress, unfinished, the other girls sometimes jumped and held each other's arms, laughing when it was over.

Students used character profiles to help fill out their character's lives and also find the wants and motivations that drive a story. Even the horse and the cat had unique personalities. Research was a constant source of inspiration. Sometimes primary sources would be mimicked such as a diary format for the book on ancient Egypt or an advertisement or letter from the time and place copied in detail. The invitation to Queen Victoria's Jubilee was fancy! The cat character lived a life similar to the Queen's and attended a cat Jubilee that mirrored Queen Victoria's. It was as if the cat was time traveling, just as we were, stepping through a portal where an ordinary house cat was transformed into a celebrated Queen of Cats.

I introduced story structure, introduction, climax, and denouement. Students learned how to foreshadow and build tension, portray a climactic scene, and create a satisfying ending. We practiced writing from a dog's point of view and an object's point of view. What might a rocking chair or a kitchen stove see, hear, and feel? We read excerpts of historical fiction with various points of view.

Pages were typed at home then trimmed to size and glued into the blank books with illustrations glued on opposing pages. Covers were adorned with a copy of a favorite illustration. Amusing, fictionalized biographical notes "About the Author" and acknowledgements were added.

The final class event was a dress-up occasion to which family and friends were invited. The author of *Nefertiti's Diary* wore gold earrings and pastel colors. The author of *Duchess Ivy's Secret* (about Queen Victoria's Jubilee) wore pink velvet cat ears and a red gown with a pearl necklace. *Mina and the Unusual*, set in pioneer Wisconsin, focused on a fictional incident of the first black family to arrive there. The author wore a blue checked gingham shirt over a white skirt carrying a straw handbag. *The Boy Who Almost Got Away*, a fictional account of Edgar Allen Poe's boyhood in England, was illustrated mainly in black and white. The author dressed up for her reading in somber gray and white with a flowered sweater. *Christina and the Plague*, set in 1600's London, inspired the author to carry a lace fan and wear white gloves.[1]

The final entry in my son's book, *First Mouse in Space*, is the end of the astro-mouse's diary.

> This all just keeps getting better. I am the first mouse scientist, the first astro-mouse. I am going to a place where the ground is made of cheese, and I can almost fly. This will be my last entry. Tomorrow I leave for the moon. My son will find this Journal on his doorstep, with a note stating the shuttle lift off time, date, and the amount of fuel the shuttle uses. (He was always interested in that sort of thing.). I will be the first of my kind to land on the moon. I might return, and I might not. Farewell.

Through writing, we can do the impossible! We can wear a cloak of invisibility, we can fly, and we can time travel! We can explore the details of history and make them come alive! [2]

1. Pictures of the event and the books are here: http://homeschoolnyc.com/images/gallery-historical-fiction.html .

2. See E – Historical Fiction Curriculum and Resources

Chapter Twenty-Four

Playwriting for Children and Teens

P laywriting is the ultimate course when it comes to taking a creative approach to personalized, game-based learning. I refer to my playwriting class as Writing On Your Feet. It's not your typical writing class with everyone seated at desks or tables. I don't even have tables in the room!

We begin with a traditional warm-up game and then jump right into games that develop setting and character. Theater games access intuition, which makes it easier to come up with ideas. In the first weeks, ideas are flowing, sometimes running into each other.

I am committed to helping each student write the play they want to write. It might be a comedy or full of stage combat, or it might be a musical or an historical drama. My hope is that whatever is in the heart of the student will come out on the page and onto the stage. When we discuss what makes a good play, one of the answers is when the writing comes from the heart. I encourage my students to let each character speak from the heart.

Prompts have come from photos of settings and people, their own random scribblings, overheard snippets of conversations, improvised scenes in class that went wrong, and games that led to scenes we never could have predicted. Countless times a student has come to me asking for permission to try a new idea even though they have already developed part of a play. Their new idea will arrive at the next class in the form of a scene that fellow students will volunteer to perform. At some point, the playwright may ask to see a different ending or invite audience suggestions in order to try something else. We are always going back to the drawing board and discovering something new. Plays are written and rewritten right up to performance.

Halfway through the playwriting course, we call in professional actors to read finished drafts of student plays. In the class following the actors' reading event, students become directors of their own plays and are cast as actors in each other's plays. The course is a triple win for my students and for me. I witness students become playwrights, directors, and actors. They will accomplish each part of the journey with professional standards and take well-earned bows as authors, actors, and directors.

Nothing else I teach has the transformative power of playwriting. We transform an empty stage into ... a beach, an English garden, a canoe on a river, a battlefield, a breakfast cafe, a city sidewalk, a spaceship. The playwrights themselves become transformed. Students who never thought they could write a play, who never acted before, or who never thought they could do these things well, surprise themselves. Parents often murmur after the student performance, "Who knew? Who knew they could do *this*?"

Students return again and again, some taking playwriting throughout middle and high school. These students become seasoned actors and writers, developing skills beyond what most college courses offer. This is playwriting with a real-life outcome. Student work will be read professionally and then performed in front of a live audience.

This is a course where I always lose myself in the work and then float on air when it's over. Witnessing so much transformation, I get to experience it too. Theater can cast a special glow over any audience, transforming everyone in the room. When theater is created from the hearts of children and teens, it exudes a rare and magical glow. [1]

---

1. See F – Playwriting For Teens

Chapter Twenty-Five

Exploring Repressed Desire

Playwriting for Teens

I t was more than halfway through playwriting class on a fall day in a large rehearsal studio on Manhattan's upper west side when Sean whispered in my ear that he had an idea for a scene. Most of the students had already started writing their play, but Sean hadn't developed a setting or characters yet. Usually students send their work to me in advance or speak to me at the start of class about an idea for a scene, and I make time for peer students to improvise a scene for the author. In this way, ideas are born, and plays are revised. It's not writing that happens quietly at a desk; it's writing that's noisy with spoken words and vivid with movement, writing on your feet. Without knowing the nature of Sean's scene but wanting to encourage a reluctant writer, I impulsively agreed to see his scene right away. This wasn't the first or last time that I allowed a student to do something without knowing what the topic would be.

Sean wanted actors to play two male characters, so I asked for volunteers. Hands shot up, and Sean selected two fellow students. He whispered directions to them and took a seat in the audience. We watched a potential dating scene between two male teens. Character A asked character B for a date, and character B replied politely that he wasn't interested in guys. When the scene stalled, Sean whispered further direction, and the scene continued with character A repeating his request more insistently. Standing over character B who was seated, he pressured him, "C'mon, you can be gay if you want to." The scene made me uncomfortable. It felt close to harassment. I called "Scene," bringing it to a close.

My class, normally relaxed and respectful, exploded. Students jumped up from their chairs and verbally called out the classmate who had just summoned the courage to try out his first scene in class.

"That's all wrong! You can't do that!""It's not like that at all!""You're born that way!"It was a verbal onslaught, not the usual non-judgmental feedback, and it occurred at the end of class. There wasn't time to address what happened before we had to vacate the room. But even if there was... I... I just sat there, speechless."You? Speechless?" my husband said later, incredulous. Normally, I am not at a loss for words. "I have to admit his scene was disturbing. The line that set everyone off was, "C'mon, you can be gay if you want to,' said repeatedly by one male actor to another like he was pressuring him." I sighed. "I'm afraid I have to have a conversation with this kid."

"About what? Being gay? The class yelling at him?"

"I'm not even sure. But if I talk to him, his mother has to be there. It's too delicate a topic, and I don't want to be alone, just me and a young teenager talking about sexual orientation. A parent has to be there. And that means his mom." I knew the parents were divorced, and his father lived out of the country.

That evening, I called Sean's mom and explained the situation, detailing what had happened in class. I asked if it was okay if I spoke to her son while she was present.

"Oh, my god, yes! I can use all the help I can get!" She paused, "But really, you don't need me. Can't you do it without me?"

I was taken aback. Was this a sign of her complete trust in me? Or was she, like me, afraid to talk about this with her teen? I told her I'd feel better if she was there.

"Well..." there was a longer pause, "let me fill you in on what's been going on."

Her childhood friend of over forty years had four kids: the oldest was lesbian and two teenage twins had recently announced that one was gender neutral and the other was transgender and planning to have top surgery. Sean was 13, new to New York City and the USA, just starting to date his first girlfriend and utterly confused by someone being transgender as well as the notion of being gender neutral. As I listened to this information from his mother, I realized that the short scene in class explored questions nagging Sean. Do you become gay or transgender just because you decide to? Can you change your mind about your sexuality on a whim?

I went to sleep that night still unsure what to do. When I woke up the next morning, I was clear about one thing: the problem had happened in class, so it had to be resolved in class. I would not be able to resolve the situation working alone with one student when the entire class had been involved. This realization gave me a focus and something to do to ease the anxiety I felt about dealing with such a sensitive issue. I emailed Sean's mom with my new plan.

> *I was thinking all last night about that scene of Sean's and I decided to create a new lesson plan for playwriting inspired by the incident. We will create characters in light of sexual preference/awareness. I will use games and improv rather than a talk that could feel like a lecture. I am delighted with this idea of taking a difficult situation and using it as inspiration for good writing. As for my desire for a "witness" — I'll have the entire class!*

Sean's mom wrote back the same day.

> *Sean, as most teens, has plenty of sexual awareness questions trolling his mind. I would be grateful for any clarification that may come out of playwriting class. Actually, I believe that it would benefit the whole group of kids.*

Sean had a fantastically open Q&A with the graysexual twin in which he asked, in his very direct way, a load of questions which seem to have been met with equal frankness. Those kids are strong. In his defense, there is a lot to digest.

This was my first encounter with the word "graysexual." It was also the first time that I put sexuality at the center of a lesson plan. I replied as we continued our back and forth email.

Right now I am writing up a "Character Sexuality" lesson plan that I expect will really get the kids going. Part of me is laughing at the brazen quality of the lesson and I feel open and ready, yet another part of me is terrified. Thanks so much for your support on this.

Sean's mom's reply included her thoughts on social influence and sexuality. This helped to crystalize one of the activities I was planning, a Social Influence Questionnaire. She wrote:

...feeling forced to live a lie could easily come under the heading of "choosing to live straight or gay." And how many people have moments of curiosity? The kids are steeped in that right now, I'm sure. It is difficult to unilaterally say that homosexual or heterosexual acts are purely had by "organic inclination" without any element of choice or mental pressure. Even if the nature of a person leans one way or another, psychological circumstance can easily persuade someone to act against their nature. It happens all the time. It's akin to not speaking one's own voice in any circumstance, even as banal as ordering what everyone else is having at a restaurant so one doesn't stand out. Or having a drink because

everyone else is. We all know that it happens in sexual encounters as much as it does everywhere else.

This wise mother was fully supportive of both me and her son, yet she went further by giving me valuable information and a clear direction. I had to work fast to have the lesson ready for next week's class and two days had already gone by. Every day, I asked myself big questions in the brainstorming process. What underlying causes might make someone change how they express their sexual identity? How can we explore the influence of society and different beliefs on a person's sexuality and how they identify publicly? Perhaps we could improvise situations that might cause or release repression, more specifically, repressed desire. Thinking about it made my head ache. I needed to share these ideas without making my students uncomfortable, and I was uncomfortable enough myself. Drawing on past playwriting workshops, I planned theater games, improvisations, and scene development, keeping the focus on repressed desire.

Students arrived to the next class without apprehension, ready to play. After a warm-up game, I introduced my newly created Social Influence Questionnaire. When I asked each question out loud, students remained seated for a no answer or stood up for a yes answer. Spontaneous discussion happened during the responses, sometimes causing students to change their minds.

"Have you ever acted differently from the way you feel?" resulted in everyone standing to indicate yes. They easily recalled situations where they could not let their true feelings be known (or chose not to) in front of teachers or parents or even friends. For the question, "Did you ever act in a way intended to make someone else change their behavior?" several kids including Sean remained seated to indicate no. Fortunately, Sean's older sister was in the same class. She had stood up to say yes and as she did, she turned to her brother, questioning his decision to stay seated.

With her hands on her hips, she leaned towards him. "Really? Like every time when we visit Grandpa and he's so grouchy and you keep making faces and telling jokes just to try and get him to laugh?" Sean's shoulders relaxed. Resigned to this truth, he stood up. So did the rest who were seated. A shift happened in the room. Expanding the idea of what it means to try to influence others — that it's not done solely with selfish or mean intent — made everyone realize that we do it all the time. Any resistance to the questionnaire dissipated. The questions, comments, and students' replies in this exercise set the tone for the entire class.[1]

Students then created tableaux (frozen scenes) in two teams. One group was given the word guilt and the other group was give the word shame. Each group took turns as tableau performers and as audience. After displaying a frozen moment, a word, sound, or phrase was added, spoken by one or more of the characters with accompanying gestures. The group depicting guilt surrounded an actor who repeated, "Sorry! I'm sorry!" painfully to each member in the group. The second group showed shame by pointing fingers accusingly at a fellow actor, all saying, "Bad! Bad!" while the targeted player hung his head and moved heavily. These scenes were dramatic, direct, and disturbing, and they felt honest.

Exploring the difference between guilt and shame, the actors expressed repression from the inside and the outside, either feeling internally repressed and guilty or being the repressor in the act of shaming. One girl said shame was an internal sensation, "Feeling I am bad." Another said guilt was related to an action, "Believing this thing I did was bad." The tableaux let to conversations that helped students articulate complicated feelings. They relaxed and became bolder.

It was around this time that I realized we were already farther along than any "talk" could have taken us, and we were only just getting started. The best part was that the class was unified. Everyone was interested in exploring these ideas, and they all came together in order to do just that. No one was accusatory; there was no rift in the class. The students had achieved a sense of synchronicity and connection. It was time to improvise scenes of conflict.

On the board, we wrote a list of situations to draw from such as a gay teen who wants to come out to homophobic parents. We included a scene similar to the one that had caused the uproar. In this version, a shy, gay teen unknowingly asks a straight teen out on a date (or vice versa), and the teen wants to say no but is afraid of hurting the other person (internal as well as external conflict). Some scenes focused on the repression of creative freedom, a subject the students all felt strongly about, such as a parent or teacher telling someone why they can't become an actor or artist. Other approaches showed attempts at repressing or controlling behavior such as a spouse explaining to a partner why they can't be charitable with their time and money or announcing that they've changed their mind about having children.

Students paired off and each pair chose a scene to play. Feedback sessions were respectful and non-judgmental, focusing on what was communicated in each scene; scenes were not compared. No one mentioned the upset at the end of the previous class. We had moved beyond it, addressing the problem by expanding our perspective and exploring various points of view.

Class ended with a writing session. I handed out blank character profiles and worksheets on the theme of repressed desire. Over the years, I've created character profiles for folktales, fairytales, science fiction, historical fiction, short stories, puppet plays, for elementary through high school. But this was the first time I created a character profile that included sexual orientation. It also had spaces for whether the character was an extrovert or introvert, whether they felt repressed or freely expressive, the character's repressed desire, and what the character wanted in terms of sexuality and relationship. One character should be experiencing a major dilemma in a scene with a contrasting character who was somehow related (friend, partner, relative). As I watched my students busily writing, I felt I could finally relax. The class of separate individuals had come together, no longer at odds with each other or themselves. I could breathe again.

After the class on repressed desire was over, weeks before Sean's play was finished, his mother wrote to thank me for having the courage and insight to teach a class on character's sexuality. I was thankful for her understanding and support and grateful that I had the freedom to alter the curriculum in order to address an issue head-on, perhaps only possible outside of a traditional school in the company of homeschoolers.

Halfway through each full-length playwriting course, I host a Reading of Student Plays by Professional Actors. This event inspires student playwrights and actors in revisions and performances. The first class following this event, the playwrights all become directors of their own plays. The turning point in the course is the professional actors' readings, and for many young playwrights, it's also a turning point in their lives. It's a pinch-me moment for a student when their play is brought to life by talented professionals. For me, it's an exhausting thrill.

The families and I provide a potluck supper as a way to thank the actors for volunteering their talents. Students bring copies of their plays as well as food to share. I've learned from past experience to bring extra food and copies of the latest student drafts. Delicious smells waft through the space as I greet actors, students (current and former), families, and friends. Actors are ushered into their own room with a double stack of plays that they divvy up as they speed-read the piles. They spontaneously choose roles and then meet with each playwright to ask questions about mannerisms, accents, and other aspects of character.

A volunteer audience member, usually a parent, reads the stage notes out loud. Children sit on the floor, adults on folding chairs, with tables of food waiting behind us. For an hour or two, we are held captive by gifted performances, vividly portrayed cold readings of freshly written plays. After each play, the actors bow, and then the author rises from wherever they are sitting for an extra round of applause to the playwright. At the end of the show, there is a final group bow of all actors and playwrights. Then we gather to break bread and congratulate each other.

The collection of plays that season was stunning. *Witches of Central Park* was a fairytale love story with a bit of Romeo and Juliet and the Metropolitan Opera thrown in. *An Unarranged Marriage* had a scene written like a two-voice poem, a side-by-side duet spoken by two players. *Life on Mars* was a surreal drama full of uncertainty and double meanings. In *The Royal Flush*, a mafia family encountered murder and mayhem. A play titled *Schopenhauer? I Hardly Know Her!* poked fun at Nietszche. In *Processing*, caged computer programmers planned a revolt. The final group bow of beaming playwrights elicited thunderous applause.

A former student came over to say goodbye and whispered in my ear, "Wanna know which one was my favorite play?" I smiled and nodded. "It was his," he pointed at Sean. Two other former students paused to say goodbye and echoed the same comment, noting "that play about the soccer player." All of the plays were good, but Sean's had stood out.

Titled *Two Left Feet*, Sean's play was about an estranged father-son relationship. The son was a professional soccer player who traveled the world; the father was a dancer who wanted his son to work in his dance studio in Colombia. The actor playing the father adopted a Spanish accent for his character. During the reading, he added religious gestures, punctuating words with movements that heightened the father's attempts to pressure his son. In a climactic moment, the son proclaimed, "Dad, I can't be the man you want me to be. I'm a better footballer than I am a dancer, and I have to be who I am." In the end, the characters remained estranged.

Watching everyone milling around congratulating each other, I knew I had achieved my goal, a unified class that worked and grew together with freedom of expression from every individual in the group. I had conquered my sheer anxiety, my terror about putting sexuality front and center in a class of teens. More important, I had diffused a potentially permanent divisive moment for the whole class. I no longer felt the need to relax and breathe. Instead, I felt proud, which is not my usual state of mind.

My husband always asks me, "Was it a good class?" I usually hesitate before I say, "I guess so, " or "I guess the kids think so.""But you?" he asks."Well, it wasn't awful." My standards may be too high for me to reach. No two classes are the same, and I look at every one to see how I can improve. Yet, this time was no normal, everyday effort. I had kept myself up nights writing and rewriting a new curriculum, thinking and rethinking about what this particular class needed. The focus may have been sexual orientation and repressed desire, but the greater focus is always creating a safe space for freedom of expression for every student on an intensely personal level. That's a lofty goal, one that sometimes eludes me. I am self-critical after every class. To be honest, I trust in the children. I believe in the students. It's myself I have doubts about.

Yet, this time I ended up feeling strangely proud of myself. Not because the plays were outstanding — they often are. But because I had run towards and embraced something scary and difficult, something that most teachers would have ignored or denied or run away from. The result was a sense of cohesion with an elevated spirit and an internal buoyancy that I could feel from each student, from the class as a whole, and within myself.

> You must be true to yourself. Strong enough to be true to your-
> self. Brave enough to be strong enough to be true to yourself.
> Wise enough to be brave enough to be strong enough to shape
> yourself from what you actually are.   ~ Sylvia Ashton-Warner,
> *Teacher*

Writing can be a transformational process, where we catch a glimpse of our true selves. Teens are in the throes of discovering who they are. Writing can spark an awakening that leads them to themselves. Sean not only found himself in his play, but he also found a truth that touched others. He was no longer on the outskirts of the class or at odds with them. He had earned his place as an integral member, highly valued by his peers.

I still get a lump in my throat when I recall the words he wrote, when a son tells his father, "I can't be the man you want me to be. I have to be who I am." I am forever surprised by the power of language, that so few words can say so much to so many.[2]

---

1. See the Social Influence Questionnaire in Appendix H.

2. See F – Play-Writing For Teens

Chapter Twenty-Six

Lit Clubbing

"Have you read *all* of *Harry Potter*?" Liza asked my son in the back seat of the car as we drove through the Bronx. Four books of the series had been published, and everyone was Potter-crazy.

"Yes," my son nodded seriously.

"Which was your favorite?"

"Don't have one." He resisted having favorites.

"Mine was the third." Liza paused then added with emphasis. "That's because the author finally let him fail." My eyes darted to the rear view mirror to take in this petite nine-year-old. "And when she let him fail, he became *so* much more interesting," She looked out the window. My mind churned— this was a child! Discussing character development at an adult level! And then I heard her sigh, "I wish I had someone I could talk about books with."

That was the moment when I knew I had to do it. I had to start a Lit Club, a group that got together just to talk about books they were reading.

I'd considered it for a while because my son wasn't reading much. He lingered and procrastinated and didn't finish the books he chose. I had read everything out loud to my first son, from birth through age 12, because of a vision problem that was finally fixed at age 13. Was I going to have to read everything aloud to my second child, too? I took him to a vision therapist, and he checked out just fine. So what was the problem? Was he a daydreamer, unable to stay focused for long enough to read a novel? Or did he dislike sitting still so much he'd leave any book in the dust? I thought a literature discussion group might offer the focus he needed. Maybe he'd finish a book if he knew other kids had read it and were planning to talk about it. I had a busy life and was less likely to make time for something my kid resisted. He would rather be volunteering on the river or hiking through the woods than reading, so I had tabled the idea. But when Liza expressed such interest and insight, I heard her longing for the very thing I'd been avoiding. As I weaved the car through city traffic, I knew I had to do it.

A group of homeschooled kids joined us at the library one weekday morning for Laurie's Literature and Poetry Club. We sat in the children's section and talked about how to choose a book. I piled suggestions on the table while kids pulled books off the shelves. "Ohhh, I love this one!" a girl said, placing *Island of the Blue Dolphins* on top of *And Now Miguel* and *The Wind in the Willows*. We looked at front and back covers, noticed awards, read blurbs and opening paragraphs, identified genre and style, and asked if anyone had read a book by that author. We whittled the pile down to one (or so) nomination per person, and voting began. Students were welcome to thumb through the books as they wrote down their first, second, and third choices. I took the votes home, promising to announce the results soon and to do my best to honor each child's first or second choice.

In the remaining time in the library, we explored the poetry shelves, searching for poems about ourselves. All the kids found a poem that reflected a part of themself, except for Liza who was still sitting on the floor by the shelves. "I can't find anything about me," she said wistfully. Together we thumbed through poetry anthologies, and suddenly she stopped at a page with a short poem about moving away. She nodded slowly, seriously. "I just moved here, to the city, and I miss my friends," she whispered. Clutching the book, we returned to the table to begin a new project, the Self-Portrait Anthology. Students copied over their chosen poems, added comments about why or how it was about them, and put them into personalized folders for the purpose of collecting poems about themselves. They would each create an anthology that was about them.

After the children left the library that day, I eyed the stack of nominated books with concern. What if a book I didn't want to read or discuss was voted onto the list? Looking at the titles, I chose the one I was least interested in, took it home, and read it that night. I was surprised to discover that there was a lot to like in the book, with moving themes of loss and family. I realized that I would be able to tackle any book, no matter how far removed from my own interests. I could always find something I could relate to or explore further. Over time, I grew to realize that this was the same expectation I gave to my students.

The next day, I emailed the voting results with our proposed reading list for the next several months. Every child had their first or second choice represented. And my sneaky plan worked! My son started reading at the same pace as the other kids. I never had to remind him. He was always ready for the group, often with a humorous quip about the book.

Naturally, not everyone liked every book. One day Felipe, who had been with the group from day one, announced he wasn't going to read *Harriet the Spy*. Everyone else was ready for the discussion, but Felipe slid his chair back from the table and crossed his arms. "It's not my kind of book, so I decided not to read it."

"That's fine," I acknowledged. "We're glad to have you here anyway, and maybe you'll enjoy the discussion."

We started going around the circle. Each person brought up what interested them. One talked about why they liked or disliked a certain character, another asked for a word or passage to be explained, another raised an ethical question. Is it okay to spy on people? The question was echoed and added to. Is it okay to spy on your friends? When is it okay, and when isn't it okay? What about reading someone's diary? How would you feel if your parents read your diary? These questions had everyone weighing in. Going around the circle, it was Felipe's turn. He just shrugged and mumbled, "I didn't read the book."

"Does that mean you don't have an opinion about whether or not it's okay for your parents to read your diary?"

Felipe's body language changed in an instant. No longer the laid-back shrug, he was now learning forward, alert. Oh, he had an opinion, all right. "No one, not even my parents, should read my diary!"

Students went on to say when it might be appropriate or even necessary for someone to peek at private writing, for example if dangerous warning signs were present. Our round table discussion was well-rounded with everyone's view given respect. We were off and running, laying a foundation of exploration and open discussion. I had no idea that Lit Club, the first homeschoolers' class I organized and led, would become the longest running course I ever taught. Twenty years later, I was still leading Lit Clubs.

At first, I questioned my own ability to discuss a book that wasn't my choice, and that is exactly what Felipe experienced. When the group welcomed and appreciated his comments, he became a full participant even though he hadn't read the book. In that moment, perhaps Felipe discovered what I had just learned. There is always something interesting! We just have to look for it! I don't think it ever crossed Felipe's mind to skip a lit club selection again.

Over time, the group moved from the library to a parent's apartment and then to my living room, where my son co-hosted. The kids were now teens and ended the class by going out for pizza before heading off to other activities. I would hear the book discussion continue down the hall and into the elevator, knowing they would still be talking about *Don Quixote* over pizza.

Other parents asked me to lead book discussions for their groups: a mother and daughter book club that met monthly in a basement apartment on the upper west side, a homeschooling co-op's weekly classes in a stone church, a group of teens who wanted to explore great novels in an upper east side apartment, an all-girls group that met weekly in a local park or a parent's apartment in poor weather. Each course began with open selections, recommendations, nominations and voting, a democratic process that accepted every student's choice as valid. The results had something for everyone. When a student didn't like a book we were reading, they knew their choice would come soon. If a student typically read one genre (such as fantasy or mystery), they were now exposed to more genres and other types of literature in a friendly, engaging manner.

One year, sixteen kids signed up for Lit Club. That first session taught me about class size. At home that evening, when I tried to tally the votes I realized that two students must have voted twice. I had trouble figuring out who since they hadn't included their names on the vote. I thought they had probably changed seats, which made it harder to remember who was who. Kids were getting up and down a lot that day, and some of them moved around. I scratched my head trying to figure it out when I realized it was a simple problem of too many. In a smaller group, I would have remembered the preferences expressed during the discussion and nomination portion of the class. This group was so large that the members probably hadn't had enough time to share their views and discuss the books. I asked myself if I was hosting an adult book club in my home how many would I invite? The answer came right away: eight—enough to fit around a dining room or coffee table, even have dinner together, a large enough group to provide a good discussion but small enough to give everyone the luxury of time, the ability to leisurely explore ideas and speak their minds. Sixteen students was too many, but it was large enough to split into two groups of eight kids each, which is what I did, separating them by age. In a more controlled environment, where a teacher has no say over the number of students, I suggest asking a co-teacher or volunteer parent to help divide the class, with each group voting on its own reading list. Every child can have a first or second book choice read by their group!

I started each class by ascertaining how much of the book had been read. If the group had read ahead of the suggested number of pages we might discuss more; if some students read less than the others, I would ask how they felt about spoilers, or we might decide that there was so much to talk about that a lesser portion was plenty. Students knew that the more they read, the more books we'd discuss, but they also understood that the discovery of the many layers in a book can take time. If the reading pace of the group slowed down, I asked why. There's always a reason such as exams or rehearsals or maybe some readers have a problem with that particular book. Everyone understood that to function as a group we needed to respect and accommodate differences.

I quickly learned the fallacy of using teachers' literature discussion guides, which are formulaic and even demeaning and distrustful, talking down to the student and quizzing them to see if they've read the book. I had to find my own

questions and my own style, putting the students first. The best questions are
about things we want to discuss or figure out. A good discussion can lead to
literary analysis, larger societal issues, and deep personal insights. With younger
students, I try to include art or music or use the books to inspire writing poetry
or another creative activity in order to enhance the experience.

A group ages 8-10 selected a classic from my childhood, *The Cricket in
Times Square* by George Selden. I read the book in advance and planned related
activities. We studied the science of mice and cats and especially crickets. We
read about the mythology and meaning of the cricket in China. We looked at
images of a two-dollar bill, a cricket cage, Times Square in the 1950's, Grand
Central Station, and the New York City subway system. We discussed stereo-
types in light of the author's racist depiction of Chinese men. We listened to
recordings of music mentioned in the book and learned about music and the
physics of sound as we made handmade kazoos and imitated a cricket's rhythms.
Children wrote nature poems about crickets and rain and sound word poems
about the city. Some of these ideas are surely in a good literature guide for this
book, perhaps alongside the standardized quizzes and worksheets that can ruin
the experience and are best ignored. But no lit guide on this book could have
predicted what turned into a year-long focus for the class.

In one discussion, students asked me why Mama and Papa in the book had
difficulties with language and needed their son's help. I explained the parents
were probably immigrants who came from Italy to New York City. Then the
kids asked, "What's an immigrant?" I explained it's when you're from someplace
else. At some point, we were all immigrants. The children denied this. "I'm from
right here, from New York City!" A red-haired girl countered, "Well, I'm from
someplace else–Texas !" I pointed out that the original inhabitants of New York
City were the Lenape and Manahatta Indians and asked if anyone in the class
was Native American. No one raised a hand. We all came from someplace else, I
told them, but it was probably their grandparents or great-grandparents or more
distant ancestors who came to this country first. I encouraged them to go home
and ask their parents, "Who came to this country first in our family?"

One by one, they brought in their family immigration stories. A few kids shared family trees; some interviewed grandparents and great-grandparents and brought in the interviews to share; some showed old photographs. One parent sent me a link to a historic home in Charleston, South Carolina, posted for sale on Zillow, that they discovered had belonged to a sea captain ancestor of theirs. This mom thanked me again and again because without the questions sparked by our classroom discussion she would have never researched her family or found out about her ancestor or seen the images of his home built in the 1700s. While this family couldn't afford to buy the historic home, they planned to visit it and take a tour. You never know where a question will lead! History had come to life for all of my students and their families, sparked from the pages of a book that is never recommended as a resource on immigration or genealogy.

Presenting historical background information to Lit Club students can have a profound effect. In a middle school class on *To Kill a Mockingbird*, I started by passing out lists of Jim Crow laws from southern states and asking students to each choose one to read out loud. Most had no idea these laws had existed and were noticeably shocked.

"You mean my best friend and I couldn't have gone out for a soda together?!"

"You mean my parents couldn't have gotten married?!"

"We couldn't have even had this class!"

I wanted to set the stage for the book so students would understand just how dangerous it was to be a Black man at that time and place, especially if he was alone in a room with a white woman.

Reading *The Prince and the Pauper* by Mark Twain, we looked at an old print of London Bridge, over-crowded with shops and dwellings, a small, squalid city all its own. Here we clearly saw the stark poverty of Tom Canty and his family in dramatic contrast to the life of the prince where countless servants stood in line just to hand him his stockings.

When journeys to far-off places occurred in books, maps were spread across the table. When objects were central to a story, I introduced a similar object to handle. With *Lord of the Flies*, we started each session by blowing an actual conch shell. While discussing *Dragonwings* by Laurence Yep, students sipped cups of green tea, for many a new experience, bringing the flavor and aroma of the book into the room. Field trips were planned or suggested. The Metropolitan Museum has a Kids' Gallery Guide (on-line for free download) on *The Mixed-Up Files of Mrs. Basil T. Frankenweiler*, a young adult bestseller about a brother and sister who run away and hide out in the Metropolitan Museum. Whenever possible, look at photographs, watch a video, examine objects, or, best of all, go there in person!

As the original Lit Club group members grew up, some moved on, and new teens joined; book choices matured, and the level of discussions became more intense. Often a theme emerged over the course of a year, and we would find ourselves reading about identity or family or war again and again. One day, we discussed the Garden of Eden (the Bible story), since it had been present as a metaphor in several books that year. One deeply religious girl believed firmly in the literal version of the story. She felt it was a warning to women and that we are all forever punished, expelled from paradise because of Eve. Other students rejected this literal view and took a more symbolic view, which was hard for the religious girl to fathom. I asked the group if the Garden of Eden was a symbolic garden and not an actual garden, what might it stand for? One student suggested it could be a garden of the mind. Then I asked, if the garden is in the mind, can the mind experience sin? If people have thoughts they consider sinful (such as wanting to hurt someone or do something they know is wrong), can they ever regain the innocence they had before they had these thoughts? Can you ever un-think those thoughts so it's as if you never had them? Solemnly, the group shook their heads no. Does everyone, at some moment in their life, have bad or sinful thoughts? Slowly, they nodded yes. If that's true, is childhood a Garden of Eden that we are all born into and ultimately expelled from? There was silence as everyone contemplated the idea.

Questions like this are not designed to elicit group agreement but to encourage students to think. The religious girl's views did not change, but she was tolerant of her fellow students' differences in attitude and opinion, and the rest of the group treated her politely even though they disagreed. Varying points of

view were always given respectful consideration. A teen Lit Club student wrote
about this in his college essay.

> *When we read Jonathan Swift's Gulliver's Travels, we were*
> *turned off by the laborious quality of the novel. Laurie took plea-*
> *sure in our opinions even though she adored this classic. She also*
> *introduced us to novels we all loved, like Harper Lee's To Kill*
> *a Mockingbird. When students had opposing opinions on J.D.*
> *Salinger's Catcher in the Rye, Laurie honored everyone's view.*
> *This was an environment where I could voice my openhearted*
> *opinions and hear different viewpoints. Entering a burgeoning*
> *growth, I became an intelligent reader.   ~Marcel*

When one Lit Club student said he had never heard of Alfred Hitchcock and
another had never heard of the Marx Brothers, I announced a course called Introduction to American Comedy in Film. We watched Charlie Chaplin's artful
playfulness in *The Gold Rush*, the Marx Brothers zaniness in *Duck Soup* (with
the famous mirror scene), roared through *Some Like It Hot*, and were struck
silly by *Arsenic and Old Lace*. I followed this course with an Introduction to
Hitchcock, master of mystery in both sound and imagery. We watched *The Lady
Vanishes*, *The 39 Steps*, *Rear Window*, and *Strangers On a Train*, munching
popcorn and chatting before and after each movie. In successive years, I offered
a Film and Drama Club, where we read plays and books and then watched film
adaptations. We waded through the deep moods of Tennessee Williams and
did a deep dive into Shakespeare's comedies and dramas. One group voted on
Shakespeare plays as a separate category, choosing two Shakespeare plays every
year. Plays are meant to be heard and need to be read out loud. Students no
longer had to read the books in advance if we read them aloud in class, but it
was still to their advantage. Each scene was cast at its start. This way if everyone
wanted to play Hamlet, everyone had a chance. But if you wanted to play a certain character in a certain scene, you needed to read the play in advance in order
to know which scene. Those who read *Macbeth* before the others could reserve

the best speech by Lady M., and those who were familiar with *A Midsummer Night's Dream* could choose, in advance, Bottom's funniest scene or Puck's most mischievous moment. We warmed up by playing the Shakespearean Insult Game. Teens loved openly insulting each other in ways that made them double over laughing. This got them comfortable with Shakespearean English, gave them a fresh vocabulary of insults, and developed camaraderie in the group.

Besides Shakespeare, we read (and watched) comedies like *Harvey* by Mary Chase, and *The Odd Couple* by Neil Simon, and dramas by August Wilson, Herb Gardner, and other great playwrights. Piles of scripts from the performing arts library branch covered my coffee table. For film viewings, my dining area was turned into a movie theater with students pushing the dining table into a corner and setting the chairs in rows as I put out bowls of popcorn. We allotted extra post-movie time to talk.

These classes felt like a party! I always enjoy a good conversation, and some of my favorite topics are books and movies. A good movie or a good book can lead to so much! I savored the talks, the books and movies, regardless of age group or reading level.

In my son's senior high school year, I broke the Lit Club voting tradition, just once. I told my son it was our last year together, and for the first time, I wanted to choose the reading list. I wanted to share my favorite books from my teenage years and introduce some controversial authors. The group agreed, and for the only time in Lit Club history, there were no nominations and no vote. This was our reading list: *Don Quixote, Part One* (Edith Grossman translation)*; Candide; The Crock of Gold, Part One* by James Stephens; *Frankenstein* by Mary Shelley; *The Sorrows of Young Werther* by Goethe; *Heart of Darkness* by Joseph Conrad; *100 Years of Solitude* by Gabriel Garcia Marquez; short stories by Dostoevsky, Tolstoy, Nikolai Gogol (*The Nose* and *The Overcoat)*, Anton Chekhov, Franz Kafka (*Metamorphosis*), Thomas Mann (*Death in Venice)*, James Joyce (*The Dead)*, D.H. Lawrence, E.M. Forster, Somerset Maugham, and Katherine Mansfield. We went on to read *The Great Gatsby* and *The Old Man and the Sea*, two short American novels that we squeezed into the last month.

At the end of each year, we always vote on our favorite book of the year, and that year it was *Don Quixote* by a wide majority. We laughed all the way through that classic! Why is *Don Quixote* no longer taught in high school? Big novels take up too much time in a test-driven curriculum. We luxuriated in the humor and character of this great classic, cited as the first comic novel in history and surely the precursor of every comic duo like Laurel and Hardy.

In one class that year, the session on Mann's *Death in Venice*, we went around the circle of students more than twice. Each time one boy, normally an active participant, paused, shook his head pensively, and passed. It was Felipe, who had joined the group at age eleven and was now a grown teen getting ready to go off to college. Every time his turn came, we all looked expectantly at him, eager to hear what he had to say, and accepting it when he skipped his turn. Our two hours were almost up, so I called it a day. Just as we were standing to gather our things and leave, Felipe said, "Oh! Now I remember what I wanted to say!" We all looked at him as he added, "It was the color red!"

"Ohhhh!" the group responded in unison. "The color red!" As if we were a single body moving in slow motion, we sank back into our seats. One at a time, we went around the circle to talk about red in the story. It was suddenly so obvious! How could we have overlooked it? Red was everywhere! And it meant so much! Passion, love, anger, blood, danger, life, death! We gathered our Lit Club minds and worked to unearth the deeply layered meanings in an elusive story. Time seemed to stop as we ignored dismissal, dancing together through endless variations of the color red.[1]

---

1. See G – Literature Discussion Curriculum

Chapter Twenty-Seven

Let's Get Lost!

The physical is the known, and through it we may find our
way to the unknown, the intuitive, and perhaps beyond to the
human spirit itself.   ~Viola Spolin, Improvisation for the
Theater

On a recent autumn day with clear blue skies, my sister and I took an
excursion down a back road in Maine. She had silenced the phone in
her lap with the GPS route, and I suddenly realized we had gone past our
destination. I let her know, "We're lost."

"Oh good!" her voice rose with glee. "That's the best part!"

"I agree!" Laughing, I continued driving, never thinking that we should stop
and turn around to aim towards our preplanned destination.

My sister was referring to "the best part" of our childhood travels with our
mother. We'd pile into the car with our mother at the wheel saying, "Let's get
lost!" It was our way of exploring a new place. Once we spent a summer in
Hawaii, when my father taught at the University in Oahu, and every day, we
tried to get lost. It was impossible to lose our bearings on the island, and we
always ended up on a dead end or the main road. But in the process of trying
to get lost, we marveled at brightly-colored flowering trees dotting a hillside,

or a hidden road that suddenly revealed glorious views of the ocean, or people picking coffee from tall trees on an estate at a dead end.

As an adult, I played the same game with my children. To explore a new place, we would get in the car, and at every intersection a different passenger got to choose which way we'd go. "Hurry up!" I'd say as we paused at a red light, encouraging impulse over logic, and someone would call out left or right or straight ahead, and off we'd go. In this manner, we visited mountain streams, drove past meadows full of wildflowers, and stopped alongside the road to pick wild berries or listen to a waterfall.

When I was little, I had freedom all too rare for kids today. In Wisconsin in the 1950s at age five, I walked myself to and from kindergarten and in my free time wandered beyond our backyard. I crossed quiet streets, roamed through neighbors' yards, and visited a pine woods to gather pinecones to bring home. How was I able to wander so freely, unaccompanied, and get myself back home? Why did I never feel lost?

One summer when I was twelve, my mother, sister, and I traveled through the south of France. Every morning, our mom let us know the next destination. She delegated tasks to us. My sister had the job of selecting tourist attractions to visit, using the French-language Michelin Guide. She didn't know much French when we started, but by the end of our trip, she could read the language fairly well. My job was to map the route and to let my mother know where to turn right or left. Each morning, she unfolded the map in my lap, pointed out where we were and where we were headed. I'm a bit ashamed to admit that it never once occurred to me to go the most direct way. Instead, I chose the route that I thought looked most interesting. I quickly realized squiggly lines were mountain roads where the driving might be scary but, in my opinion, the scenery was worth it. Once I directed my mother on a circuitous, coastal route without any foreknowledge that it was a long, narrow dirt road through a swamp. Flood warning signs in French dotted the road telling drivers to get out of the area if it rained. Once, we encountered an oncoming car, and both vehicles had to get their side tires wet in order to pass. My mother gripped the wheel and cursed at me, "It's like driving between two gigantic pots of bouillabaise!

Never again!" Bouillabaise was the local seafood stew, and it felt like we were swimming in it! She forgave me when we entered the town through a Medieval arch that transported us back in time. We looked overhead as we drove through, dumbstruck. We never would have driven through that venerable town entrance if we'd taken the conventional route or relied on GPS for directions.

In March 2016, the *New York Times* published an article on Wave Piloting[1] that reminded me of the essential value of getting lost. Wave piloting is the ancient art of open water navigation, now practically extinct. The Polynesian diaspora has mystified many historians. How could boats leave Polynesia in three different directions and end up establishing new communities in Hawaii, New Zealand, and Easter Island? Today, without modern navigation equipment, a boat could easily miss those islands in the vast ocean waters. But in ancient times, Polynesian wave pilots had gone straight to these destinations. It takes keen awareness and experience to locate "roads" or "highways" that exist within the ocean waves. I was fascinated to read about how this was done and even more fascinated when I learned that the key to acquiring this art is getting lost! **The apprentice must get lost before he can feel his way back and understand where he is.**

When I taught map-making to children, I asked them to draw images of their commute from home to my class. "Draw a scary place. Draw a silly place. Draw a landmark, a place you would recognize." One girl came to me and said she didn't pass any scary or silly places. I told her not to worry; she would take the commute again and could look for some.

At our next class, she was jumping with excitement. "I had no idea we drove past a cemetery!" she said with wide, spooky eyes. And then she twirled, "Going round and round on the highway ramp felt very silly!" She paused. "And we passed a landmark! A post office!" She then confessed that she had spent previous commutes looking at her phone, not out the window. She had been driving to her destination with little to no awareness of where she was. Her thrill at discovering details of the route was the thrill of connecting with the world around her.

Travel is a common metaphor for life. We are all on a life journey. Our learning experiences will influence the direction that journey takes. How can we know where we are going if we never look, if we fail to pay attention to the journey? How can we see beyond the path if we don't explore as we create our own route?

Today, people rarely look at a map larger than their phone. Seeing such a small area, they can't know if there's an enormous lake just north of where they are or if there's an old growth forest a few miles off the highway that's worth the detour. They won't catch all the place names that evoke a certain culture and history. They will miss the flavor of the place. Destinations are now reached by following the robotic voice of GPS, so there is no longer any reason to remember landmarks or recall details, no need to pay close attention to the journey. People can travel mindlessly, ignoring the larger world around them. Perhaps most disturbing is that when we rely on GPS, we never actually know where we are.

Just as GPS chooses the route to our destination and the traveler becomes unaware of what lies beyond, standardized education limits learning to such an extent that children are unaware of what is possible. They grow to hate learning, seeing it as enforced and personally meaningless. A student that feels disconnected from learning is likely to feel disconnected from the world and from themselves. Personalized education becomes a meaningful journey that the student can appreciate and build on. They can discover their direction. They can know who and where they are.

What if we stopped being afraid of losing our way and stopped dreading mistakes? What if we celebrated getting lost? What if we embraced making mistakes and getting lost as our greatest learning experiences? After all, these are the moments that change our perspective and teach us where we are. Just like the apprentice, we need to be able to get lost before we can know where we are. Out of our comfort zone, in unknown territory, we experience something new in our environment and, in the process, discover something new within ourselves.

On that autumn day in Maine, my sister and I drove until the road ended and parked near a lighthouse on the shore. We got out and walked to a bench, where we sat and watched the surf. We could have sat there for hours, mesmerized by the salt spray and the energy of the waves, two sisters quietly enlivened by the roar of the ocean. Soon, we got back in the car, retraced our path, and found our original destination, now comparatively boring. We knew the best part of our day had already happened. We had shared the blissful experience of getting lost and discovering what matters most.

---

1. "The Secrets of the Wave Pilots," New York Times, March 17, 2016.

Discussion And Activity Guide

To Be Used Alone Or In Groups

Q uestion #1 refers to chapter Hearing & Listening.

1. The five senses and the intuition (often referred to as the sixth sense) are pathways for learning, ways in which we gather information and make connections. Which of these six pathways do you rely on most for learning? Which pathway do you use least? Why? Which pathways did you use most when you were a child? Which pathways are used most in school?

Questions #2, 3 and 4 refer to the chapter Games: My Not-So-Secret Weapon.

2. Think back to before age five or six, before you attended school. Close your eyes, and take a few moments to recall yourself playing at a young age. What games did you play? Alone and with others? Did you invent any games? Imagine yourself engaged in play at this age. After you open your eyes, reflect on your work and lifestyle today as an adult. Do you recognize any connection between your early play experiences and your adult life? Does your work or attitude or lifestyle reflect your early choices of what, where, and how to play?

3. How do you feel when you recall childhood games and play experiences? How much do you play now? In what ways do you play? Do you wish you played more? Why don't adults play more than they do?

4. Did you play games for learning as a child? Do you play games with your students? What kinds of games? How did playing games affect the learning experiences? Which games that are mentioned in this book do you want to play and why?

Questions #5-8 are general questions about learning.

5. Think back on your learning experiences from ages preK-12. What stands out as vivid and transformative? What experiences made you see yourself or the world differently? Share at least one. Did these experiences happen in school? In a classroom? Did the experience come from a book? Was it something that already interested you before you did it?

6. Consider your post-high school learning experiences. Were any life changing? Was there an experience that permanently expanded your horizons? When and where did these experiences happen? Were you indoors? In a classroom? Or were you outdoors? Was it a hands-on experience? Was it something you were already interested in before you did it?

7. Are you actively learning now? What are you learning? How are you learning it? In what ways do you learn best? How would you change your learning?

8. Can you recall learning experiences in which your intuition was actively engaged? Or where you saw others using their intuition to learn? Share stories of intuitive learning.

Question #9 is an activity that can lead to an original, personalized lesson plan. Questions are included to serve as a non-judgmental evaluation of the experience. Use these questions to modify or build on the experience.

9. Design a learning experience on any topic, for yourself or for others, in which multiple pathways are used to gain, share, and connect information and

ideas. Include play or games that are appropriate. After leading others (or yourself) through your self-designed experience, practice non-judgmental evaluation by asking questions about the problem, not about the players. What was the focus? When were you able to stay in focus? What happened when you were in focus? What was communicated? What did you see or feel? After, did you feel different than you did before? Is there anything you would change about the learning experience if you experienced it or conducted it again?

Add your own questions and activities here.

CURRICULA and RESOURCES

A – Multicultural Geography Syllabus

Ten 90-Minute or 2-Hour Classes

For a detailed description of this curriculum, see Time Travel in the Classroom above

Typical Class Schedule for a 90-minute class (times are approximate):

10-15 minutes – Introduce place with maps, images and symbols.

Ask who has visited this place or has something to share about it. Encourage questions and information from the children.

If there is a Fun Fact sheet, this is a good time to share it.

10-15 minutes – Play a children's game from that part of the world.

10-15 minutes – Read a folktale aloud (volunteers welcome); group asks questions; discuss the tale and how it relates to the place.

20-30 minutes – Do a hands-on art activity. While students work, play traditional music from that part of the world.

10-15 minutes – Share artwork (finished or in progress to be finished later). Remind students which place will be the focus of the next class and write down any new questions.

Hand-outs or email with follow-up activities that can be done at home:

- Foods and recipes from that part of the world. Foods can be contributed and shared at in-person classes or made at home and eaten during or after a zoom class.

- Instructions to complete or duplicate art projects at home.

- Class follow-ups with links to games, information, resources, related books and movies.

Sample classes on West Africa, Egypt, India, Russia, France, Turkey, Hawaii, Mexico, Japan, Australia are included below.

These classes can be presented in no particular order. After the group selects places, start with a place that more than one child asked for, and allow more time for others to decide which place they want to learn about. Students usually prefer bouncing around the globe to sticking to one continent at a time.

Each class includes:

- maps showing borders and terrain

- images of landmarks

- fun facts

- symbols such as the flag

- great seal and motto

- national animals

- answers to student questions

If there is a second class on the same place, explore a different period of history in that place; share another story and hands-on activity. During art activities, play traditional music from that place, easily found on the Internet.

Classes

West Africa

Game: Clapping Games

Clapping games are played all over Africa. Find videos on YouTube demonstrating from Liberia and Nigeria. Pause and rewind so children can study the hand and leg movements and try to duplicate them.

Stories

"All Stories are Anansi's" or "Anansi's Hat-shaking" Dance from *The Hat-Shaking Dance: Other Ashanti Tales from Ghana* by Harold Courlander. Other Anansi stories are available online.

Food

Jollof rice, mashed peas and potatoes, groundnut sweet potato stew made with peanut or almond butter.

Hands-on Activities: Recognizing Rhythms and Making Masks

Recognizing Rhythms

Africa is a drumming culture, with rhythm in everything. Introduce some African rhythms from different African countries by playing a recording or video of examples. Ask children to raise their hands every time they hear the rhythm change.

In Africa, rhythm influences art, visible as rhythmic patterns woven into fabric. Look at examples of rhythm in African textiles. Draw rhythmic patterns on paper.

Resource: *Flash of the Spirit: African & Afro-American Art & Philosophy* by Robert Farris Thompson, with images of African textiles.

Mask Making

1. First look at images of African masks in museum collections (see resources).

2. Then lay out materials: raffia, feathers, buttons, fake hair, beads, cowrie shells, paint, markers, glue, metallic paper scraps, magazines, collage material, found objects.

3. Each student gets a paper pulp mask (have extra just in case) purchased from an art supply store.

4. After the masks are decorated, use a hole puncher to place holes in the sides for an elastic string and cut out eye holes carefully, using an X-acto knife.

These are wearable masks that can also be hung on the wall.

Mask Making Materials
- Paper pulp masks (available form DickBlick)

- Markers

- Tempera paint and brushes

- Glitter

- Glue

- Buttons

- Tinfoil

- Fake hair or yarn

- Miscellaneous items for adornment

Egypt

Mapping Skills

Display a map of Upper and Lower Egypt, and ask the students to guess which is Upper and which is Lower. This exercise challenges the mistaken belief that north is "up" and south is "down." "Up" is actually the direction that leads away from the earth, towards the moon and outer space. In this case, "up" doesn't refer to elevation but rather to the source of the Nile and the direction from which this mighty river flows; a term we use is "upriver." Once the kids are shown that the Lower part of Egypt lies to the north, ask why the southern part might be called Upper. Sooner or later, a student will guess that there are mountains or that the river comes from there.

Game: Mehen

The ancient Egyptian game of Mehen is available online.

Story

The Blue Faience Hippopotamus by Joan Grant, available online.

After reading, show the image of William, a faience blue hippo at the Metropolitan Museum, online.

Food

Pomegranates, figs, dates, yogurt and honey. Ancient Egyptian recipes can be found online at the Food Timeline for Egyptian flat bread and sesame rings. Hummus and Ful Medamas (a fava bean spread) were eaten in ancient Egypt and are still eaten today.

Hands-on Activities: Draw (or write) Hieroglyphs on papyrus scrolls or bookmarks.

Draw or write hieroglyphs.

Hieroglyphs can be copied, made using rubber stamps or printed and cut out (see resources). Students can begin by writing their names, either in hieroglyphs for Letters (sounds), or in symbols by creating their own glyphs. Papyrus is available at art supply stories. Folding it causes it to crack, so a scroll is the sensible way to use papyrus. If papyrus is not available, cut wide strips of card stock in tan, pale yellow, or orange to resemble the color of papyrus and make bookmarks.

Hieroglyphic writing is read right to left —opposite from the way English is read— and top to bottom.

Resources for Egyptian Hieroglyphic writing

The Winged Cat by Deborah Nourse Lattimore, with a page of hieroglyphics.

Fun With Hieroglyphics by Catharine Roehrig, rubber stamp kit with booklet published by the Metropolitan Museum of Art.

Multicultural Books To Make And Share by Susan Kapuscinski Gaylord, contains the papyrus name scroll activity.

Alternate Hands-on Activity: Design an Egyptian collar, template on following pages.

Wide collars were worn as jewelry by royalty in ancient Egypt. First look at images of Egyptian Collars found online. Then decorate the Egyptian Collar template. Print or copy the collar outline on card stock, decorate it, punch holes in the edges and tie a cord through each hole so it can be worn around the neck. Thin cardboard or a paper plate can also be used.

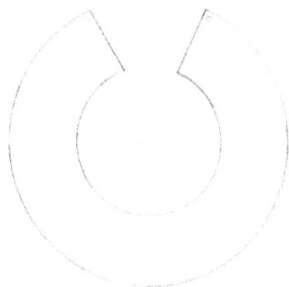

India

Game: Antakshari or Parchesi

Antakshari is a traditional game in India, similar to Geography, where the next player uses with the previous word's final letter as the starting letter. In India, one player sings a line from a song (likely a Bollywood song), and the next player sings a line from a different song, each beginning with the ending sound from the line just heard.

We played this game so the next player could begin with either the last letter or the last word of the song. (You can also play by using the last musical note.) If a player sang the line, "Twinkle, twinkle little star," it could be followed by a line from a different song beginning with the letter R or the word Star. This game was not easy but was still fun to play. "Mary had a little lamb" ended with "snow," which prompted a line starting with W, "Where in the World is Carmen SanDiego?" which prompted an O line, "Oh, holy night...."

India is the place of origin for many games, including Parchesi. A Parchesi board and instructions can be downloaded online for free. Libraries may have Parchesi available to borrow.

Story

Rama and Sita and *Story of the Stories* from Usborn's *Stories from India* by Anna Milbourne.

Or choose a Jataka animal wisdom tale, available free online.

Food

Lentil dal, kale & potato curry with garam masala, spiced chickpeas, naan or roti.

Hands-on Activity: Draw a mandala

Use a compass or trace three circular objects of increasing sizes to create templates with three concentric circles, drawn lightly in pencil. Students create rows of patterns in each ring of the circle using brightly colored markers or colored pencils. The mandalas can be drawn directly on a template or on a sheet of paper or Dura-lar plastic overlaid on top of a template. Finished mandala can be taped to a window to look like a layer of stained glass. While drawing mandalas, listen to sitar music by Ravi Shankar and traditional music.

Mandala art lessons in pdf are available online.

Materials for making mandalas

Child-friendly compass for making circles using no sharp points, called "Slide N Measure" or "Safety Bullseye" (available online)

Dura-lar to make a window mandala (attach a sheet over template using a paper clip), available from DickBlick.

Sharpie Fine Point Permanent Markers, including Glam Pop Colors set of 24, and Metallic Colors set of 6.

Russia

Game: Grandma's Bloomers

When you play Grandma's Bloomers, everyone gets to ask a question, which is answered by the next player who says, "Grandma's bloomers!" For example: What did you eat for breakfast today? What will you wear to the fancy dress ball? What do puppies prefer to play with? Prepare yourself for hysterical laughter.

Story

Vasalisa the Wise (or the Beautiful) or Peter and the Wolf, with Prokofiev's music. Resources: *Russian Fairy Tales: Palekh Painting* by Alexei Orleansky, *Women who Run with the Wolves* by Clarissa Pinkola Estes contains an excellent interpretation of Vasalisa the Wise.

Food

Blini, small crepes stuffed with jam or cheese; borscht, beet soup topped with sour cream.

Hands-on Activity: Draw in the Style of Marc Chagall

Watch clips of the Bolshoi Ballet dancing *Firebird* (on YouTube) and look at the set designs for *Firebird* created by Marc Chagall. Then look at paintings by Marc Chagall. Focus on "I and the Village." Encourage students to draw their home and neighborhood or a place they know well and might miss. Divide the paper into sections, and turn it around while drawing so some buildings and objects appear upside-down or sideways. A border on three sides can suggest the ground.

France

Game: Red Light Green Light in French.

Children play Red Light Green Light. but instead of the child who is "It" saying "One, Two, Three, Red Light!" they say: "Un, deux, trois, Soleil!" (1, 2, 3, Sun!). The child who tags "It" first takes their place, unless they have already gone. In which case, they select a new player who wants a turn. This game has been played on Zoom, with students starting at an agreed number of steps or distance away from the screen and tap the screen instead of tapping player who is "It."

Story

Well-known fairytales from France include Cinderella, Little Red Riding Hood, Puss 'n Boots, and Beauty and the Beast. I suggest a French tale from the Middle Ages about Reynard, the trickster fox, such as The Deep, Deep Well or Reynard in the Well (available free online)

For a historical focus, read Marguerite Makes a Book by Bruce Robertson, set in medieval Paris, showing how medieval books were made.

Hands-on Activities: Draw Stained Glass Windows or Make Your Own Paint.

Draw stained glass windows.

Use markers on Dura-lar sheets of acetate, a surface that accepts markers and wet materials. Tape or clip a clear sheet of Dura-lar over a template of a blank rose window or a set of concentric circles. Draw on the Dura-lar. When you're done, tape it on a glass window to see how it looks with light coming through.

For materials, see Mandala art activity for India.

Make your own ink or paint just as Marguerite does in *Marguerite Makes a Book*

- To make a rich yellow, add a few threads of saffron to a tablespoon of beaten egg white.

- To make green, take a spoonful of beaten egg white and add some parsley juice (chop the parsley finely and squeeze it through a strainer or piece of cheesecloth).

- For red or dark blue, add a few drops of food coloring or liquid watercolor or ground pastels or chalk dust to a spoon of beaten egg white.

Turkey

Game: Tongue Twisters

Tongue twisters are popular in Turkey. Try some in English (not Turkish), just for fun.

Story

The Most Precious Gift from Stories of Hope and Spirit: Folktales from Eastern Europe by Kan Keding

Food

Etliekmek (means meaty bread), or Shish kabob (skewered meat and vegetables). Shish means skewer. Recipes can be found online.

Hands-on Activity: Islamic Tile Designs

Look at photos of Turkish tiles in wall designs, and coloring pages of Islamic tiles and patterns. Use graph paper or printouts from the activity book listed below (use fig. 3 triangle grid, fig. 6 diagonal grid, in Activity 7 and Activity 10). Alternately you can use graph paper. Draw a pattern for a tile and color it in. Then copy it or reproduce it so you have four paper tiles. You can create a tessellated pattern or glue the paper tiles using rotational symmetry, or into any pattern you like. Colored pencils work well for this activity.

If you have the time, space, and materials, you can carve blocks and print them using rotational symmetry.

Art resources and materials

Art of the Islamic World: A Resource for Educators, Metropolitan Museum (free download), containing the Islamic Art and Geometric Design Activity Book.

Graph paper or printouts from activity book, colored pencils or fine point markers.

If you want to make block prints, which can be messy, you can purchase a block printing starter set with soft eraser material, available at DickBlick. For a large group, choose the carving block size, and purchase items in bulk, as well as a variety of ink colors. You will need a smooth tile or smooth washable surface (such as a piece of glass or a countertop) to apply ink to a roller, and plain paper for printing.

Hawaii

Game: String Figures

Make string figures like cat's cradle. String figures are used as part of storytelling in many indigenous cultures. Watch YouTube demos to learn how to make one.

Story

Maui Traps the Sun from *Hawaiian Myths of Earth, Sea and Sky* by Vivian Thompson, or Maui Takes On the Sun and Maui Raises the Sky, available online

Food

Pineapple, pineapple juice, papaya.

Hands-on Activities: Dance the Hula and Sing the Hukilau Song; Make Kapa Bark Cloth

Dance the hula and sing the Hukilau song with hula movements.

Hula demos for kids can be found on YouTube, where you can also see the Hukilau song performed. Song lyrics are available online.

Make Kapa or Bark Cloth from paper. Bark cloth in Hawaiian stories is known as *kapa* and in Polynesia as *tapa*. To prepare a facsimile of bark cloth, cut open a brown paper bag, crumple the paper, smooth it and crumple it again, repeating the process until you achieve a soft texture. Then decorate the fabric using Hawaiian patterns with floral and geometric shapes. When you are done, you can flatten and smooth the paper by using an iron. Place the smoothed paper between sheets of waxed paper and then in between newspaper before ironing with a hot iron.

Mexico

Game: Loteria (Mexican Bingo)

Loteria, or Mexican Bingo, sheets are free to download on the Internet. Children can use coins, paperclips, torn bits of paper, etc. as markers while playing. Make a list of all the images and call them out one at a time, checking off each item called. When someone gets every image in a row (in any direction), they call out *Loteria!*, which means they've won. In my classes there are no losers, so we keep playing until everyone has won Loteria! This game is easily played in a video class, if students print a Loteria sheet and find or make markers in advance.

Story

The Day It Snowed Tortillas by Joe Hayes. Listen to master storyteller Joe Hayes tell the tale on YouTube.

Or read The Chili Patch also known as Goat in the Chile Patch, available online.

Food

Corn (or flour) tortillas; refried beans and cheese tacos in soft tortillas. Mexican hot chocolate. This is where hot chocolate originated! Make your own by adding cinnamon to cocoa.

Hands-on Activities: Decorate Jaguar Masks; Paint in the Style of Frida Kahlo

Color and decorate jaguar masks and Day of the Dead masks.

Resources follow for printable pages for this project. If you print on card stock and punch holes between the edge and the eyes, you can tie a string and make it a wearable mask. Regular paper works too, but not as well.

Paint in the Style of Frida Kahlo.

We looked at images of Diego Rivera murals and paintings by Frida Kahlo. For inspiration, we looked closely at two by Kahlo, "Still Life" and "Frame." "Still Life" shows fruit with a parrot, is a still life you can create at home. I suggested drawing any fruit with a stuffed animal. "The Frame" is a self-portrait, which means the artist needs a mirror, or if you're on Zoom just look at the screen while you work. Decorate the border, perhaps with flowers and animals that you like or that live near you, to create a vibrant frame. Use bright, vivid colors. Children can choose to make a still life or a self portrait with frame.

Art Resources

Jaguar and Day of the Dead mask templates found online.

Frida Kahlo and Diego Rivera: Their Lives and Ideas, 24 Activities by Carol Sabbeth

Suggested materials: card stock, hole puncher and string, brightly colored markers or paints, printer paper.

Japan

Game: Rock Paper Scissors "Jan-Ken-Pon"

The original version of Rock Paper Scissors is Jan-Ken-Pon. Gu means stone, choki is scissors, and pa is paper. We begin by shaking a fist (stone) and saying Saisho Wa Gu (beginning with stone), Jan Ken Pon. Then we count one, two, three; on three, everyone shows their choice with their hand. If you tie (showing the same), then you say Aiko de sho, which means tied. If you win, say the word in Japanese, such as Pa! (Paper!) or Gu!(rock!). We took turns saying the words while the entire class played together, everyone trying to beat the speaker. Alternately, students could pair up and play a few rounds. Demos are on Youtube.

Story

Peach Boy, from *Japanese Children's Favorite Stories for Children* edited by Florence Sakade. Peach Boy (Motomaro) is also available online.

Food

Sushi, such as nori-wrapped rice and cucumber. Ramen (noodle soup) garnished with half a hard-boiled egg and chopped scallions.

Hands-on Activities: Origami; Design a Kimono; Write a Haiku

Make Origami

Make a simple paper cup which you can actually use, an easy activity. For a slightly harder (intermediate) activity, fold a jumping frog using a green (or any color) index card. This becomes a toy because you can make the frog jump. Kids can have a contest to see which origami frog jumps the farthest. A difficult fold is the flapping crane or blow-up crane. If time allows, students can make all three.

Origami Resources

Origami cup and jumping frog are found online with demos on YouTube. *Easy Origami Animals* by John Montroll. John Montroll's original origami designs are demoed on Instagram.

Kimono Art

Design your own kimono. Look at images of kimonos and discuss the patterns and scenes on the fabric. Pass out a blank outline of a kimono on paper that students can decorate any way they like. Reproducible kimono template is on the following pages.

Kimono Art Resources

Kimonos in the Brooklyn and Metropolitan Museums can be viewed online.
    Kimono template is on the following pages. Colored pencils or any medium can be used.

Haiku Poetry

Write a haiku poem, or write several. Haiku can be included in the kimono design or written on origami. Resources for teaching Haiku follow.

Haiku Resources

Haiku lessons for all ages are available free online at the Haiku Foundation.
    Haiku: One Breath Poetry by Naomi Wakan
    Haiku by Patricia Donegan

Origami and Haiku Inspired by Japanese Artwork, from the British Museum

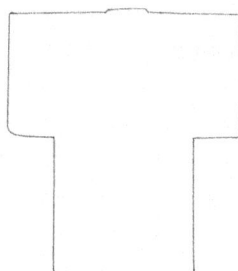

Australia

Game: Bite a cookie into an Aussie shape

Bite the biscuit into an Aussie shape. You can do this with an Anzac biscuit, but it's easier with an arrowroot cookie or slice of bread. Carefully eat away just enough to leave the shape of Australia. Have a map of Australia visible to all students and extra cookies or bread. Alternately, bite the food into the shape of an Australian animal such as a kangaroo, koala, or echidna (display animal pictures). Those not wanting to use food can tear a piece of paper into the desired shape. (Try doing this activity another time using your own state or country!)

Story

How the Kangaroo Got Her Pouch, from *Stories from the Billabong* retold by James Vance Marshall, with dot painting illustrations.

More aboriginal animal stories from the Dreamtime can be found online and in libraries.

Food

Anzac biscuits, like an oatmeal cookie with coconut, were sent to Australian soldiers in WWI because they lasted a long time. Today they are a national treat eaten on Australia Day. Recipes are online.

Hands-on activity: X-ray Dot Drawings

First listen to a didgeridoo, aboriginal music that has a deep vibrational sound (there are many choices on YouTube). This sets the tone for creating aboriginal x-ray dot drawings, named *x-ray* because they show the inside of an animal. Didgeridoo music can be played as background music while students draw. Look at aboriginal art, focusing on images of animals that show internal organs along with patterns of lines and dots. Start by tracing the hand, which is the earliest form of art found in petroglyphs and caves and fill the hand outline with patterns. Then choose an animal and do the same, drawing an outline and filling it with patterns. Have images on display of Australian animals (kangaroo, koala, wallaby, kookaburra, etc.), or students can draw any animal they like. Use large sheets of drawing paper and markers or colored pencils.

Imaginary Country Worksheet

N ame of Country:

Language:

Currency (money):

National bird:

National mammal:

National flower:

National tree:

Natural resources:

Foods:

What this country is known for:

Draw the flag:

Meaning of colors and symbols on the flag:

Motto:

On a sheet of paper, draw a map of your imaginary country. Name the cities, rivers, mountains and other geographical locations. Then write a story that could be a folktale from this country.

Multicultural Geography Resources

Includes language arts, history, math, art, and cultural understanding
Additional online resources are available at LaurieBlockSpigel.com.

Geography

- National Geographic website for kids.

- National Geographic Magazines for adults and for kids

- *Smart Kids Picture Atlas: Essential Facts About Every Country* by Roger Priddy

- *Geography for Every Kid* by Janice Van Cleave (hands-on activities that include earth science)

- The United States of America: A State-by-State Guide by Millie Miller and Cyndi Nelson

- KidsDiscover Magazine: Maps issue, available to order from their archives.

- See the central fold-out, "The WORLD'S not Flat???" for a comparison of world maps; also includes the orange peel activity and map of Mikey's Room, a humorous look at a kid's room introducing geographical terms.

- *Mapmaking With Children: Sense of Place Education for the Elementary Years* by David Sobel, an essential classic for teachers in geography education for the young.

- *Geography for Every Kid* by Janice Van Cleave, quick and easy hands-on activities.

- Free map downloads available online including Peter's Projection and other World Maps, Many Ways to See the World.

Games Around the World

- *Let's Play: Children's Games from Around the World* by Nancy Dickman

- The Multicultural Game Book by Louise Orlando

- *Games of the World*, published by UNICEF

- YouTube search for "[country] + children's games"

Holidays Around the World

- *A Calendar of Festivals* by Cherry Gilchrist, stories about international holidays

- Celebrations Around the World: A Multicultural Handbook by Carole S. Angell

Foods Around the World

- Food By Country: Website with foods of many countries linked by location, including some history, photographs and recipes:

- Food timeline online with recipes from around the world throughout history.

- *How to Make a Cherry Pie and see the USA* and *How to Make an Apple Pie and see the World* by Marjorie Priceman. These books can inspire humorous poetry or prose about taking a nonsensical journey in order to make a particular dish.

Folktales Around the World

- World of Tales, folktales from around the world online.

- Ten versions (there are many more!) of Cinderella from around the world, found online.

- Glass Slipper Gold Sandal: A Worldwide Cinderella by Paul Fleischman, combines Cinderella tales from several countries into a single story, with illustrations reflecting each culture.

- *Mooncakes to Maize: Delicious World Folktales* by Norma J. Livo, food-related folktales.

- *Between Heaven and Earth: Bird Tales From Around the World* by Howard Norman

- *Trick of the Tale: A Collection of Trickster Tales* by Tomislav Tomic

- *Stories from the Silk Road* retold by Cherry Gilchrist, includes a map of the Silk Route or Silk Road.

- Usborne's Stories From Around the World

Art and Hands-On Activities

- Discovering Great Artists by MaryAnn Kohl and Kim Solga

- Metropolitan Museum art books for educators, free to download on-line.

- For Kids series on history and art, with 21 (or more) hands-on activities in each book.

- Art from Many Hands: Multicultural Art Projects by Jo Miles Schu-man

- Brown Bag Ideas From Many Cultures by Irene Tejada, projects made from brown paper bags.

- *World Cultures Through Art Activities* by Dindy Robinson

B - Puppetry Activities and Syllabus

For a detailed description of this curriculum, see Puppets in the Snow above

Three Steps to Introduce Puppetry

From *Puppetry: How to Do It* by Mervyn Millar

STEP ONE

Warm up! Stretch! Breath!

Players begin with deep breathing. Inhale, stretch, and collapse. Stretch and collapse individual body parts including fingers (balling, unrolling, typing, or drum-tapping), shoulders and face. Then stretch the voice with the breath. Even if doing table-top puppets, you may have to crouch, kneel, or stretch. Crawl on the floor! Become alert to physical sensations of emotional states such as guilt or joy. Show various emotional states in the face and then the body and then in movement.

STEP TWO

Practice with things, like sticks or twigs, spoons or kitchen objects, apple on stick through a plastic bag weighted with other apples (viewable in TED talk video)

STEP THREE

Perform with objects.

Additional Activities

- Play warm-up games and games to increase sensory awareness. See curriculum outline (below).

- Read through one or more story/fable. Select one or more for the group to perform.

- Make puppets and create characters for a performance.

- Large paper puppets can be made from a roll of brown paper, tearing off a six-foot length and bending it in half in a long U-shape that is then bent and squeezed to form a figure with a head from the central loop, with shoulders, arms and legs. Smaller puppets can be made in the same way, or using cardboard tubes, sticks, paper plates, etc.

- If making a large paper puppet that will require two players to manipulate, play MIRROR before working together. If three performers are required, play three-way mirror.

- Read through and then improvise the story using puppet characters.

Two-Day Puppetry Workshop Syllabus

(Time for each activity is in parentheses, in minutes)
For a detailed description of this course, see chapter 17, Puppets in the Snow.

DAY ONE (10am-4pm)

1 0am - 4pm (duration of activity is estimated in minutes in parentheses)

Introduction (5-10))

Name labels (5)

Write out name tag and sticker for each child, take pictures of each to memorize their names that night. (Day two they won't have name tags.).

Name Game (5-10)

If the group is new to each other, play the Name Game. Everyone walks around the room passing by their fellow players saying their own name out loud to each person they see. Then the group is side-coached to say the name of whoever they are walking past (instead of their own). This is a quick way to learn everyone's name.

Warm-ups (10-15)

- Pussy Wants a Corner (or Kitty Wants a Corner)

- Body stretches

- Facial expressions: sad, scared, happy, angry, surprised and confused

- Body expressions: tired, sad, angry, scared, shy, happy, confused, surprised

- Space Walk #1 (Spolin). Feel the Space. (10-15)

- Additional games (Spolin) if time allows, for pairs:

- Tug of War

- Three Changes (then six, then nine)

- Mirror

- Games that introduce puppetry skills (one hour or more)

- On floor, Hand Animals (Millar p. 17) (30)

- Hand Animal Variations with weight and moods.

- If time allows, Hand Animal Encounters.

Hands Alone (Spolin) (20-30).

Pull a couch away from the wall to use as a stage or flip a table onto its side or add a skirt or low-hanging tablecloth to a table. Play Hands Alone hiding the player's body behind the stage.

If time allows play variations of Hands Alone: using only the hands, show moods and feelings through actions, such as eating cereal, playing an instrument, gardening, walking a dog, dancing, etc. This is good to play following afternoon warm-ups.

Lunch break (one hour)

If children finish lunch early, play some games!

Warm-up games (20-30 minutes)

- Lemonade / New York (Spolin) with a focus on professions (Who game)

- Additional games if time: What Are You Doing? and Give and Take.

Puppetry skills games (30+ minutes)

- Hand Encounters (if there wasn't time in the morning).

- Give out Oobi Eyes. (Children can choose colors. Have extra on hand.)

- Oobi Eyes Encounters on stage (players work in pairs). (20-30 minutes)

- If time allows: Sticks and Stick Encounters. (30 minutes)

Art (one hour or more)

Make puppets. Distribute materials. Show possible combinations and applications.

Writing (20-30 minutes)

- Ask the students, "Does your puppet have a name?" Write down answers.

- Pass out Puppet Character Sheets, and make sure students understand each line.

- Those who are ready can start filling one out for each puppet character.

- Explain homework (don't worry - homework is optional)

- Finish making your puppet(s).

- Complete a character sheet for each puppet you make.

- Bring the completed sheets back tomorrow to use in a game we will play!

Closing circle game (if time): Crazy Compliments or Machine (10-20 minutes)

Crazy Compliments (10-15, more if group is large).

To play this game, each person says a crazy compliment to the person next to them who must answer "Thank you," and then that person does the same back.

The first receiver turns to the next person and repeats the process. Example: Player A: "I really like your shirt because it reminds me of when I went to the Grand Canyon and almost fell in!" Player B: "Thank you!" Player B compliments Player A who thanks B and then B compliments C and so on, until the last player compliments A who compliments that player back and the game is over.

Machine[1] (10-20 minutes) in two groups, a good game for improvised teamwork.

If there is additional time, students can take their puppets and Oobi eyes outside for unstructured outdoor play.

Children each take home two sets of Oobi eyes, puppets in various stages of completion, a character sheet for each puppet, and copies of AESOP Tales or other tales which can be adapted or improvised into puppet plays.

DAY TWO (10am - 4pm)

Warm-up games (15-20 minutes)

Who Started the Motion?
    Red Light Green Light - as animals
    Space Walk - Include/Occlude, Sole Support/ Feel the Space Support You.

Character and Setting Development (20-30 minutes)

Puppets wake up slowly and explore the room
    Explore your puppet's moods and feelings (interests, fears, etc.)
    Work on character sheets. Complete homework.

Game - Character Interviews (one hour +)

Conduct Puppet Interviews. First the student reads the character sheet aloud (or asks a volunteer to read), then the puppet introduces itself with the maker creating the puppet's voice and movements. This can be done using a puppet stage or the puppet maker can sit in a chair and let the puppet perform on the arm of the chair or on the maker's knee. Questions are taken from the audience (fellow players and teachers). The puppet character can call on any raised hand. Here the puppet finds its voice and the maker learns more about their character. The maker does not use their own voice until the puppet has completed the interview and left the performance area. Interviews are 5-10 minutes each.

After puppet interview, the puppet maker can add to its character sheet.

Lunch break (one hour)

Puppet Interviews - continued (45 minutes or longer)

Meet every puppet and hear its voice. Each player introduces at least one puppet. If time allows, a maker's second puppet can be interviewed. (In a longer course, interviews can be spread out over several classes, allowing time for games and writing in between interviews.)

Puppet Encounters (Millar p. 24) (30 minutes)

Puppets meet other puppets and react to each other. Relationships are formed between puppets.

Weather Exercise (Spolin p. 107) in two groups (20-30 minutes)

This activity develops the where or setting.

If time allows, other "where" games to play:
- Where with Three Objects

- Build a where

Warm-up games to select before performance (10-15 minutes)

- (Often the first traditional game of the course is played again now.)

- Pussy (or Kitty) Wants a Corner

- Playing Catch

- Give and Take

- Extended Sound (helpful for children to share their voices with the audience)

Final performance (5 min.+- per player or pair; total time one hour +-)

Students choose a partner or teacher assigns pairs of number to the kids. Example: in a group of 12, number students 1-6 twice and each number finds its partner. Each pair chooses a where and a physical activity for their puppet characters. Then they perform an improvised scene where the characters (puppets) interact with each other and the setting while engaged in a physical activity.

Side-coach suggestions

Remember where you are. React to the place. Focus on the activity. Speak in the *puppet*'s voice. Feel the emotion in the *puppet*'s face. Feel the emotion in the puppet's body.

Final Take-Home

At the end of workshop students take home finished puppets and character sheets, two sets of Oobi eyes, and selected tales for puppet shows.

Additional games that can be added to a longer puppetry workshop

Warm-up games (group games and games in pairs)

In pairs:

- Three changes (then six, then nine),
- Mirror,
- Tug of War

Circle games, half the group plays while the other half observes as audience

- Playing Catch
- Extended Sound
- Give and Take

Entire class playing in open space

- Space Walk (variations)

- No Motion

- Space Shaping

- Space Object Games

- When I Get to California (with space objects)

- Taste and Smell

- Transformation of Objects

Sensory and Where games (developing setting)

- Sending Hearing Out

- Taste and Smell

- Seeing a Sport

- Build a Story (two teams, half of the class observes as audience)

Who games (developing character)

- Walks without attitude

- What Age Am I (also called Bus Stop)

- Physical Exaggeration (Spolin p. 244), good for creating & physicalizing superheroes

- Gibberish games (good for communication, can develop Who and also Where)

Allow for non-judgmental self-evaluation and feedback after every game and exercise.

Use the Spolin phrases straight out of the book for side-coaching and evaluation.

Character development worksheet, applicable to puppetry or any form of writing, follows.

---

1. Instructions to play Machine are in Chapter 17.

Puppet Character Questionnaire

N ame:

Nickname:

Age:

Gender:

Occupation:

Type of being (human, animal, fairy, alien, fantasy creature):

Appearance:

Mannerisms/Attitude (way of speaking, posture, gestures):

Quirks and habits:

Family members:

Best friend:

Describe where s/he lives:

Talents, abilities, or powers:

Faults:

Good points:

Fears:

Secret:

What s/he wants more than anything else:

Obstacles to that want (what is in the way of getting those wants?):

Draw a picture of your character.

Puppetry Resources

***Puppetry: How to Do It* by Mervyn Millar.**

T he ultimate book on puppetry, with everything you need to know to teach a workshop and create a magical experience.

TED Talk online by Mervyn Millar, "This is Your Brain on Puppetry"

***The Sophisticated Sock: Project Based Learning Through Puppetry* by Karen Konnerth**

Puppetry Games

- *Theater Games for the Classroom* by Viola Spolin - see suggested games below

- Character Development Resources

- Character Trait Print-Outs are online at ReadWriteThink for grades 3-5 and 6-8.

Resources on Emotions

- *The Emotion Thesaurus: A Writer's Guide to Character Expression* by Angela Ackerman and Becca Puglisi, 2nd ed.

- Video clips showing physical movements and behavior, and explanations of negative and positive emotions are online at Emotion Typology.

Stories for Puppet or Story Theater Performances

- Indigenous Tales from Native America, Africa, aboriginal Australia, etc., available in libraries and online at Gutenberg and other sites.

- AESOP tales online, illus. by Milo Winter.

- *Aesop's Fables Coloring Book*, published by Dover

AESOP tales suggested for performance

- The Lion and the Mouse (two players)

- The Dog and his Reflection (one player, two if one is the reflection, playing mirror)

- The Fox and the Crow (two players)

- Two Travelers and a Bear (three players)

- The Shepherd Who Cried Wolf (whole class: shepherd, sheep, wolf, villagers)

- The Two travelers and the Purse (whole class?)

- The Town Mouse and the Country Mouse

- The Fox and the Crane (practice with space objects first) (two players)

- Nursery rhymes suggested:

- Jack Be Nimble Jack Be Quick (one player)

- Simple Simon (two players)

- Little Miss Muffet (two players)

- Pussycat and Queen (3 players)

- Hey Diddle Diddle the Cat and the Fiddle (five players)

- Little Bo-Peep (one player and sheep)

- Hark! Hark! (whole class)

- Hot Cross Buns (whole class)

Note: multiple players can participate in scenes with one or a few players. For example, everyone can be Jack jumping over a candlestick.

Making Puppets, Materials and Kits

- Kit: "Make Your Own Sock Puppets," by Creativity for Kids, with materials for three soft hand puppets appropriate for preschoolers. Add your own objects, such as buttons, stickers, pipe cleaners, ribbon and anything else you might use to adorn a puppet. Additional socks and other materials can be used for the puppet body.

- Oobi Eye Finger Puppets (available online)

- Creative Canvas Hand Puppets available at DickBlick.

- Faber-Castell Make Your Own Sock Puppets (with self-adhesive add-ons) from DickBlick.

- Tulip Dual-tip Fabric Markers, from DickBlick.

- Wiggle eyes in assorted shapes, sizes and colors

- Felt squares in a variety of colors

- Buttons, fabric scraps, pipe cleaners, yarn

- Glue and small brushes

- Scissors

- Socks, clean used or new, tube socks are preferred

- Found objects such as seashells, pinecones, twigs, bits of costume jewelry, etc.

Additional online resources are available at LaurieBlockSpigel.com.

C - Board Game Course Syllabus

For a detailed description of this curriculum, see Board Game Land above

Make Your Own Board Game for Ages 8 and Up

Intensive schedule, 20 hours over four days (24 hours including lunch breaks).

Activity times are estimated.

Alternate time schedules follow.

This curriculum is described in detail in chapter 18, Board Game Land.

DAY ONE

Morning

10:00-10:15

W arm-up, traditional children's circle game, Pussy Wants a Corner (or Kitty Wants a Corner)

10:15-10:30

Discussion of favorite games

10:30-11:00

Show examples of board games, differences in design and how they are played. (Monopoly, Parchesi, Chutes & Ladders, Candy Land, Life, Scrabble, Chess, Checkers, Risk, Clue, etc.)

11:00-11:30

Board game materials are shown - game boards (framed and blank), cards, pawns and dice. (Materials purchased from Bare Books.) Students select the topics they want to learn more about, which their games will be based on.

11:30-12:30

Research materials handed out (folders, pads and pencils) and different types of research are discussed (see resources that follow).

   The game-making process is outlined:

- Choose the focus of the game (topic)

- Do research, take notes for fact cards, turn notes into closed-ended questions for Q & A

- Figure out how your game will look and how it will be played

- Design and decorate your game board

- Write instructions on how to play your game

Lunch break (one hour)

Afternoon

1:30-1:45

Warm-up circle game - "Extended Sound" if class needs to communicate more; "Dog and Bone" if class needs to listen more.

1:45-2:30

Students discuss their chosen topics, and each topic is approved by the teacher. Topics that are too broad or vague are narrowed down or made clearer. Individual research begins with library books, magazines (such as Zoobooks and Kids-Discover) and computers with Internet access. Students are encouraged to use several different resources for research, not just the Internet. Recommendations are made for reliable Internet sites, such as National Geographic, NASA and the San Diego or Bronx Zoo). Wikipedia should only be used as a stepping stone to more reliable sources. Students each write at least three facts in the form of Q and A (as many as they like). Individual assistance is offered.

2:30 -3:00

Game: Stump The Class[1]
   Students ready with questions can volunteer.

3:00-3:50

Sketch a preliminary design for your board.

3:50-4:00

Closing circle game (5-10 minutes if time allows): Crazy Compliments

Silly compliments are told by each student to the next, always thanking them before creating another silly compliment for the next player. The teacher begins to set the example, such as "I like your hair because it reminds me of the time I almost flew to the moon." "Why, thank you. I like your shoes because they look like my grandma's fancy teapot."

Alternate Closing Game: Machine (see Part of a Whole in Spolin), 10-15 minutes, for one or two groups of 6-10 players.

Students, one at a time, when they are ready, enter the stage area (empty floor space) and each create a sound with a movement, repeating it continuously, while other students enter the stage and add their own sound and movement. When the group is all on stage, simultaneously making sounds and movements, they have become a machine. Side-coach changes in speed, volume and pitch, ending either in slow motion to a grinding halt, or in triple time at a furious pitch that explodes. Then ask students (audience and players) what kind of machine they thought it was. Go through the movement and sound one more time to see it as the machine they stated.

DAY TWO

Morning

10:00-10:15

Warm-up circle game: Who Started the Motion?
   or Three Changes (doing 9 changes in total) in pairs
   (both games develop observational skills)

10:15-10:30

Go over the chosen topics - some students might have changed their topic.
Students select either a blank or framed board. Individual problems about game
design are discussed.

10:30-11:30

Research and write facts as Q and A or work on game board design.

11:30-12:30

Play Stump the Class. Show game board designs.
   Lunch break (one hour)
   Afternoon

1:30-1:45

Warm-up game: entire group plays an intellectual game based on facts, either
Mammal, Bird or Fish (also known as Beast, Bird or Fish) or Birds Fly[2]

1:45-3:30

Work on individual research and fact cards. Design fact cards. These can be
marked with a symbol that appears on the game path, indicating that the player
picks a card with that symbol when landing on that square. The symbol usually
reflects the topic. Rubber stamps or stencils can be used to apply the symbol to

a stack of cards fairly quickly or the symbol can be drawn by hand. Continue to work on game design and fact cards.

3:30-4:00

Game: Stump the Class or Machine[3] (if it has not yet been played)

DAY THREE

Morning

10:00-10:30

Stump the Class (select those who haven't played it yet) or Quick Numbers.

10:30-12:30

Game instructions are discussed. Examples from actual games are shown. Students are encouraged to read game instructions at home. Specific points include how to begin; if there is a winner, how you win; how the fact cards are used in the play; the meaning of symbols on the board and cards; if the game is cooperative how players must cooperate in order to succeed; variations on the game such as an easier or harder version. Those who are ready write a first draft of their instructions and try it out on other students. The goal is for instructions to need no explaining, so children are free to play other games on Game Day.

Lunch break (one hour)

Afternoon

1:30-1:45

Game: Name Six

　or Guggenheim for older kids, a writing game

1:45-3:30

Work on completing fact cards and board game design. Pawns and dice are given out, along with replacement materials (cards, pads, folders, boards) if needed. Game instructions are written or revised.

3:30-4: 00

Game (if time allows): Stump the Class or any game requested by the kids.

DAY FOUR

Morning

10:00-10:15

Warm-up game: Red Light Green Light as animals

　or Silent Crambo (also known as Dumb Crambo) with the group in two teams.

10:15-12:30

Game boards are completed and decorated. Instructions are tested and revised. (No one wants to have to explain their game on Game Day when they could playing everyone else's games.)

Lunch break (one hour)

Afternoon

1:30-2:15

Final touches are put on games. Instructions are finalized. Games are set up.

2:15-2:30

A final warm-up game is often played at the start Game Day, usually repeating the first game played, Pussy (or Kitty) Wants a Corner, or the children can select their favorite group game.

2:30 -4:00

GAME DAY!

Family and friends are invited to play the board games!

Alternate schedules and time lengths

This twenty-hour course can also be taught in 15 or 16 hours over the course of several weeks, using time at home as needed for additional research, game design, making game cards, decorating the board, writing, and revising instructions.

Weekends offer the possibility of on-site research such as observing at a zoo or pet store or interviewing an expert. I have taught this course in eight weeks of two-hour classes and in ten weeks of 90-minute classes, with the final class as Game Day.

Small groups range in size from 7 to 12 kids. Larger groups may require an assistant. With 20 students in Sydney, Australia, several adults volunteered, making a child/adult ratio of approximately 4:1, which is more than ideal.

---

1. See Chapter 18 for a description of this game.

2. Both games are in *Handbook for Recreational Games* by Neva Boyd

3. Instructions in Chapter 18.

Board Game Materials and Resources

Game Board Materials

B oards, dice, pawns, cards, available online from Bare Books. Students may need several stacks of cards. If errors occur, an extra board may be needed. They may opt not to use the dice or pawns and to create their own pawns.

Decorating Materials

- Stickers and templates of geometric shapes are available at Bare Books.

- Rubber stamps can be found with images of animals, plants, outer space, and more. Rubber stamps save time if you want to mark fact lots of cards and game spaces.

- Permanent markers, in fine, medium and wide tips, come in all colors including metallics.

Research Resources

- Library books

- Magazines and periodicals

- Photographs

- Film and video

- Internet,

- Interviews and Experts

- Observation (such as zoos, birdwatching, sports, etc.)

- Museums

- Historical sites

- Specialized collections and specialized libraries, archives

Circle Games for Warm-Ups

- Handbook of Recreational Games by Neva Boyd, available online.

- Theater Games for the Classroom by Viola Spolin

- Improvisation for the Theater by Viola Spolin, 3rd edition

Images and History of Board Games

- Monopoly and other images of early board games can be found online at the National Toy Hall of Fame and other sites.

- Images of Board Games Made by Students can be found online at HomeschoolNYC.

- Additional online resources are available at LaurieBlockSpigel.com.

D - Interview Course Syllabus

16 hours delivered in 8 classes

A detailed description of this course is in Interviewing: The Lives We Live above Games and the order of activities are subject to change. Flexibility is important. Class interviews might take ten minutes or a half hour. Games are also unpredictable in their time length. This course has been taught over eight or ten weeks of 90-minute or 2-hour classes with a few hours of homework each week.

Class #1

Warm-up game:

Quick Numbers or Name Six.

Define "interview."

Invite children to share any personal interview experiences. Ask them what types of interviews they've heard about (college interviews and job interviews may come up).

Share interview examples from newspapers and magazines.

How does an interviewer prepare?

Discuss three stages of each interview:

1. preparation and organization, including locating an interviewee and arranging to meet or communicate with them.

2. the actual interview

3. writing up the interview, including post-research and revision.

How would you prepare to interview a children's author? A scientist? A relative?

Brainstorm questions. Make lists of questions.

Conduct a group interview with a parent or volunteer.

During this first practice interview, model the process, greet the person, and introduce them, take notes, and thank them at the end along with the class. Encourage students to raise hands and ask questions. That evening, write up the interview and share it with students in the next class.

At the end of class, if there's time, show a book of interviews from a previous class or share a published interview (perhaps of a child or teen) that can be read aloud by students taking turns.

Student homework:

Email two interviews to the group to read (see interview resources).

Teacher's homework:

Type up class interview for the next class. Prepare handouts of published interviews.

Class #2

Warm-up games:
  Telephone or Dog and Bone (both games build listening skills)
  Space Walk - See and Be Seen / Include and Occlude
  Share finished group interview from previous class.
  Read it together and discuss.
  List any new questions they'd like to ask. Amend question list.

How else might they change the interview process or prepare differently?

Discuss three parts of every written interview:

Beginning, middle, and end: i.e. introduction, body, and closing.

Show different formats of interviews:

Questions and Answers written in two voices.

Prose paragraphs written from the interviewer's point of view.

Read examples of interviews.

Focus on openings and closings. Discuss the nature of the questions.

Second classroom interview

Pass out materials, steno pads and pencils.

Guide a follow-up interview with same person who was the first class interviewee, with new questions.

Or interview another volunteer.

Everyone takes notes.

Conduct peer interviews in pairs.

Students are free to ask whatever they like. Students are encouraged to take notes.

Peer Interview Feedback (if time allows).

Invite students to share their experiences. What did they learn about their classmate? How were their comfort levels? Could anyone have been made to feel more comfortable? What suggestions do the students have? How might they change this interview experience? (This can be done in the following class.)

If time, play Trinterview as a group.

Alternate closing game: World's Worst Interviewer.

Student Homework:

Each student writes up their notes for group classroom interviews and peer interviews and emails their notes to the teacher.

Choose a relative to interview. Prepare a list of questions for them. Send the questions to the teacher. Schedule the interview.

Teachers Homework:

Teacher compiles the group interviews to share in class.

(Peer interviews will receive feedback in pairs in class.)

Class #3

Warm-up game:

Extended Sound or Mirror Sound

Discuss peer interviews.

What did you learn about each other? Did you have more questions you wanted to ask? Write them down, and ask the person later, during or after class.

Share previous group interview, reading aloud together (voluntarily).

Set guidelines for non-judgmental feedback. Avoid "like" and "don't like." Avoid rephrasing the interviewer's questions. Instead, comment on what stayed with you, made you think or feel, or that you related to personally.

Go over list of questions for relatives.7

Share immigration questions and other relative questions.

Read an interview written by a student or a professional interview with an elderly person.

Play a closing game, if there's time, such as Telephone or Alphabet Story.

Student Homework:

Conduct an interview with an elderly relative (if you have not already done so). Take notes. Write it up and send it to the teacher.

Class #4

Warm-up game:

Sending Your Hearing Out or Listening to the Environment

Class interviews a volunteer interviewee.

Students prepare to interview non-relatives, a family friend or neighbor.

How will they each select someone they have met but don't know well? Write down their plans.

Class brainstorms questions and helps fellow students find interviewees.

Create a list of questions appropriate for this type of interview.

If time, read and discuss an interview of a neighbor or "ordinary" person. (See resources.)

Closing game, if time allows, World's Worst Interviewer. (if not yet played).

What's the rudest or most insensitive way to interview someone? Act it out! This game is hilarious.

Student Homework:

Schedule an interview with a non-relative. Do research, write questions, make an appointment.

Read one or two interviews or watch video clips of interviews (documents or links emailed to students by teacher).

Class #5

Warm-up game:

What is my thought like? or Silent Crambo

Share relative interviews.

Ask students what they felt good or strong about in the process, and the writing, and where they feel unsure.

Share revision guidelines.

Begin revising the first interview.

Play a closing game, if there's time, such as How Am I Like that?

Student Homework:

Conduct the second interview and write it up. Revise first the interview.

Class #6

Warm-up game

   New York / Lemonade (in two teams, groups each mime a profession)

   Plan the third and final interview, focused on a chosen profession.

The entire class and community helps students find people in these professions willing to be interviewed. Students have this week and next to complete this interview and revise their work.

Student Homework:

Prepare for the third interview. Research, write questions, and make arrangements for the interview. Conduct the interview and write it up.

   Revise second interview.

   Send all finished work, including photographs, to teacher for the final project, a book of interviews. (Submitting work early makes the final project go more smoothly.) Ask for a student to volunteer to make a cover or use some of their photos. Deadline for all submissions, photos, and cover is a week before the last class.

Class #7

Warm-up game:

   Choose a game on your list that there wasn't time to play.

   Final group interview in the classroom.

This might be a profession that several students found interesting. We have had parents who were actors, playwrights, musicians, writers, teachers, psychologists, and family friends visiting from Greece, Germany, Japan, and England.

   The group takes notes and sends them to teacher. This final collaborative interview can be compiled by the teacher and added to the book.

   Discuss book title.

Take nominations.

Students will vote by email on their first, second, and third choices for the title.

If they cannot come to a group decision, they can each make their own title page and use different titles. The teacher can make one title page for everyone and offer a blank sheet (the same cover image with no title) so they can make their own.

Share interviews by students that are finished or in process.

Complete third interview if not yet completed.

Revise all interviews. Send in finished work and photos.

Deadline is 5 days before final class, allowing time for teacher to compile and print the book.

Student Homework:

Complete all interviews and revisions and send all work by the deadline.

Teacher homework:

Book is completed by teacher in the final week. Photos of interviewees can be included.

Class #8

Warm-up game:

Students choose the final game, often the first game (in this case, Quick Numbers).

Final interviews are shared along with the process.

What would they change if they could?

Completed book is passed out.

Students can bind or put the books together in class and make covers.

If the front cover is copied in black and white, students can color it. If they asked for a blank cover, they can title it.

Family, friends, and interviewees are welcomed.

Selections from the book are read aloud by students.

Everyone is publicly thanked for their help and support.

If there's time, we play a final game, Good, Bad and Ugly Advice with audience questions or a game of Trinterview.8 Both games can include the guests.

Students go home with their own book of class interviews, complete with photos and a cover.

Interview Questions Created by New York City Homeschoolers

N ot all questions are right for every interviewee. Create your own list of questions!

For Immigrant Grandparents

- When did your family first come to this country?

- How did you come?

- How long was the journey and what was it like?

- How did you feel when you got here? Were you lonely? How did you make friends?

- How did you find work? What was your first work experience here like?

- What was the hardest part of leaving your home country?

- What was the hardest part about living in a new country? What was the best part?

- Do you identify with being from here or from your previous country? As American or as _____? Or both? Which identity is stronger? How much of the new culture have you adopted? How much of the old culture did you bring and keep alive?

- Which place did you like living in more? Why?

- What are your favorite traditions or holidays? Why?

- What parts of your former country's culture do you miss?

- How many places did you live in the US? Where did you live?

- What are the advantages and disadvantages of living in the US or in your place of origin?

- Do you miss any foods or special dishes that you used to eat before you came to the US?

- How do the markets and foods there compare to the ones here? Which do you prefer?

- Is there any place else where you would like to live or travel to?

- What would you change about your life here today?

Immigration History

- Where is your family originally from?

- How were they treated there? What was their life like?

- Why did they decide to come to the United States?

- When did they come?

- How many came here together and who were they? How old were they?

- How did they come (by ship or plane)?

- Did they stop at Ellis Island?

- How difficult was their journey?

- What language(s) did they speak when they got here?

- How did it feel when they arrived? How did it feel to leave their home?

- What were their professions?

- Where did they settle? Did they live in New York?

- Are there special foods, music or customs that you still have in your family that came from your place of origin?

- Did you ever go back and visit?

Childhood

- What did you want to be when you were a kid?

- Tell me a childhood memory, perhaps something funny or embarrassing.

- What is your earliest memory?

- Did you have any pets? Any siblings? What was your relationship with them?

- Did you have a best friend? What do you remember about him/her?

- What kinds of games did you play as a child?

- Did you have a favorite teacher or a special learning experience you could tell me about?

- Tell me about a teacher you didn't like.

- What did you wear to school? What did you eat for lunch?

- Did you go to church or temple or a mosque? What did you wear and how did you have to behave?

- How did you celebrate holidays? Share a holiday memory.

Work (Profession)

- What kind of work do you do? What are some of the things that you do at your workplace?

- How did you choose this profession?

- How did you learn to do your job?

- How old were you when you first got started?

- Do you like your job? Why?

- Why are you working at two jobs?

- Tell me about your job as a parent. What is it like taking care of your children?

- Why did you retire?

- What did you learn from your work?

- If you could change your job, how would you change it?

- If you could do something else or something different, what would that be?

Resources For Interviewing

*C*lassroom Interviews: A World of Learning by Paula Rogovin, a first grade teacher in New York City public schools creates a year-long curriculum from spontaneous interviews. Filled with inspiring examples, applicable to any age.

Interview, Edit and Shape: A Step by Step Guide, by the NY Times.

Foxfire Book Series by Elliot Wigginton. A high school teacher and his students, living in the Southern Appalachian Mountains, interviewed elderly residents to create a magazine. They chronicled oral histories and photographed vanishing practices, preserving Appalachian heritage. The project spawned 12 volumes in a book series, the Foxfire Museum in Georgia, and Foxfire Magazine with student contributions. I shared two interviews from Volume One with my students, "Making a Hamper Out of White Oak Splits" and "Soapmaking."

Published Interviews from newspapers and periodicals, including interviews with teens and people students might know, such as:

"It All Started With a 12-Year-Old Cousin: A Conversation with Salman Khan," by Claudia Dreifus, NY Times, Jan. 28, 2014 (interview with the scientist who founded Kahn Academy) https://www.nytimes.com/2014/01/28/science/salman-khan-turned-family-tutoring-into-khan-academy.html

"On the Baseball Beat: At 12, Landing Interviews with Major League Players," by Corey Kilgannon, NYTimes October 6, 2013.

"Character Study," by Corey Killgannon, NYTimes 2015-2018, a column about "ordinary" New Yorkers, such as: tow trucker driver, female tugboat deckhand, ship photographer, saxophone repairman, safecracker, veterinary acupuncturist, digger of buried artifacts, teenage birder, sidewalk fruit vendor and many more.

Foxfire Book Series selected chapters (see above)

Games

- *Handbook of Recreational Games* by Neva Boyd, available online.

- *Theater Games for the Classroom* by Viola Spolin

- Warm-up games

- (Most games are in the books listed above by Spolin and Boyd)

Awareness:

- Quick Numbers awakens a tired group (group in line or circle)

- Pussy Wants a Corner (or Kitty Wants a Corner)

- Space Walk (increases intuition and relaxation)

- Listening skills: (also see games listed in Appendix J)

- Telephone - group game in a line

- Dog and Bone

- Sending Your Hearing Out

- When I Go To California (verbal memory game)

- When My Ship Goes to London (verbal memory game alphabetical)

- Observation skills and fostering collaboration:

- Mirror (in pairs)

- Three Changes done in pairs (done three times, nine changes in total)

- Space Shaping (alone, then in pairs, then two groups)

- New York / Lemonade (two groups)

- Verbal and communication skills:

- Name Six

- Silent Crambo

- Extended Sound

- How Am I Like That? (game of comparison and metaphor)

- What Is My Thought Like? (game of comparison and metaphor)

Interview Games:

- World's Worst Interviewer

- Good, Bad and Ugly Advice

- Trinterview

How To Play Trinterview

Created by middle school students in one of my interview classes, this game is for three or more players. Trinterview comes from the words Trio and Interview. It is a good group warm-up game for interviewing.

Three or more players sit in a circle (or at a table or in a car). They each take a turn asking a simple, closed-ended question, like a yes/no question, which other players answer one at a time. Nonsense questions and answers are welcome. Repeating questions or answers is not allowed. Variation for a small group (say, three to four players): don't use "yes" or "no" and skip those answers for more interesting ones. In an earlier chapter, there is an example from when my class played the game.

E – Historical Fiction Syllabus

For examples of teaching writing historical fiction, see Time Travel in the Classroom above.

Primary and Secondary Resources

A primary source is some sort of evidence that was written, created, or produced during the time under study. Primary sources offer an eyewitness or inside view of a time or event. Examples include letters (or e-mails and texts), diaries, receipts, autobiographies, interviews, news articles, video, film, official records or minutes, photographs, speeches, relics, cookbooks, clothing, architecture, paintings, plays, songs and music, poetry, and novels.

- Plato's Republic— women in ancient Greece

- The Declaration of Independence— U. S. history

- African-American Poetry (1750-1900)— U. S. history & literature

- *Night* by Elie Wiesel and *Diary of Anne Frank*— experiences of Jews in World War II

- Film footage and photos of Civil Rights marches in Alabama in the 1960s— US history

- National Security Data Archives— U. S. history, declassified documents

Secondary Sources

A secondary resource contains information taken from primary resources and may provide interpretation and analysis. Secondary sources are one step removed from primary sources.

- Britannica Online encyclopedia

- American National Biography (database)

- Literary criticism analyzing a play, poem, novel or short story

- Magazine or newspaper articles about past events or people

- Political commentary analyzing an election or politician (via Lexis-Nexis database)

- Textbooks

Note: some of these secondary sources, such as encyclopedias and textbooks, may be tertiary with content drawn entirely from secondary sources.

Online Sources

- New York Public Library Online Research Catalog:

- National Archives

- Free Online Resources for Primary Documents

Photos of student work in historical fiction are online at HomeschoolNYC.

Materials for Writing Historical Fiction

- Clear poly reusable envelopes large enough to hold the following: a 9 X 12 pad and pencils for note-taking, magazine articles, clippings, copies made from reference books, etc. This is the "grab-n-go" envelope for library visits and research sessions. It can hold all notes for this project.

- Blank Books— affordable blank books in a variety of sizes available online at Bare Books. Student can choose the size and thickness of the blank book, hard or soft cover, portrait or landscape format. Or they can choose a blank comic book or make a book by hand. Creating a cover design, and inserting the story, completes the historical fiction children's book project.

Additional online resources are available at LaurieBlockSpigel.com.

Selected Historical and Period Fiction

For Elementary School

The Magic Tree House by Mary Pope Osborne (series)

The Time Warp Trio by Jon Scieszka and Lane Smith (series)

For Middle School

USA

Little House on the Prairie (series) by Laura Ingalls Wilder.

The Captain's Dog: My Journey with the Lewis and Clark Tribe by Roland Smith

The True Confessions of Charlotte Doyle by Avi

Little Women by Louisa May Alcott

Rascal: A Memoir of a Better Era by Sterling North

Roll of Thunder, Hear My Cry by Mildred Dr. Taylor

Out of the Dust by Karen Hesse (written in poetry)

The Education of Little Tree by Forrest Carter

England

Adam of the Road by Elizabeth Janet Gray
   Catherine, Called Birdy by Karen Cushman
   At the Sign of the Sugared Plum by Mary Hooper (London 1665, the Plague)
   The Secret Garden by Frances Hodgeson Burnett
   The Prince and the Pauper by Mark Twain
   Splendors and Glooms by Amy Shiltz (Victorian England)

Germany, WW II

The Book Thief by Markus Zusak

Japan

A Samurai's Tale by Erik C. Haugaard

For Teens and Adults

O Pioneers by Willa Cather (selections are appropriate for middle school)
   Novels by Jane Austen
   A Tale of Two Cities by Charles Dickens
   Doctor Zhivago by Boris Pasternak
   The Amazing Adventures of Kavalier and Clay by Michael Chabon
   East of Eden by John Steinbeck
   A Tree Grows in Brooklyn by Betty Smith
   Their Eyes Were Watching God by Zora Neal Hurston
   The Joy Luck Club by Amy Tan

Historic Event – What's Beyond?

This worksheet can be used for fictional prose or playwriting, for teens or any age.

Drawn from the work of David Shookhoff of the Manhattan Theatre Club, and Viola Spolin.

Historic Person or Event on the Verge of Triumph or Disaster

- Choose an historic event that will remain "beyond" and write it below.

- Research the event for important details. Take notes on a separate sheet.

- Name two characters for your story, below.

- Choose a setting and an activity, something physical the characters are doing.

- Have the characters hold what's beyond in focus —an event that either just occurred or is about to occur— without speaking directly about it.

- The story ends when the event beyond is brought into focus.

C reate two characters, on the verge of triumph or disaster, related to this event. Keep the event in the immediate past or future. The event may occur in a place other than the setting for this scene. Allude to the event without stating it directly. The characters may be famous or not.

Focus on the human drama

- Setting of the event (what's beyond)

- Characters and their relationships

- Characters' intentions and conflicts

- Characters' different life attitudes

- Tension leading up to, or the aftermath of, the event

- Use details taken from your research. If possible, include a significant object.

Historic event

Character #1 NAME: Age: Appearance:
    Relationship to event:
    Relationship to character #2:

    Character #2 NAME:Age: Appearance:
    Relationship to event:
    Relationship to character #1:
    Significant Object:

Character Profile for Historical Fiction

To create a fictional historical story and find a fictional point of view

Name:

Age:

Gender:

Occupation:

Time period:Location:

Personality traits:

Appearance:

What is usually carried or worn:

Habitat/dwelling, economic status (home, neighborhood, room):

Family members, roommates, pets:

Most important person or being:

Reason for being (purpose in life):

Deepest wants (be specific):

Obstacles to main want:

Fears:

Secrets:

Event that triggers the start of their adventure (Why this day/time? Why now?):

Draw a picture of this character on another sheet of paper.

F - Playwriting for Teens - Repressed Desire Workshop Syllabus

Three-Hour Workshop

Inspired by the workshops of David Shookhoff of the Manhattan Theatre Club

For curriculum examples, see Exploring Repressed Desire (Playwriting for Teens) above

Workshop Outline

Warm-up games

Walk with different parts of the body leading,

- Walks Without Attitude

- Space Walk— See and Be Seen / Include and Occlude / Sole Support (Viola Spolin)

Social Influence Questionnaire[1]

- Stand up for every yes answer; remain seated for no.

- Discuss with a non-judgmental approach.

- What makes people feel uncomfortable about sex?

- Ask participants for possible responses to this question and make a list.

Answers might include being pressured to have sex, being in public, public displays of affection, having to explain to a child about sex, or not feeling comfortable with one's own sexuality.

Different Views

Draw a continuum line on the board, and place homosexuality at one end and heterosexuality at the other, explaining that this could be a circle, not a line. A character could be anywhere along that line, midway being bisexual. Discuss. Mention Native American view that a homosexual person has two spirits (male and female), and a heterosexual person has one. Question: If you had one or two invisible spirits, how would you know? Draw another line to indicate how society sees you, to underscore the fact that you are viewed differently without than within.

Repression vs. Expression

Draw another continuum line and put repressed (or introverted) at one end and total freedom of expression (or extroverted) at the other. These concepts can be expressed in two different lines. Repressed is different from introverted, and freely expressive is different from extroverted. Then, discuss possible sources for repression (sexual, artistic, or altruistic) or trapped desires. Ask for examples of characters who are introverted and characters who are repressed. How are they different? Do the same with the concepts of freedom of expression and extroverted behavior. Can someone be repressed and extroverted? Or introverted without feeling repressed desires?

Tableaux

In groups of three or four players, assign each group a word or phrase. Allow for a plan and rehearsal for each group to strike a pose. In a small class, or with limited time, eliminate, you can just use the first two and last two cards on the list, omitting 3 and 4.

Cards say:

- masculine

- feminine

- repressed feelings

- freely expressive

- guilt

- shame

Guide students to be subtle, "Show, don't tell." Groups see only their own card. The focus is on the dramatization of the word or phrase on the card. Tableaux are shown first silently and then with a sound (word, phrase or sound) uttered by one or more of the players in that group. Students are given 2-5 minutes to plan, choose their sound or words, and rehearse once or twice. Each group sits when ready, and then they perform their tableau one at a time. Evaluation: audience (other groups) try to guess the word or phrase that is being shown. If they cannot guess that group has the chance to strike their pose again and to exaggerate the pose. If it is still too hard to see, that group can reassess their choices and try to dramatize the word or phrase in another way.

Improvise Conflict

Improvise one or more of the following scenes of conflict. Contrast and conflict should come out, but humor is allowed to come out too. Students can add ideas to this list. Do as many scenes as there is time for, perhaps three. The focus is on building conflict between two characters. Afterwards evaluate by asking the audience: What was the nature of the conflict? What was the outcome or the implied outcome? Did one person win over the other or was there a stand-off?

If there is time, share a list of the following scenes (both on sexuality and on other repressed feelings), and let students select a few they would like to see. One at a time, ask for volunteers for each scene, performing as many as time allows. Briefly discuss each scene using non-judgmental feedback guidelines.

Scenes of Conflict on Sexuality

- A gay teen wants to come out to his conservative, homophobic, or religious parents.

- A teen contemplates getting sex change surgery in a conversation with another teen who is against the idea.

- A shy, gay teen unknowingly asks a straight teen out on a date (or vice versa), and the straight teen needs to say no but is afraid to hurt the other person.

- A husband or wife confesses to their spouse a repressed sexual preference.

- A straight teen asks his/her gay parent for advice about dating. A parent lectures their teen about dating.

- Homophobic parent asks teen to stop seeing a gay friend.

- A dating young couple discuss that one wants to have sex and the other one doesn't.

Scenes on other repressed feelings
- Parent explains to child why s/he can never be an actor or artist.

- Spouse explains to partner why s/he can't be charitable with their income and/or time.

- Teacher/director explains to student why s/he can't be a singer.

- Spouse explains s/he has changed his/her mind about having children.

- Spouse explains why s/he wants to quit his/her job.

Writing

Hand out worksheets[2]. Read worksheets aloud with class and ask if there are any questions. Allow students 15-20 minutes of writing time to complete the profiles and one monologue. Students may do less or may write both monologues. They can continue working on this at home and use the monologues as a basis for a two-character scene.

Performance of Student Work

Perform written scenes as improvised cold readings with volunteer players, allowing the playwright the chance to see the scene. Discuss using nonjudgmental feedback. This activity can be continued during the next class, as monologues become scenes.

Alternate Schedule

To divide this 3-hour workshop into two workshops:

- Assign the writing to do (the first monologue) outside of class. Distribute the handouts for homework at the end of the first session. Complete the rest of the activities in the second session.

- Start second class with a traditional warm-up that combines movement with words, like Kitty Wants a Corner, or Playing Catch followed by Extended Sound, or Give and Take Warm-Up using movement and sound (all games are in Spolin).

- Ask how the homework went. Determine if the class needs to perform another conflict scene, perhaps one from the second category of scene or a scene suggested by a student.

- Monologues are performed on a voluntary basis, one for each playwright. If questions occur, the character profiles can also be shared. Practice non-judgmental feedback after each one.

- Allow 15-20 minutes writing time for a second monologue or, for students who have already written a second monologue, for a two-character scene with dialogue, using the two monologues for inspiration. Monologues can be woven together, lines can be used, or none of the lines can be used. Volunteer players can improvise the scenes (no rehearsal) when they are done. Perform as many as there is time for. Practice non-judgmental feedback.

---

1. Find more resources on using this question in Chapter 22.

2. See worksheets in Chapter 22.

Playwriting Resources

Playmaking for Children by Daniel Judah Sklar

Find Your Voice: A Methodology for Enhancing Literacy Through Re-Writing and Re-Acting by Gail Noppe-Brandon

Theater Games for Rehearsal by Viola Spolin

Improvisation for the Theater by Viola Spolin

Manhattan Theatre Club (Manhattan Theatre Club (MTC) has videos and online guides for playwriting, for teens and adults, from the education department led by David Shookhoff. Free workshops include the Family Matinee and Write Now! programs for teens and professional development workshops for teachers. These often include food and theater tickets after an artist-led workshop, all free.

Additional online resources are available at LaurieBlockSpigel.com.

Character Worksheet – Repressed Desire

Complete two contrasting character profiles.

Include their sexual preference and level of repression/expression, introversion/extroversion.

It can help to have two contrasting photos or drawings of the characters. Sketch them on a separate sheet of paper or find clippings that look like your characters.

Write a monologue for character A.

Show your character in a major dilemma: whether or not to leave a lover, become a fugitive, have an operation, leave home, change professions, etc. Reveal their love relationship and/or repressed desires as a key part of their dilemma.

Write a second monologue from the standpoint of contrasting character B.

This character could be the lover, the pursuer, the closed-minded parent or child, the opposite sex, an alternate double or doppelganger, etc. This character responds to the first character's monologue and provides contrast.

Write a third scene where the characters meet.

Provide contrast that is physical, psychological, emotional, and/or spiritual. Allow for potential transformation in one or both characters. Remember to write in each character's voice, from their point of view, and realize that others may not see them that way. Behavior usually changes when you are alone (as in a monologue) compared to when others see you (as in a dialogue). Draw on the emotional content of the monologues and feel free to use all or part or none of the lines as you create a dialogue.

Revise your scene.

If possible, watch an improvised performance of your scene before you revise it.

Use the Revision Guidelines.

Optional: add a song, perhaps a duet, to the scene.

Character Profiles – Repressed Desire

Character A

Name:
Relationship to Character B:
Gender & pronouns:
Age:
Profession:
Appearance:
Sexual orientation:
Marital/dating status:
Introvert/extrovert; repressed/freely expressive:
Most recent problem with a relationship:

Dwelling:
Cohabitants:
Most important person/being:
Repressed desire:
Deepest want:
Want in terms of sexuality or relationship:
Fear:

Secret:

Character B

Name:

Relationship to Character B:

Gender & pronouns:

Age:

Profession:

Appearance:

Sexual orientation:

Marital/dating status:

Introvert/extrovert; repressed/freely expressive:

Most recent problem with a relationship:

Dwelling:

Cohabitants:

Most important person/being:

Repressed desire:

Deepest want:

Want in terms of sexuality or relationship:

Fear:

Secret:

Social Influence Questionnaire

Stand up if the answer is yes; stay seated if the answer is no.

H ave you ever...

Yes / No

1. felt misunderstood?

2. acted differently from the way you felt?

3. behaved like you were someone else?

4. been mistaken for someone else?

5. felt like you couldn't be yourself?

6. been embarrassed?

7. felt ashamed?

8. been expected to do something you were not comfortable doing?

9. Did you do it?

10. been asked to do something you were not comfortable doing?

11. Did you do it?

12. acted in a way intended to make someone else change their behavior?

13. Did it succeed?

14. behaved in a way that surprised you?

15. acted in a way that you didn't understand?

16. If your life were on television, would you behave differently? How?

Non-Judgmental Feedback Guide

Inspired by the work of Aretha Sills

U se these questions to pose to an audience after reading your work aloud. Alone, read your work aloud with a pencil in hand at least a few days after writing. Then ask these questions of yourself.

Questions

When did you feel something while listening or reading? When did your own emotions bubble up? What moment was that in the story? What were you feeling?

Which moments in the story stayed with you? Is there a part you kept thinking about?

What images or scenes were vivid?

Did any phrases, details, or ideas jump out at you?

When or where were you surprised?

What moments made you want to keep reading or listening? Where were you hooked?

Did you relate to any parts on a personal level? Did some parts remind you of personal memories?

Was there a significant object that was important to the story? Did certain images, objects, or phrases develop a deeper meaning?

Did any themes emerge? Theme is about the inner story, not the plot but the deeper meaning. Common themes are love, loss, family, coming of age, leaving home. There are more. What themes did you notice?

Tips

Avoid saying what you like or don't like, which is often a matter of opinion or taste, and not necessarily helpful to the writer. Instead, say how a scene or moment made you feel or how you related to it. This information can be very helpful to the writer.

Instead of focusing on approval or disapproval (is it good or not?), give yourself the freedom to feel the story and explore the characters, setting, and ideas. Look at the writing as a work in progress.

G - Literature Discussion Curriculum and Guidelines

For ages eight to adult. Weekly discussions range from one to two hours. Depending on the size and difficulty, a book can take one or two weeks to a few months to read and discuss.

For a description of this course, see Lit Clubbing above

Class One - Introduce and share books, nominate, vote

Assignment Before First Class (for Students and Teacher)

E veryone is encouraged to bring in one or more books to nominate to create our reading list for the term or year. Give them a week or a period of time that includes a weekend. The teacher also brings in a stack of recommended books.

Class Size

Limit the size of the group to 12 students, eight if the group meets for just one hour. If you have no control over the class size, get volunteers to help and divide the class into appropriately-sized groups, each small enough to share nominations, voting, and the creation of a reading list.

Nominations

Students can recommend more than one book, but each student is limited to one nomination. They can nominate a book they have read before and want to reread and discuss with the group, a daunting book that they don't want to read alone, or any title that intrigues them. Nominations are voluntary; some students might pass. When recommending or nominating, make sure that the group looks at the cover and reads the blurb or back cover out loud as well as the opening paragraphs. If anyone is familiar with the work of that author, they are invited to share their experience and opinion.

The teacher introduces recommended books and adds them to the pile of possible nominations. The teacher does not nominate any titles. Nominations and voting are the exclusive rights of the students.

After the nomination process, the teacher hands out paper (maybe large index cards) and pencils. Students vote by writing down their first, second, third choices, and so on, preferably listing five or more choices, numbered so you are sure which is first and which is second. (One student once put their top choice at the bottom, like a count-down list, and after that, I always asked for the choices to be numbered.) Collect the votes, and let everyone know the results will be e-mailed in a day or so.

E-mailing the results takes any disappointment out of the classroom and allows time for students to adjust to the voting list. Don't delay the voting results; send them as soon as possible so students have time to get the first book.

Reading Pace

Ask the group about their reading pace. How many pages do they think they usually read in a half hour? How many days a week do they usually read? If they don't know, have everyone read one page silently and see how long it takes. Slower readers may be willing to spend more time reading at home in order to keep up with the group. A faster reading pace means more books can be read, and the group may be motivated to read more to get to their choices. They can also choose to read a complicated book more slowly. Not every book will have the same reading pace.

Additional First Day Activity

Have a short, short story available to read out loud together and discuss in case there is time left over on day one. Nominations and voting often occupy the entire first class.

Homework for Teacher

Tally the votes. This can be complicated. I make a grid with student's names along the top and book titles on the side, placing the number of preference (1 for 1st choice, 2 for 2nd, etc.) in the corresponding box on the grid.

Once the vote is tallied and you can see the leading selections, choose the order in which the books will be read and discussed. The majority choice does not have to come first— it might come second or third. I choose a book that is widely available, perhaps free online and on shelves in local libraries so we can start without delay. I also might choose a first book I am already familiar with to give myself more time to read and research any books that are new to me. Even if I have read the book before, I read it again along with the students.

The next day voting results are emailed to the class. Put the first book to be read in bold at the top of the page. If there is a link to the book online, include the link. Audio books are acceptable, and preferred by some readers, so include an audio link if available. State the suggested number of pages to read for next class based on the reading pace the class has set and the knowledge that students might obtain the book just a few days before class. Remind students to bring their copy of the book with them, along with any questions or comments.

Read as much of the first book as you can and prepare some questions and background information designed to intrigue the students and make them think.

Homework for Students

Obtain the first book and start reading! Try to read the suggested assigned amount (maybe the first few chapters or 20 pages), or as much as you can. Bring any questions and comments that occurred to you during or after the reading. Taking notes will help you to remember your questions and comments.

Class Two - Discussion Process

Be ready with a warm-up game that can be played while students arrive, such as Quick Numbers or a Word Association game where each player says the next associated word (either randomly or relating to a chosen topic), or How Is It Like Me? (Boyd p.97)

Ask each student how many pages they read. If someone wasn't able to read the book, read the first chapter out loud together (voluntarily take turns) and discuss that chapter. If not everyone has a copy, people can take turns reading from the same book.

Invite students to share questions and comments with the group. The teacher may have to start this process with the first question. Ask what they found interesting (more sample questions follow) and give them time to respond. Don't worry about moments of silence. Was there something in the book they could relate to personally? That reminded them of someone or some place? Was there anything that surprised them? That they didn't understand?

Or found disturbing? Did anyone have a favorite character or scene? Why was it their favorite?

Homework Explained

Their homework is not to just read the book but to imagine having a dialogue with the book. The student's job is to discover what they find interesting or worth asking about or sharing. Show examples of your own notes (maybe penciled in margins of books you own or marked with post-it bookmarks or noted on a large index card) showing thoughts and questions. I might use marks or symbols such as a question mark at a place I don't understand, or an exclamation point where I am surprised. Don't just go through the motions of reading. Pay attention to how the book makes you feel. We want to hear about what matters to you! Students may need to be reminded of this approach throughout the year. They have a lot of power in what gets discussed!

Collaborative Assignments

At the end of each class, ask how much they would like to read for the next class. If the teacher has read ahead, students can be alerted to notice something coming up by giving them a thoughtful question posed in advance.

Overview of Successive Classes

Repeat the process of Class Two, with a warm-up game, a quick assessment of what has been read by the students, and a round of questions and comments that, with the teacher's help, keep a discussion going.

Share background information on the author's life and the setting of the book as well as information on customs and fashion of the era to deepen the understanding of the book. Experiences that awaken the senses can help bring the book to life such as listening to music played in the book (or during that era), tasting food, or handling an object. For example, in one class on *Don Quixote*, we munched on olive oil rolls and Manchego cheese, probably what the two main characters ate on their adventures.

After more than one book is read, books are often compared naturally as part of the discussion. This becomes an introduction to comparative literature, where ideas and styles are compared and discussed, including the styles of different eras or countries.

When the book is a student's first choice, that student may want to bring in some of the background material. Any student who is interested can research a story or author and introduce that material to the class.

Warm Up Games

These games can relax the group, make communicating easier, and help kids want to arrive on time!

- Quick Numbers (makes tired minds alert)

- Guggenheim

- Name Six

- Geography

- Word Ladder (on a board for all to see)

- Stinky Pinky (rhyming riddle game)

- Silent Crambo (also called Dumb Crambo)

- How Is It Like Me? (creating metaphors)

- Who Am I? (using characters from history and fiction)

- Build-A-Story

- The Casting Game with books the group has read. What famous actor should play the part of (choose a character from a group book has read)?

- Shakespearean insult game (for any period English) - sample games are online.

General Questions for Any Book

Opening Questions

- What parts stayed with you? What did you end up thinking about later?

- Was there a part you related to or a character you identified with?

- Did any scene or character remind you of a personal experience?

Questions That Help Predict and Understand the Story

- What do you think will happen next?

- At the end of a cliff-hanging chapter. What would you do if you were the character in this circumstance?

- Basic Questions to Help Untangle a Complex Story

- Who is the protagonist? (Or hero or antihero, the main character?)

- What does the hero want? What obstacles are in the way of these wants?

- Do the obstacles change the hero's direction or the hero's wants?

- Who is the antagonist (villain or person representing obstacles)?

- What does the antagonist want? What obstacles are in the way of these wants?

- Does the main character face internal conflicts or obstacles?

- Does the antagonist have to deal with internal struggles?

Reflective and Thematic Questions

- Whose story is it? Is it the main character's (protagonist's) story?

- How do the characters change?

- Which character in the story changes the most?

- Did you notice any recurring motifs or symbols?

- What themes emerged in the book?

- Is there a deeper meaning beneath the plot?

Questions can lead to interesting disagreements. Here are two times when the group was split over whose story it was. In *Ronia the Robber's Daughter* by Astrid Lindgren, readers decided that the father changed the most while other characters didn't change much. Does this mean it's really the father's story and not Ronia's story? The class was divided. In *To Kill a Mockingbird*, is it Jem's story or Scout's? It's told through Scout's eyes, from her point of view. But it begins by talking about Jem. He is the main character in the opening and closing of the book. Reread the opening and ending; notice who narrates and whose point of view is in control. Then ask, whose story is it? Is the narrator telling her own story or someone else's?

Resources for Literature Exploration and Discussion

*D*econstructing *Penguins* by Lawrence Goldstone and Nancy Goldstone

Should be Burn Babar? by Herbert Kohl

Oprah's Book Club online. Some of Oprah's books have excellent resources, such as 100 Years of Solitude.

Metropolitan Museum Gallery Guide for Mixed-up Files, available online.

Biographies of authors and historical background information.

Library lists of recommended books and award winners, Newberry award winners for children, Pulitzer and Nobel Literature prize winners for teens and adults.

Additional resource mentioned in chapter 23, Lit Clubbing:

The Self-Portrait Anthology poetry project is from *Awakening the Heart* by Georgia Heard (p35), a classic guide to teaching poetry in elementary and middle school.

Book Selections

Elementary and Middle School

Novels and Classics

- *Charlotte's Web* and *Stuart Little* by E. B. White

- T*he Secret Garden by Frances Hodgson Burnett*

- *Ronia the Robber's Daughter* by Astrid Lindgren

- *Because of Winn Dixie* by Kate DiCamillo (and other titles)

- *The One and Only Ivan* by Katharine Applegate

- *Love that Dog* (and other titles) by Sharon Creech

Mystery

- *Three Times Lucky* by Sheila Turnage

- *Holes* by Louis Sachar

- *The Westing Game* by Ellen Raskin

- *A Series of Unfortunate Events* (series) by Lemony Snicket

- *The Great Cake Mystery* by Alexander McCall Smith, set in Botswana

Historic and Period Fiction

- *The Secret Garden* by Frances Hodgson Burnett

- *The Prince and the Pauper* by Mark Twain

- *The Book Thief* by Marcus Zusak (also for teens)

- *Treasure Island* by Robert Louis Stevenson

- *Anne of Green Gables* by Lucy Maud Montgomery

- *Little Women* by Louisa May Alcott

- *The Call of the Wild* by Jack London

- *Rolling Thunder, Hear My Cry* by Mildred D. Taylor

- *Splendors and Glooms* by Laura Amy Schiltz

Fantasy and Science Fiction

- The Chronicles of Narnia by C. S. Lewis

- *Archer's Goon* by Diana Wynne Jones

- *Howl's Moving Castle* by Diana Wynne Jones

- *The Night of Wishes* by Michael Ende

- *The Neverending Story* by Michael Ende

- *The Wizard Children of Finn* by Mary Tannen

- *Artemis Fowl* by Eoin Colfer

- *The Phantom Tollbooth* by Norton Juster

- *Mary Poppins* by P. L. Travers

- *The Cat Who Wished to Be a Man* by Lloyd Alexander

- *The Wizard of Oz* by L. Frank Baum

- *Peter Pan* by J. M. Barrie

- *The Tale of Despereaux* by Kate DiCamillo (and other titles)

- Percy Jackson and the Olympians by Rick Riordan

- *A Wrinkle in Time* by Madeleine L'Engle

Memoir

- *Cheaper by the Dozen* by Frank Gilbreth and Ernestine Gilbreth Carey

- *My Family and Other Animals* by Gerald Durrell (excerpts)

- *Rascal* by Sterling North

High School

Historical and Period Fiction

- *Jane Eyre by Charlotte Bronte*

- *My Antonia* and *O Pioneers* by Willa Cather

- *Lord of the Flies* by William Golding

- *To Kill a Mockingbird* by Harper Lee

- *Doctor Zhivago* by Boris Pasternak

- *Anna Karenina* by Tolstoy

- *A Tale of Two Cities* by Charles Dickens

- *A Tree Grows in Brooklyn* by Betty Smith

- *Their Eyes Were Watching God* by Zora Neal Hurston

- *East of Eden* by John Steinbeck

- *The Grapes of Wrath* by John Steinbeck

- *Catch 22* by Joseph Heller

- *The Amazing Adventures of Kavalier and Clay* by Michael Chabon

Mystery

- *The Murder of Roger Ackroyd* by Agatha Christie (and other titles)

- *The Hound of the Baskervilles* (and other titles) by Sir Arthur Conan Doyle

- Short stories of Edgar Allen Poe

- *The Blessing Way* (and other titles) by Tony Hillerman, mysteries set on the Navaho Reservation

Science Fiction and Fantasy

- *1984* by George Orwell

- *Brave New World* by Aldous Huxley

- *Stranger in a Strange Land* by Herbert Heinlein

- *The Hitchhiker's Guide to the Galaxy* by Douglas Adams

- *Watchmen* by Alan Moore

- *Slaughterhouse-Five* by Kurt Vonnegut

- *The Hobbit* by J. R. R. Tolkein

Memoir

- *Dust Tracks On A Road* by Zora Neal Hurston

- *My Life and Hard Times* by James Thurber (humor)

- Travels with Charley by John Steinbeck

- *Scoundrel Time* by Lillian Hellman

- American Short Story Authors

- Washington Irving

- Nathaniel Hawthorne

- Edgar Allen Poe

- Mark Twain

- Kate Chopin

- Essays of Henry David Thoreau and Ralph Waldo Emerson

- "The Book of the Grotesque" and "Hands" from *Winesburg, Ohio* by Sherwood Anderson

- "A Christmas Memory" and "Miriam" by Truman Capote

- "The Killers" and "The Short Happy Life of Francis Macomber" by

Ernest Hemingway

- *Vampires in the Lemon Grove* by Karen Russell

- Short stories by Ray Bradbury

- American Short Novels

- *The Great Gatsby* by F. Scott Fitzgerald

- *The Old Man and the Sea* by Ernest Hemingway

World Literature for mature teens (my selections - the only time there was no vote)

Novels

- *Don Quixote* by Cervantes (Edith Grossman translation)

- *Candide* by Voltaire

- *Le Grande Meaulnes* (The Wanderer) by Henri Alain-Fournier

- *Fathers and Sons* by Ivan Turgenev

- *Notes from Underground* by Fyodor Dostoevsky

- *One Hundred Years of Solitude* by Gabriel Garcia Marquez

- *Frankenstein* by Mary Shelley

- *The Crock of Gold* by James Stephens, Part One (available online)

Short Stories and Novellas

- "Boule de Suif" and "False Gems "(or The Necklace) by Guy de Maupassant

- "The Nose" and "The Overcoat" by Nikolai Gogol

- "Ivan the Fool" (and other tales) by Leo Tolstoy

- "The Lady and the Dog" by Anton Chekhov

- *Metamorphosis* by Franz Kafka

- *Death in Venice* by Thomas Mann

- *Heart of Darkness* by Joseph Conrad

- *The Dead* by James Joyce

- *The Rocking Horse* by D. H. Lawrence

- *Miss Brill* by Katherine Mansfield

- *African Stories* (selections) by Doris Lessing

Plays (after reading aloud, each can be followed by a film version)

Shakespeare

- *A Midsummer Night's Dream*

- *Much Ado About Nothing*

- *Twelfth Night*

- *Romeo and Juliet*

- *Hamlet*

- *Othello*

- *Macbeth*

Period Comedy / Drama

- *Cyrano De Bergerac* by Edmund Rostand

- *Tartuffe* and *The Miser* by Moliere

- *The Rivals* by Sheridan

- *The Importance of Being Earnest* by Oscar Wilde

- *The Seagull* by Anton Chekhov

Comedy

- *The Front Page* by Ben Hecht and Charles MacArthur

- *The Odd Couple* by Neil Simon

- *A Thousand Clowns* by Herb Gardner

- *The Real Inspector Hound* by Tom Stoppard

Drama

- *Death of a Salesman* by Arthur Miller

- *Ma Rainey's Black Bottom* by August Wilson

- *Fences* by August Wilson

- *Top Girls* by Caryn Churchill

- *Top Dog/Underdog* by Suzan-Lori Parks

- Tennessee Williams

- *The Glass Menagerie*

- *Cat On a Hot Tin Roof*

- *Who's Afraid of Virginia Woolf*

H - Theater-Themed Curriculum Resources

For a detailed description of this curriculum, see High School Theater All-Subject Curriculum above.

General Resource

- *Longman Anthology of Drama and Theater: A Global Perspective* (compact edition) by Michael Greenwald, Roger Shultz, and Roberto Pomo. An overview of the history of theater with plays from around the world. Includes maps and timelines. Used as a college text.

Shakespeare

- *Tales from Shakespeare*, seven plays in comic format by Marcia Williams. For elementary ages.

- *Shakespeare for Kids: His Life and Time, 21 Activities* by Colleen

Aagesen and Margie Blumberg. Hands-on activities for elementary and middle school.

- *The Usborne World of Shakespeare* by Scholastic. Internet linked. For all ages.

- *Shakespeare: His Work and His World* by Michael Rosen and Robert Ingpen. An introduction to Shakespeare and his plays.

- *Discovering Shakespeare's Language* by Rex Gibson and Janet Field-Pickering. Activity sheets and lessons for middle and high school.

Additional online resources for thematic curriculum are available at LaurieBlockSpigel.com.

See also Puppetry Resources, Playwriting Resources, and Theater Games.

I - Animal-Themed Curriculum

For a detailed description of this curriculum, see Whale and Animal Curriculum above.

Focusing on a favorite animal can include all major academic subjects from K-12+. This focus works well with elementary school ages, when most kids love animals, and many have a favorite.

For a group experience, each child can choose an animal to become an expert on. They can share facts about that animal by playing Stump the Class[1], and do any of the following activities as a group.

Reading

- Classic animal tales such as *Winnie the Pooh*, *Charlotte's Web*, *Just So Stories*

- Folktales such as animal pourquoi tales

- Myths and legends such as animals in constellation myths from various cultures

- Enchanted animal fantasies such as the *Chronicles of Narnia*.

- It is possible to focus on a single animal in children's literature, such as the mouse or dog or cat. For example, there are many books with fictional mice.

- More mature reading for teens such as *Moby Dick* or *Watership Down.*

- Nonfiction animal literature includes naturalist's accounts (*Never Cry Wolf* by Farley Mowat; Sy Montgomery's *Soul of the Octopus* and *The Good Good Pig*)

- Animal memoirs (books by Gerald Durrell and Sterling North)

- Research on animals, animal science, field guides, and animal reference books.

Writing

- Brainstorm and research animal questions for fiction and nonfiction writing

- Essays on animals in the news and science

- Stories including fables, pourquoi tales, fantasies with imaginary or mythical animals (such as unicorns and dragons)

- Nonfiction pet stories and memoirs

- Poetry (acrostics, haiku, ballads, odes, silly rhymes, concrete animal shape poems and more)

- Letters to authors of animal books and penpal letters with pet owners

- Interviews with people working with animals such as farmers, trainers, vets, pet store workers, groomers, dog walkers, zookeepers, and animal scientists (possibly by email)

- Humorous writing including from the point of view of a pet or other animal comics.

Social Studies, History and Geography

- Animal origins

- Migrations

- Folktales showing animal's relationship to that land and culture

- Animals in art throughout history (cave paintings, Ancient Egyptian sculpture, Medieval bestiaries and unicorn tapestries, contemporary illustrations, and comics, etc.)

- Symbolic meanings of animals in various cultures (state and national birds and animals, folklore, beliefs, superstitions)

- Human uses and practices (shearing wool, making cheese, hunting, working and farm animals)

- Dietary practices showing cultural and historic use

- Field trips including zoos, sanctuaries, seeing eye dog training school, and more

Math

- Weight and measurement of animals from birth to adult

- Life span

- Distance of migration as well as speed

- Quantities of food consumed

- Population growth

- Speed of movement

- Speed and height of jumping or flying

- Measuring and comparing using a variety of methods.

Science

- Biology including anatomy

- Habitat and environment

- Camouflage

- Hunting

- Evading predators

- Animal behavior

- Evolution of the species

- Mammal (including human) biology

- Interspecies interactions and friendships

- Modern experiments such as genome research and cloning

- Uses of animals in medicine

- Endangered and extinct animals

Art

- Creating and viewing animal art:

- Drawings, paintings, sculpture, puppets, and masks by great artists such as Calder's Circus, Picasso's Gorilla, Chagall's horses and birds

- Art from cultures around the world such as African sculpture, Native American carvings

- Egyptian tomb paintings and statuary

- Making animal art from a variety of different mediums

- Illustrating animal tales

Music

- *Peter and the Wolf* by Prokofiev introduces orchestral instruments with a different instrument for each animal. Do musical instruments sound like animals?

- *Carnival of the Animals* by Saint-Saens, includes selections titled Royal March of the Lion, Hens and Roosters, Wild Donkeys, Elephants, and more. Act out the animals to the music in either of these famous compositions. Do animals each have their own rhythm?

- Create your own animal music. What sort of music might bring to mind a hummingbird? Or a crow?

- Which animals are known for their sounds? Examples include crickets and cicadas, warblers, wolves, lions.

- Which animals are named for their sounds? Some birds are named after their call.

- Make simple instruments such as a kazoo, drum, maraca, and simple string instruments to imitate animal sounds and rhythms.

Physical Education

- Trips to the zoo will have you walking all day. Act out animal behavior or play animal charades (become a cat, pigeon, hawk, squirrel, buffalo)

- Create your own animal field guide for your block or local park or backyard (a project that uses all major academic subjects)

- Birdwatching can include nature hikes

- Build a bird feeder or birdhouse (includes math)

- Create a hummingbird garden

- Participate in the annual backyard bird count

---

1. The game Stump the Class is described in Chapter 21.

J - Resources on Listening, Giving and Taking, and Games

For a detailed description of this curriculum, see Hearing and Listening above.

Listening and Listening/Hearing Games

Native Plant Stories told by Joseph Bruchac (also in *Keepers of Life* by Michael J. Caduto and Joseph Bruchac), with a chapter on Giving and Taking.

Handbook of Recreational Games by Neva Boyd, with over 300 children's games, online.

Listening games in this book include:

Beckon or Silent Circle, Knocking, Jingle the Keys, Animal, Dog and the Bone, Good Morning, Whistle Talk, Interpreting Rhythms, Throwing Light, Quick Numbers, Singing Proverbs, Proverbs, Crambo, Polite Conversation, Singing Syllables, Dumb (Silent) Crambo.

Theater Games for the Classroom: A Teacher's Handbook by Viola Spolin

Listening games in this book include:

Listening to the Environment, Sending Hearing Out, Dog and Bone, When I go To California, Knocking, What am I ... Hearing?, Dumb Crambo, Singing Syllables, Give and Take warm-up and game, Mirror speech, Gibberish Games (chapter: Communicating with Sounds), Three-Way Conversation, Relating an Incident Adding Color, Building a Story.

Improvisation for the Theater by Viola Spolin, 3rd Edition

Listening games in this book include:

Listening to the Environment, What Am I Listening To?, Gibberish games, Give and Take, Relating an Incident Adding Color, Throwing Light, Building a Story, Contrapuntal Argument, Dubbing, Mirror Sound, Mirror Speech, Three-Way Conversation, Unrelated Conversation, Dumb Crambo (also called Silent Crambo), Singing Syllables, Contact, Silent Tension.

Spolin Theater Game Workshops, taught by Aretha Sills (granddaughter of Viola Spolin), in person and via Zoom. Courses include Improv for Educators, and Improv for Writers.

Tips for Listening are in chapter 11, Hearing and Listening.

Resources on Giving and Taking

From chapter 12, Giving and Taking.

Roots of Survival: Native American Storytelling and the Sacred by Joseph Bruchac

(Giving and Taking)

Theater Games for the Classroom: A Teacher's Handbook by Viola Spolin

Improvisation for the Theater by Viola Spolin, 3rd Edition (contains games not in

other editions)

Handbook of Recreational Games by Neva Boyd, with over 300 children's games.

Spolin Theater Game workshops taught by Aretha Sills, in person and via Zoom,

including Improv for Educators and Improv for Writers.

Resources on Games and Learning through Play

For a detailed description of this curriculum, see Games: My Not-So-Secret Weapon above

Learning Through Play

- Theory of Play, essay by Neva Boyd (mentor of Viola Spolin), free online.

- Peter Gray's column in Psychology Today, Freedom to Learn:

- Magical Child by Joseph Chilton Pearce

- Play: How It Shapes the Brain, Opens the Imagination, and Invigorates the Soul by Dr. Stuart Brown, founder of the National Institute for Play.

- Stuart Brown's TED talk, Play is More Than Fun.

- Playing for Keeps: Life and Learning on a Public School Playground by Deborah Meier, Brenda S. Engel, and Beth Taylor.

- Spark: The Revolutionary New Science of Exercise and the Brain by John J. Ratey.

- Free Play: Improvisation in Life and Art by Stephen Nachmanovitch.

- Handbook of Recreational Games by Neva Boyd (Viola Spolin's mentor), out of print. Over 300 games including categories: Intellectual Games, Sense Games, and Games Requiring Voluntary Control of Impulses. Available online.

- Kids Play: Igniting Children's Creativity by Michele Cassou.

- Life, Paint and Passion, and Point Zero: Creativity Without Limits by Michele Cassou. The author also has a video on YouTube on children's creativity.

Games

- Theater Games for the Classroom, and other titles by Viola Spolin

- Handbook of Recreational Games by Neva L. Boyd

- Online classes taught by Aretha Sills.

All games in the next three categories are in Spolin and Boyd, listed above. This is a partial list.

Games that Increase Alertness

- Quick Numbers

- Red Light Green Light

- Extended Sound

- Dog and Bone (or Beckon)

- Who Started the Motion

- When I Go to California

Games that Increase Sensory Awareness

- Listening to the Environment

- Sending Hearing Out

- Sending Sight Out

- Seeing a Sport

- Give and Take

- Taste and Smell,

- What Age Am I?

Animal-Themed Games

- Pussy (or Kitty) Wants a Corner

- Animal Sound

- Guess What Animal I Am?

- Dog and Bone

- Birds Fly

- Bird-Beast-or-Fish

- Animal Geography

Math Games

- Math For Love, a website with free games and games for purchase designed by a math teacher who loves math and aims at critical thinking.

- Family Math by Jean Stenmark

- Math manipulatives for all ages at hand2mind.

Writing Games

- The Grammar of Fantasy by Gianni Rodari (contains the Fantastic Binomial game)

- The Adventures of Dr. Alphabet by Dave Morice (Word Grids, Haiku Maze)

- Wishes, Lies and Dreams by Kenneth Koch

- Favorite Poetry Lessons by Paul Janeczko, with instructions for a Word Box

Writing Games found online

- Stinky Pinky rhyming game

- Dictionary Game

- Word Ladder

- Shakespearean Insult Game (prep for Shakespeare or writing a medieval scene)

Commercially-Sold Writing Games

- Bananagrams, Scrabble, Boggle, Pictionary

- Storymatic Kids! (there is also a version for teens & adults)

- Fabula Deck for children

Classes on Games for Teaching and Writing

Aretha Sills workshops, Introduction to Improvisation, Improv for Educators and Improv for Writers, online and in various locations. Additional online resources are available at LaurieBlockSpigel.com.

K - Student-Centered Education Resources

How to Choose Resources

There are a vast number of resources for any topic, and choices can feel overwhelming. Pay attention to what works well for your child or student. Be prepared to make choices with the student, using the child as a guiding star. Communication and partnership in learning is key to finding the right resources.

Additional online resources are available at LaurieBlockSpigel.com.

All Subjects

Classroom Interviews: A World of Learning by Paula Rogovin, first grade teacher, creates a complete curriculum using spontaneous interviews, techniques applicable at any age.

Starting from Scratch: One Classroom Builds Its Own Curriculum by Steven Levy, a fourth-grade class builds a curriculum with a child-led approach and a focus on the process.

Make Just One Change: Teach Students to Ask Their Own Questions by Dan Rothstein and Luz Santana. This brainstorming process removes the usual reluctance to question a subject or idea, leading to greater focus and personalization in research and writing.

Language Arts

Handwriting

- Loops and Other Groups by Mary Ann Benbow (an occupational therapist), cursive for all ages, with an introduction that includes exercises for small motor skill control and other writing difficulties. Visual keys for groups of letters make it fun. The test of your skill is if you can write the letter with your eyes closed. It is possible to teach first graders cursive with this method.

- Handwriting Without Tears by Jan Olsen (an occupational therapist), popular handwriting curriculum for printing and cursive. Also has a pre-writing readiness program for pre-K and K.

- Writing and Understanding Poetry

- *Wishes, Lies and Dreams: Teaching Children to Write Poetry*, and other books by Kenneth Koch, using the ideas and words of the children.

- *Awakening the Heart: Exploring Poetry in Elementary and Middle School* by Georgia Heard, individualized projects such as heart mapping, and the self-portrait anthology (referred to in the chapter Lit Clubbing).

- *Poetry Everywhere* by Jack Collum and Sheryl Noethe

- *A Kick in the Head,* and *A Poke in the Eye,* and other titles by Paul Janeczko

Writing Stories

- *The Grammar of Fantasy: An Introduction to the Art of Inventing Stories* by Gianni Rodari, contains the fantastic binomial game, which inspires story writing in children.

- Writing Magic: Creating Stories That Fly by Gail Carson Levine

- What a Writer needs by Ralph Fletcher, with beginnings and endings

- How to Write Your Life Story by Ralph Fletcher, written to the child

- *What It Is* by Lynda Barry, creative brainstorming techniques in writing, using timed sessions to produce flow, written for adults but applicable to all ages.

- Multi-Genre Research Projects, personalized projects with various voices and points of view, creative nonfiction on history and social studies.

- *A Teachers' Guide to the Multigenre Research Project: Everything You Need to Get Started* by Melinda Putz

- *The Multigenre Research Paper: Voice, Passion and Discovery in grades 4-6* by Camille A. Allen

- *Writing with Passion: Life Stories, Multiple Genres* by Tom Romano

- *Fearless Writing: Multigenre to Motivate and Inspire* by Tom Romano

- Vocabulary Video Contest for ages 13-19

- *New York Times* annual vocabulary video contest is as much fun to watch as to enter. Find videos at the New York Times and YouTube. Try making these videos at home without a contest and having a reveal party.

History and Social Studies

African and African-American History

- *Africa's Great Civilizations*, video series hosted by Henry Louis Gates, Jr.

- African-American Research and History Websites: Black Past and The History Makers: The Digital Repository for the Black Experience.

- *The Warmth of Other Suns* by Isabel Wilkerson. True stories of three African-Americans examine the Great Migration from the early 20th Century until about 1970. Researched history with personal narratives.

Native American History

- *1491* by Charles C. Mann, dispels commonly held myths about Native Americans before European settlement.

- Native American culture from the National Indian Education Assoc., pre-K togr. 8: NIEA website.

- Native American Tribal Nations Map, with original locations and tribal names, available online in pdf.

- Native American history and culture lessons and activities online, from Smithsonian National Museum of the American Indian, pre-K-college:

United States History

- *The History of US* by Joy Hakim, a series for elementary grades that speaks directly to the reader without pandering.

- *For Kids series*, with hands-on activities, on many historic figures and topics, such as *Mark Twain for Kids*, and *California History*, from Chicago Review Press.

- KidsDiscover Magazine, for ages 7-12, issues on science and social studies topics, child-friendly with lots of pictures and a few games.

- Cobblestone Magazine, American history for ages 9-14.

- Colonial cookbooks and more, from Townsends.

- *Kids On Strike!*, and other Y/A books by Susan Campbell Bartoletti.

- *Taxes, the Tea Party and Those Revolting Rebels: A History in Comics of the American Revolution* by Stan Mack.

- *Lies My Teacher Told Me: Everything Your American History Textbook Got Wrong* by James W. Loewen

- *Rethinking Columbus* and other books for K-12 that combine social justice with academic subjects, from Rethinking Schools.

- *A People's History of the United States* by Howard Zinn, a contrast to most history texts that are told from the conquerors' point of view (for teens and adults).

- *Eyewitness to America: 500 Years of American History in the Words of Those Who Saw It Happen* by David Colbert (for teens and adults).

- *The Cartoon History of the United States* by Larry Gonick, for teens and adults.

US Government

- Landmark Supreme Court Cases seasons one and two, online at CSPAN.

- C-SPAN US Government and Social Studies lesson plans online at CSPAN.

- The Most Perfect Album: 27 Constitutional Amendments interpreted in music by contemporary artists, available online. Each is different, with its own style.

- Educating for American Democracy initiative has a Roadmap for American Democracy, online with free Learning Resources (lesson plans, primary sources, videos)

World History

- For Kids series, with 21 (or so) hands-on activities, on many historic figures and topics, such as *Leonardo Da Vinci: His Life and Ideas* by Janice Herbert, Chicago Review Press.

- *Picture the Middle Ages Resource Book* by Linda Honan, with hands-on activities.

- KidsDiscover Magazine back issues on history and social studies (USA and beyond)

- *The Cartoon Guide to World History* by Larry Gonick.

Historian Skills

- Resources to help develop news literacy online at NewsLit.

- *Reading Like a Historian*, history curriculum for grades 6-12 created by Stanford University, available online.

- What's Going on in This Picture? Online interactive research at the New York Times Learning Network.

Theater Arts that can Include Social Studies and History

- *Dorothy Heathcote: Drama as a Learning Medium* by Betty Jane Wagner

- *Collected Writing on Education and Drama* by Dorothy Heathcote

- Dorothy Heathcote videos on YouTube including setting up a shoe factory.

- *Theater of the Oppressed* by Augusto Boal (for teens)

- Books by Viola Spolin

Recommended historical fiction in Appendix E.
Resources for multicultural geography in Appendix A.

Science

- *Who's Afraid of Spiders?: Teaching Elementary Science* by Selma Wasserman and J. W. George Ivany, a child-led approach with a complete K-6 science curriculum.

- *Science for Every Kid* (series on many sciences) by Janice Van Cleave, short chapters with hands-on activities, for ages 7-12.

- *Zoobooks Magazine*, for elementary ages, animal science.

- *KidsDiscover Magazine*, for ages 7-12, issues on science topics.

- Cornell Lab K-12 bird education, with free lessons for K-12.

- *Foraging With Kids: 52 Wild and Free Edibles to Enjoy with Your Children* by Adele Nozedar.

- *A Year of Forest School: Outdoor Play and Skill— Building Fun for Every Season* by Jane Worroll, combines nature science with Phys. Ed., art, and more.

- *The Cartoon Guide to Physics* by Larry Gonick, visual guide for high school physics.

- *The Cartoon Guide to Chemistry* by Larry Gonick, and other titles.

Math

- Math for Love, website with free games and lessons, and award-winning games for sale, aimed at build creative thinking skills.

- Family Math by Jean Stenmark, math games for the whole family.

- *Everyday Math Literature* book lists for K-6 as well as games and resources from the University of Chicago online at EveryDayMath. Click on grade in the sidebar.

- Hands-On Equations Learning System by Dr. Henry Borenson, algebra for grades 3 and up, game-like visual approach to algebra.

- *Geometry for Every Kid* by Janice VanCleave, and other titles.

- *Calculus By and For Young People Worksheets* by Donal Cohen.

- Ten Things All Future Mathematicians and Scientist Must Know But Are Rarely Taught by Edward Zaccaro

- Cartoon Guide to Calculus by Larry Gonick.

Games, see Appendix J.

Personalized Education and Homeschooling

- *Teacher* by Sylvia Ashton Warner (and other titles). A pioneer in child-led learning, Warner created readers for Maori children using their own words and stories.

- *Pedagogy of the Oppressed* by Paolo Freire (and other writings by this author)

- *Educating for Human Greatness* by Lynn Stoddard, lists universal educational goals, none of which are curriculum.

- John Taylor Gatto, "Classrooms of the Heart" video, as well as books and articles.

- *Turning Points: 35 Visionaries in Education Tell Their Own Stories* by Jerry Mintz and Carol Ricci.

- *The Teenage Liberation Handbook: How to Quit School and Get a Real Life and Education* by Grace Llewellyn, written to the teen, available free online.

- *Classroom Interviews: A World of Learning* by Paula Rogovin, shows how to create a complete curriculum using spontaneous interviews in a first grade class. This approach can be applied to any age.

- *Make Just One Change: Teach Students to Ask Their Own Questions* by

Dan Rothstein and Luz Santana, excellent brainstorming technique for essay writing, and board game.

- *Living By Wonder: The Imaginative Life of Childhood* by Richard Lewis and other titles.

Early Childhood

- *The Sun's Not Broken There's Just a Cloud in the Way: On Child-Centered Teaching* by Sydney Gurewitz Clemens, and other titles. https://eceteacher.org/

- *Reggio Emilia and The Big Crowd Project,* article online.

- Reggio Emilia Alliance and Resources online at ReggioAlliance.

- Poem "100 Languages" (of children) by Loris Malaguzzi, founder of Reggio Emilia, online at reggiochildren.

Outdoor Learning for Pre-K and elementary grades

- Forest and Nature School in Canada curriculum guide at childnature.

- *How to Set Up a Forest School* from the Forest School Association.

- Seasonal outdoor curriculum from Forest School for All, for ages 2-6 and 5-10.

- *A Year of Forest School: Outdoor Play and Skill— Building Fun for Every Season* by Jane Worroll, combines nature science with Phys. Ed., art, and more.

Alternative Education Resources

AERO has annual conferences, a bookstore, alternative school map, training and assistance to create democratic schools and homeschool learning centers, online at Education Revolution.

Materials

Game board materials, blank puzzles and calendars, blank books, online at Bare Books.

.

Works Cited

Ashton-Warner, Sylvia, Teacher, Simon & Schuster, New York, 1986.

Boyd, Neva, *Handbook of Recreational Games*, Dover Publications, New York, 1973.

—- and Paul Simon ed., *Play and Game Theory in Group Work*, Jane Addams Graduate School of Social Work, University of Illinois, Chicago, 1971.

Bruchac, Joseph and Michael J. Caduto, Keepers of Life: Discovering Plants through Native American Stories and Earth Activities for Children, Fulcrum Publishing, Colorado, 1997

Bruchac, Joseph, *Native Plant Stories,* Fulcrum Publishing, Colorado, 1995.

Cassou, Michele, *"The Flowering of Children's Creativity,"* video

Freire, Paulo, "The Banking Concept of Education" https://wrt120.digitalwcu.org/wp-content/uploads/2017/09/freire.pdf

—- *Pedagogy of the Oppressed*, Bloomsbury Academic, New York 2018

McGilchrist, Ian, The Master and His Emissary: The Divided Brain and the Making of the Western World, Yale University Press, 2019.

Pearce, Joseph Chilton, *Magical Child*, Plume, USA, 1992.

Shakespeare, William, *Hamlet.*

Spolin, Viola, Improvisation for the Theater, 3rd edition, Northwestern University Press, Illinois, 1999.

—- Theater Games for the Classroom: A Teacher's Handbook, Northwestern University Press, Illinois, 1986.

Tingley, Kim, "The Secrets of the Wave Pilots," The New York Times, March 17, 2016

Acknowledgements

I am grateful to my fellow teachers, writers, homeschooling parents, and friends who volunteered to be part of my feedback panel. The constant support and flow of intuitive feedback of Shauntay William, fellow writer, was indispensable to the process. I met Shauntay through an Improv for Writers class taught by Aretha Sills. Aretha's classes have been a well of inspiration and information for this book. Invaluable feedback came from my family, my husband Jerry, son Solomon, and my beloved daughter-in-law Lindsey, whose notes were always insightful. Many homeschooling parents supported and assisted me in this project including Jackie Bellis, Janet Jaros, Nicky Harper, Mary O'Riordan, Ellen Barnett, and others. Former students shared stories and gave feedback including Maya Jaros, Marcel Hidalgo, Caoilin Ramsey, Artemesia LeFay, Fredi Guevara-Prip, Valentina Giovannini, and others. Thanks to the Maine Writers & Publishers Alliance for connecting me with talented feedback partner Emma Bouthillette. I am indebted to Andi Cumbo and Caroline Topperman of Mountain Ash Press for their expertise, insights, professionalism, and enthusiasm for my work. I am deeply grateful to everyone, including many not mentioned here, who supported the journey that led to this book.

About the Author

Laurie Block Spigel homeschooled her two sons in New York City, where she created the website HomeschoolNYC.com as an informational resource for homeschooling parents, and taught popular classes to homeschoolers. Laurie lectured at homeschooling and alternative education conferences, wrote articles, and published a HomeschoolNYC newsletter. In 2006, she published *Education Uncensored: A Guide for the Aspiring, the Foolhardy and the Disillusioned*, part memoir and part homeschooling guide, with an explanation of what's wrong with America's educational system. Today, Laurie's homeschooled sons are college-educated, married, lifelong learners. Laurie now lives with her husband and cat in Maine, not far from her younger son and daughter-in-law. She continues to write, teach, and advocate for homeschoolers and child-led, self-directed, game-based learning. Find Laurie's current work at LaurieBlockSpigel.com.

www.ingramcontent.com/pod-product-compliance
Lightning Source LLC
Chambersburg PA
CBHW070118100426
42744CB00010B/1854